CW00542591

EMPIRES OF THE DRAGON

THE FAR EAST AT WAR

Written by Nik Gaukroger & Richard Bodley Scott,
assisted by James Hamilton, Rudy Scott Nelson,
Paul Robinson, Thom Richardson & Duncan Head

First published in Great Britain in 2009 by Osprey Publishing Ltd.

© 2009 Osprey Publishing Ltd and Slitherine Software UK Ltd.

Osprey Publishing, Midland House, West Way, Botley, Oxford OX2 0PH, UK
443 Park Avenue South, New York, NY 10016, USA
E-mail: info@ospreypublishing.com

Slitherine Software UK Ltd., The White Cottage, 8 West Hill Avenue, Epsom, KT 19 8LE, UK
E-mail: info@slitherine.co.uk

All rights reserved. Apart from any fair dealing for the purpose of private study, research, criticism
or review, as permitted under the Copyright, Designs and Patents Act, 1988, no part of this publication
may be reproduced, stored in a retrieval system, or transmitted in any form or by any means, electronic,
electrical, chemical, mechanical, optical, photocopying, recording or otherwise, without the prior
written permission of the copyright owner. Enquiries should be addressed to the Publishers.

A CIP catalogue record for this book is available from the British Library

ISBN: 978 1 84603 690 3

Rules system by Richard Bodley Scott, Simon Hall and Terry Shaw
Page layout and cover concept by Myriam Bell Design, France
Index by Michael Parkin
Typeset in Joanna Pro and Sleepy Hollow
Cover artwork by Peter Dennis
Photography by Curteys Miniatures, The Assault Group, Perry Miniatures & Bear's Den Miniatures
All artwork and cartography © Osprey Publishing Ltd
Project management by JD McNeil and Osprey Team
Technical management by Iain McNeil
Originated by PDQ Media, Bungay, UK
Printed in China through Worldprint Ltd

09 10 11 12 13   10 9 8 7 6 5 4 3 2 1

FOR A CATALOGUE OF ALL BOOKS PUBLISHED BY OSPREY MILITARY AND AVIATION
PLEASE CONTACT:

NORTH AMERICA
Osprey Direct, c/o Random House Distribution Center, 400 Hahn Road, Westminster, MD 21157
E-mail: uscustomerservice@ospreypublishing.com

ALL OTHER REGIONS
Osprey Direct, The Book Service Ltd, Distribution Centre, Colchester Road,
Frating Green, Colchester, Essex, CO7 7DW
E-mail: customerservice@ospreypublishing.com

FOR DETAILS OF ALL GAMES PUBLISHED BY SLITHERINE SOFTWARE UK LTD
E-mail: info@slitherine.co.uk

Osprey Publishing is supporting the Woodland Trust, the UK's leading woodland
conservation charity, by funding the dedication of trees.

www.ospreypublishing.com
www.slitherine.com

CONTENTS

INTRODUCTION

This book covers the widest geographical area and time span of all the *Field of Glory* companion volumes. Armies are included from some of the earliest periods of recorded history in Asia and covering an area of land from the Indus in the west to Korea and Japan in the east. Despite this vast period and expanse, many of the armies are linked through their interaction with the steppe cultures, which provided some of the stiffest military challenges and some of the greatest military leaders of all time. Even those areas not directly influenced by the steppe interacted with those that did and thus military methods were often similar over a wide area.

CHINA

During the period covered by this book China was ruled by a number of Imperial dynasties that claimed to have the backing of the gods,

"The Mandate of Heaven", to rule what they considered to be the civilised world. However, such dynastic rule was not continuous and there were often periods of civil war and fragmentation between the dynasties, and not all the rulers were even Chinese. From time to time China was ruled, partly or wholly, by foreign peoples such as the Xianbei who founded a number of the so called Northern Dynasties and, of course, most famously by the Mongols when Genghis Khan's grandson Khubilai Khan founded the Yuan dynasty.

Inevitably, warfare was an integral part of the state's function from the earliest dates. Armies started off quite small and were mostly foot soldiers, but from about 1300 BC, under the Shang dynasty, chariots started to be used by the nobility and were to dominate the battlefield for half a millennium.

Han Close Combat Foot

From around 500 BC the size of armies started to grow dramatically. It is for good reason that from this point onwards until the start of the Qin dynasty in 221 BC, the period is known as the Warring States period, as warfare between the various Chinese kingdoms was almost continuous. Eventually the ruthless and well-organised state of Qin under Yíng Zhèng succeeded in defeating all its rivals at which time Zheng proclaimed himself "First Emperor of Qin" (Qín Shìhuángdi).

The victory of Qin over its rivals coincided with the rise of the Xiongnu, the first of the really dangerous steppe nations that were to fight against the Chinese for most of the rest of their history. The Chinese were never really able to find a satisfactory answer to the fast moving, mobile and hard-hitting horse archers other than to try and copy them. The most successful Chinese dynasties were those such as the Tang that could themselves field large numbers of similar cavalry.

However, China did not just look to the north, and throughout the period was slowly, but surely, also expanding southwards from the initial Shang ruled areas on the Yellow River. This brought it into contact, and conflict, with a number of south-east Asian peoples who were themselves influenced by Chinese military methods and technology. Eventually the rise of the Ming dynasty in 1358 showed that the south of China had finally eclipsed the north, although the greatest military threats still came from the north, as the construction of the Great Wall shows.

The Great Wall today. Taken from Fortress 57: The Great Wall of China 221 BC–AD 1644.

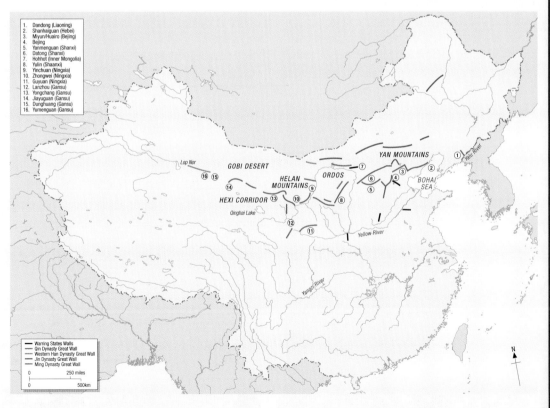

1. Dandong (Liaoning)
2. Shanhaiguan (Hebei)
3. Miyun/Huairo (Bejing)
4. Bejing
5. Yanmenguan (Shanxi)
6. Datong (Shanxi)
7. Hohhot (Inner Mongolia)
8. Yulin (Shaanxi)
9. Yinchuan (Ningxia)
10. Zhongwei (Ningxia)
11. Guyuan (Ningxia)
12. Lanzhou (Gansu)
13. Yongchang (Gansu)
14. Jiayuguan (Gansu)
15. Dunhuang (Gansu)
16. Yumenguan (Gansu)

— Warring States Walls
— Qin Dynasty Great Wall
— Western Han Dynasty Great Wall
— Jin Dynasty Great Wall
— Ming Dynasty Great Wall

0   250 miles
0   500km

THE STEPPES

The Eurasian Steppe, stretching from the borders of Hungary in the west to Manchuria in the east, was home to a vast number of separate tribes who usually associated in larger loose federations of related tribes. It is under the names of these larger groupings, such as the Xiongnu and Mongols, that the steppe peoples are generally known. The western tribes are covered in other Field of Glory Companions – this book covers those who lived east of the Aral Sea.

Throughout the period, dominance of the steppe changed hand many times as the fortunes of tribes rose and fell. As their existence was often precarious due to the limited natural resources of the steppe, tribes were often not in a position to recover from a serious reverse and so a once powerful tribe could swiftly be reduced to vassaldom by another tribe, or by one of its own subjects, if circumstances allowed.

The military power of the steppe people was based on their cavalry. Practically raised from birth to ride and shoot, they were natural warriors, and so all of their manpower could be used as an army, unlike their more sedentary neighbours. Added to this they were used to hardship in a way that settled peoples were not and were very mobile – meaning that opponents would often not be aware of when and where they would strike next. Nomad cavalry influenced, and was copied by, most of the nations they came into contact with and became the normal type of cavalry in the east.

JAPAN

Although Japan was somewhat isolated for a significant proportion of the period, Japanese armies intervened at times in Korea and, famously, were invaded by Khubilai Khan's Mongols. These relatively brief contacts with other nations and military systems heavily influenced the Japanese military and after each conflict changes were made. Horse archery and conscript armies are examples of foreign influence. Additionally, Japanese armies were engaged in wars within the islands that make up Japan.

Although the usual perception of Japanese warriors is of the samurai, early armies were in fact raised by large scale peasant recruitment. Even in the later armies, after the rise of the samurai class, non-samurai would often make up the majority of soldiers. Large scale conscript armies were introduced in the mid-7th century as a result of Chinese/Korean influence – and probably the risk of an invasion from mainland China in response to Japanese involvement on the Korean side during the Tang conquest of

Mongol Heavy Cavalry

Bushi Cavalry

Korea. As the possibility of such an invasion receded, large armies were no longer justified and warfare devolved to smaller numbers of warlords and their followers. It was from this that the samurai evolved as the warrior class that, by the end of the period, were the effective rulers of Japan – the *shogunate* – despite the fact that a hereditary Emperor still theoretically ruled Japan.

KOREA

Although very much smaller and somewhat peripheral compared to its larger neighbour, China, Korea had, at times, a significant influence on the region's history. Initially a number of competing kingdoms in the Korean "Three Kingdoms" period, a series of massive invasions from China under the Sui and Tang dynasties ended up unifying the peninsular under the Shilla dynasty. Despite the disparity in size between Shilla and Tang China, the Koreans were successful in driving out the Chinese

and securing their independence which, apart from a period of Mongol dominance, they subsequently maintained.

SOUTH EAST ASIA

The various kingdoms of south-east Asia were influenced by both India and China, although as their military was based mainly on elephants and infantry, it bore more resemblance to the former than the latter. Whilst they were often characterised as barbarians by the Chinese, many in fact had complex and sophisticated cultures. They mostly remained independent of their larger northern neighbours as the terrain was largely inhospitable jungle and northerners suffered badly from the endemic tropical diseases and unfamiliar climate.

INDIA

With the collapse of the Gupta and Kidarite Kushan Empires, and the expulsion of the Hephthalite Huns, India entered a period of

Korean Kwang-gun Cavalry

fragmentation. Whilst there were occasionally kingdoms and empires that controlled large areas, such as Vardhan in the north and the Pandyas in the south, these were often fleeting in nature and smaller scale states became the norm.

Starting from 650 AD the newly formed Muslim Caliphate began to look to India as the next step eastwards in their mission to conquer the world for Islam. Initial armies were relatively small and even the fractured states of northern India could hold them back, although the fighting was hard. Finally, in 712, led by Muhammad bin Qasim, the Arabs broke into north-west India and created the Muslim province of Sind in what is now Pakistan. Further expansion into Rajasthan was stopped by the Pratiharas and the Chalukayas, and territory was retaken in subsequent years by the local Rajput rulers.

Following this, Indian states settled back into their normal pattern of endemic warfare until the reappearance of a Muslim conqueror, in the shape of Mahmud of Ghazni. He conducted a series of terribly destructive raids into north India, carrying off vast quantities of wealth and destroying many Hindu holy sites. The Ghaznavids were succeeded by the Ghurids, who were to settle

Vijayanagarian Bombards

permanently in north India, founding the Delhi Sultanate, which was to last, on and off, until the Mughal conquest.

Whilst the north of India suffered repeated foreign invasion, from the Deccan southwards India remained mostly in Indian hands. Whilst it was also fragmented, the south threw up two major empires, the Chola and Vijayanagar, the last of which was able to successfully invade Muslim held territory.

CHINESE NAMES AND TERMS

The transliteration of Chinese into English has always been a problematic issue. There are currently two systems in widespread use. The older of these, called Wade-Giles after the Englishmen who developed it in the second half of the 19th century, was the main system used until the last quarter of the 20th century. The newer system is called Pinyin and was developed by the People's Republic of China to standardise the teaching of Mandarin Chinese in schools. It has subsequently been adopted as an ISO standard and has mostly supplanted Wade-Giles in modern works on China and Chinese history.

As nearly all new publications and web resources now use Pinyin, we have decided that it is appropriate that we do so in these lists. However, players should bear in mind that older works will still use Wade-Giles and to help avoid confusion the following table lists the alternative transliterations of many of the names and terms in our lists.

For other eastern languages such as Korean and Japanese we have used the common forms of transliteration, although again players should be aware that there are minor differences (e.g. the Korean state Shilla is sometimes referred to as Silla).

Pinyin	Wade-Giles	Pinyin	Wade-Giles
Aguda	Akuta	Rouran	Juan-juan
Bubing	Pu-ping	Shatuo	Sha-t'o
Bushe	Pu-she	Song	Sung
Chu	Ch'u	Tuoba	T'o-pa
Di	Ti	Wuyue	Wu Yueh
Fubing	Fu-ping	Xi Xia	Hsi Hsia
Ganzhou	Kanchou	Xianbei	Hsien-pei
Jin	Chin/Ts'in	Xiongnu	Hsiung-nu
Jin (Jurchen)	Chin/Kin	Yelü Abaoji	Yeh-lu A-poa-chi
Liu Bang	Liu Pang	Yelü Abaoji	Yeh-lu A-poa-chi
Nanzhao	Nan-chao	Zhao	Chao
Qi	Ch'i	Zhao Kuangyin	Chao K'uang-yin
Qiang	Ch'iang	Zhongshan	Chungshan
Qidan	Khitan/Kitan	Zhou	Chou
Qin	Ch'in	Zhu Yuanzhang	Chu Yuan-chang
Qin Shi Huang	Ch'in Shih-Huang	Zhuge Liang	Chu-ko Liang

ERLITOU-SHANG CHINESE

This list covers Chinese armies from the early Bronze Age Erlitou culture, possibly to be identified with the semi-mythical Xia Dynasty (c.1700–1500 BC), and the Shang Dynasty (1500–1046 BC) which is thought to have evolved from the same culture. These early kingdoms, based in Henan Province in central China, are known for their exquisite bronzes and divinatory inscriptions on oracle bones, as well as their characteristic slave populations. Organised armies began to appear, with divisions in to left, right and centre, and later in the Shang period light, two-horse chariots appear. Bows and dagger-axes (*ge*) of bronze dominate the finds of weapons, with spears (*mao*) and battle-axes (*fu*, *qi* and *yue*) in a minority. Bronze helmets appear in the later Shang, and shields, thought to be of wooden frames covered in leather and about 80 cm in length, are known from their bronze mounts. Shang noble burials include dagger-axes as well as bows, suggesting they fought as Swordsmen as well as archers, and the same mix of weapons is found in the later Shang chariot burials.

The dynasty is supposed to have moved its capital six times, and the last move to Yin gives its name to the later Anyang phase. The characteristic of the Anyang period is the chariot burial. One tomb at Anyang contains large quantities of spearheads and helmets, and may have been the equipment of Shang imperial guards. The central

Shang Commander

Shang warriors, by Angus McBride. Taken from Men-at-Arms 218: Ancient Chinese Armies 1500–200 BC

Shang state was small, and there were many other bronze-casting states in central China. Alliances with non-Chinese peoples are probable but not certainly recorded. The last king of Shang, Di Xin, the Zhou Wang, was reputedly given over to drinking, women and generally immoral behaviour, ignoring affairs of state. One pleasure was the Alcohol Pool and Meat Forest, in which the diners would paddle canoes in a lake of wine and eat meat hung above the water. He is said to have taken his own life when his capital fell to the invading army of the Zhou duke Wu, after the battle of Muye in 1046 BC. The Zhou army was aided by a force of Shang slaves, and many of the Shang soldiers refused to fight. His heir continued as a vassal of the Zhou until about 1035 BC.

TROOP NOTES

The Shang dagger-axe (*ge*) had a dagger-like blade on a metre-long shaft, much like a one-handed battle-axe. The most appropriate designation for its wielders is Swordsmen.

Shang Dagger-axe Men

ERLITOU-SHANG CHINESE STARTER ARMY (AFTER 1300 BC)

Commander-in-Chief	1	Field Commander
Sub-commanders	2	2 x Troop Commander
Nobles	3 BGs	Each comprising 4 bases of nobles: Superior, Undrilled Light Chariots – Bow
Guard spearmen	1 BG	6 bases of guard spearmen: Superior, Protected, Drilled Medium Foot – Offensive Spearmen
Drilled Dagger-axe men	1 BG	8 bases of drilled Dagger-axe men: Average, Protected, Drilled Medium Foot – Swordsmen
Drilled archers	1 BG	8 bases of drilled archers: Average, Protected, Drilled Medium Foot – Bow
Undrilled Dagger-axe men	1 BG	8 bases of undrilled Dagger-axe men: Poor, Protected, Undrilled Medium Foot – Swordsmen
Undrilled archers	1 BG	8 bases of undrilled archers: Poor, Unprotected, Undrilled Medium Foot – Bow
Skirmishing archers	2 BGs	Each comprising 8 bases of skirmishing archers: Poor, Unprotected, Undrilled Light Foot – Bow
Camp	1	Unfortified camp
Total	10 BGs	Camp, 12 mounted bases, 54 foot bases, 3 commanders

BUILDING A CUSTOMISED LIST USING OUR ARMY POINTS

Choose an army based on the maxima and minima in the list below. The following special instructions apply to this army:

- Commanders should be depicted as nobles.
- A Chinese allied commander's contingent must conform to the Erlitou-Shang Chinese allies list below, but the troops in the contingent are deducted from the minima and maxima in the main list.

ERLITOU-SHANG CHINESE

Territory Types: Agricultural, Hilly

C-in-C	Inspired Commander/Field Commander/Troop Commander	80/50/35	1
Sub-commanders	Field Commander/Troop Commander	50/35	0–2
Chinese allied commanders	Field Commander/Troop Commander	40/25	0–3

Troop name		Troop Type				Capabilities		Points per base	Bases per BG	Total bases	
		Type	Armour	Quality	Training	Shooting	Close Combat				
Core Troops											
Nobles	Only before 1300	Medium Foot	Protected	Superior	Drilled	Bow	Swordsmen	10	6–8	0–8	6–18
		Medium Foot	Protected	Superior	Undrilled	Bow	Swordsmen	9	6–8	6–18	
	Only from 1300	Light Chariots	–	Superior	Undrilled	Bow	–	17	4–6	6–18	
Dagger-axe men		Medium Foot	Protected	Average	Drilled	–	Swordsmen	7	6–8	0–32	12–96
		Medium Foot	Protected	Poor	Undrilled	–	Swordsmen	4	8–10	8–72	
Archers		Medium Foot	Protected	Average	Drilled	Bow	–	7	6–8	0–32	12–96
			Unprotected					6			
		Medium Foot	Protected	Poor	Undrilled	Bow	–	4	8–10	8–72	
			Unprotected					3			
Skirmishing archers		Light Foot	Unprotected	Poor	Undrilled	Bow	–	3	6–8	0–18	
		Light Foot	Unprotected	Average	Drilled	Bow	–	5	6	0–6	
Optional Troops											
Guard spearmen	Only from 1300	Medium Foot	Protected	Superior	Drilled	–	Offensive Spearmen	10	6	0–6	
Spearmen		Medium Foot	Protected	Average	Drilled	–	Offensive Spearmen	8	6–8	0–8	0–18
		Medium Foot	Protected	Poor	Undrilled	–	Offensive Spearmen	5	6–10	0–18	
Armed slaves	Only from 1300	Mob	–	Poor	Undrilled	–	–	2	10–12	0–24	
Allies											
Di, Rong or Yi allies – Early Northern Barbarians											

ERLITOU-SHANG CHINESE ALLIES

Allied commander	Field Commander/Troop Commander	40/25	1

Troop name		Troop Type				Capabilities		Points per base	Bases per BG	Total bases	
		Type	Armour	Quality	Training	Shooting	Close Combat				
Nobles	Only before 1300	Medium Foot	Protected	Superior	Drilled	Bow	Swordsmen	10	4–6	0–6	
		Medium Foot	Protected	Superior	Undrilled	Bow	Swordsmen	9	4–6		
	Only from 1300	Light Chariots	–	Superior	Undrilled	Bow	–	17	4–6	0–6	
Dagger-axe men		Medium Foot	Protected	Average	Drilled	–	Swordsmen	7	6–8	0–8	*6–18
		Medium Foot	Protected	Poor	Undrilled	–	Swordsmen	4	8–10	0–18	
Archers		Medium Foot	Protected	Average	Drilled	Bow	–	7	6–8	0–8	*6–24
			Unprotected					6			
		Medium Foot	Protected	Poor	Undrilled	Bow	–	4	8–10	0–24	
			Unprotected					3			
Skirmishing archers		Light Foot	Unprotected	Poor	Undrilled	Bow	–	3	4–6	0–6	
Spearmen		Medium Foot	Protected	Average	Drilled	–	Offensive Spearmen	8	6	0–6	
		Medium Foot	Protected	Poor	Undrilled	–	Offensive Spearmen	5	6		
Armed slaves	Only from 1300	Mob	–	Poor	Undrilled	–	–	2	8	0–8	

EARLY NORTHERN BARBARIAN ALLIES

- The commander should be depicted as nobles or warriors.

Barbarian Warriors

EARLY NORTHERN BARBARIAN ALLIES

Allied commander		Field Commander/Troop Commander						40/25		1	
Troop name		Troop Type				Capabilities		Points per base	Bases per BG	Total bases	
		Type	Armour	Quality	Training	Shooting	Close Combat				
Nobles	Only from 1350 to 1050 BC	Light Chariots	–	Superior	Undrilled	Bow	–	17	4	0–4	
	Only from 1125 BC	Heavy Chariots	–	Superior	Undrilled	Bow	–	20	4		
Warriors with dagger-axe or sword	Any date	Medium Foot	Protected	Average	Undrilled	–	Swordsmen	6	8–12	8–24	
	Only from 700 BC	Medium Foot	Protected	Average	Undrilled	–	Impact Foot, Swordsmen	7	8–12		
Archers		Medium Foot	Unprotected	Average	Undrilled	Bow	–	5	6–8	6–24	
		Light Foot	Unprotected	Average	Undrilled	Bow	–	5	6–8		

EARLY ZHOU CHINESE

The Zhou Dynasty lasted from 1122 to 255 BC. Originating as a Shang vassal kingdom in modern Gansu province, duke Wu of Zhou defeated the last Shang king at the battle of Muye in 1046 BC, establishing the Western Zhou dynasty, named after its capital Hao, close to the site of modern Xian. A strong military system based on the Six Armies of the West and the Eight Armies of Chengzhou conquered a large empire in north central China. Civil war in 771 BC led to the defeat of the Western Zhou king by his former queen's father, the Marquis of Shen, with the aid of the Rong tribes and the allied states of Zheng, Liu and Qin. His son, Ji Yijiu, was established as king. Soon afterwards, the capital was sacked by northern barbarian invaders, and, in 722, was moved to Luoyang in the east, after which the later Zhou is known as the Eastern Zhou.

Zhou control was limited, and the period 722–481 BC, known as the Spring and Autumn period after the annals of the state of Lu of that time, and the following Warring States period, 475–221 BC, were ages of constant conflict between effectively independent states, most dominant of which were Qi, Qin Jin and Chu. It was during this time that Sunzi (Sun Tzu) wrote his Art of War.

In addition to the wars between the states, there were continual campaigns against the 'barbarian' tribes of the north and west, the Rong, Di and Yi. These were largely subsumed into the expanding territories of the states by the late 7th century, after which campaigns

Zhou chariot, by Angus McBride. Taken from Men-at-Arms 218: Ancient Chinese Armies 1500–200 BC.

against displaced tribes continued, but no more alliances are recorded.

This list covers the armies of the Zhou Dynasty and the various independent states from 1122 to c.350 BC when massed crossbowmen and cavalry started to appear in Chinese armies.

TROOP NOTES

Zhou forces were dominated by four horse chariots, crewed by a driver and warriors armed with the dagger-axe and bow (and later in the period, the crossbow). At Muye in 1046 BC the Zhou forces are recorded as 300 chariots accompanied by 3,000 *huben* ('Tiger guards') and 45,000 other infantry.

Dagger-axes (*ge*) became longer and were wielded with two hands, so we interpret them as

heavy weapon. Spears (*mao*) continued in a subordinate role, while bronze straight swords (*qian*) appeared later in the period.

Zhou Commander

EARLY ZHOU CHINESE STARTER ARMY (AFTER 700 BC)

Commander-in-Chief	1	Troop Commander
Sub-commanders	2	2 x Troop Commander
Chariots	2 BGs	Each comprising 4 bases of chariots: Superior, Undrilled Heavy Chariots — Bow
Dagger-axe men and supporting archers	2 BGs	Each comprising 8 bases of Dagger-axe men and supporting archers: 4 Average, Armoured, Drilled Medium Foot — Heavy Weapon, 4 Average, Armoured, Drilled Medium Foot — Bow
Spearmen and supporting archers	1 BG	9 bases of spearmen and supporting archers: 6 Average, Armoured, Drilled Medium Foot — Offensive Spearmen, 3 Average, Unprotected, Drilled Light Foot — Bow
Poor quality dagger-axe men and supporting archers	1 BG	8 bases of poor quality Dagger-axe men and supporting archers: 4 Poor, Protected, Undrilled Medium Foot — Heavy Weapon, 4 Poor, Protected, Undrilled Medium Foot — Bow
Detached archers	1 BG	8 bases of detached archers: Poor, Unprotected, Undrilled Medium Foot — Bow
Skirmishing archers	2 BGs	Each comprising 8 bases of skirmishing archers: Poor, Unprotected, Undrilled Light Foot — Bow
Camp	1	Unfortified camp
Total	9 BGs	Camp, 8 mounted bases, 57 foot bases, 3 commanders

BUILDING A CUSTOMISED LIST USING OUR ARMY POINTS

Choose an army based on the maxima and minima in the list below. The following special instructions apply to this army:

- Commanders should be depicted in chariots.
- The total number of bases of dagger-axemen in the army cannot be more than twice the total number of bases of archers and vice versa.
- A Zhou Chinese allied commander's contingent must conform to the Early Zhou Chinese allies list below, but the troops in the contingent are deducted from the minima and maxima in the main list.

EARLY ZHOU CHINESE

Territory Types: Agricultural, Developed, Hilly

C-in-C		Inspired Commander/Field Commander/Troop Commander					80/50/35		1	
Sub-commanders		Field Commander/Troop Commander					50/35		0–2	
Zhou Chinese allied commanders		Field Commander/Troop Commander					40/25		0–3	

Troop name		Troop Type				Capabilities		Points per base	Bases per BG	Total bases
		Type	Armour	Quality	Training	Shooting	Close Combat			
Core Troops										
Chariots		Heavy Chariots	–	Superior	Undrilled	Bow	–	20	4–6	6–18
Dagger-axe men and supporting archers	Only before 700	Medium Foot	Protected	Average	Drilled	–	Swordsmen	7	All, 2/3 or 1/2	0–24
	Only from 700	Medium Foot	Protected	Average	Drilled	–	Heavy Weapon	8		
			Armoured					10		
	Any date	Medium Foot	Protected	Average	Drilled	Bow	–	7	0 or 1/2	6–9 / 0–24
	Only from 700	Medium Foot	Armoured	Average	Drilled	Bow	–	9		
	Any date	Light Foot	Unprotected	Average	Drilled	Bow	–	5	0 or 1/3	12–64
	Only before 700	Medium Foot	Protected	Poor	Undrilled	–	Swordsmen	4	All, 2/3 or 1/2	8–48
	Only from 700	Medium Foot	Protected	Poor	Undrilled	–	Heavy Weapon	5		
	Any date	Medium Foot	Protected	Poor	Undrilled	Bow	–	4	0 or 1/2	8–10 / 8–48
	Any date	Light Foot	Unprotected	Poor	Undrilled	Bow	–	3	0 or 1/3	
Detached archers		Medium Foot	Protected	Average	Drilled	Bow	–	7	6–8	0–24
			Unprotected					6		
		Light Foot	Unprotected	Average	Drilled	Bow	–	5	6–8	0–8	12–64
		Medium Foot	Protected	Poor	Undrilled	Bow	–	4	6–8	8–48
			Unprotected					3		
		Light Foot	Unprotected	Poor	Undrilled	Bow	–	3	6–8	0–18
Optional Troops										
Tiger guards, *huben*	Only before 770	Medium foot	Protected	Superior	Drilled		Swordsmen	9	6–8	0–8
Spearmen and supporting archers	Any date	Medium Foot	Protected	Average	Drilled	–	Offensive Spearmen	8	All or 2/3	0–9
	Only from 700	Medium Foot	Armoured	Average	Drilled	–	Offensive Spearmen	10		6–9
	Any date	Light Foot	Unprotected	Average	Drilled	Bow	–	5	0 or 1/3	0–18
	Any date	Medium Foot	Protected	Poor	Undrilled	–	Offensive Spearmen	4	All or 2/3	0–18
	Any date	Light Foot	Unprotected	Poor	Undrilled	Bow	–	3	0 or 1/3	8–9
Convicts, prisoners of war		Mob	Unprotected	Poor	Undrilled	–	–	2	10–12	0–24
Volunteer swordsmen or tribal allies	Only from 700	Medium Foot	Protected	Average	Undrilled	–	Impact Foot, Swordsmen	7	8–10	0–20
Allies										
Shang Chinese allies (Only before 1034) – Erlitou–Shang Chinese										
Di, Rong or Yi allies (Only before 622)– Early Northern Barbarians										

EARLY ZHOU CHINESE ALLIES

Allied commander		Field Commander/Troop Commander					40/25		1	
Troop name		**Troop Type**				**Capabilities**		**Points per base**	**Bases per BG**	**Total bases**
		Type	Armour	Quality	Training	Shooting	Close Combat			
Chariots		Heavy Chariots	–	Superior	Undrilled	Bow	–	20	4–6	4–6
Dagger-axe men and supporting archers	Only before 700	Medium Foot	Protected	Average	Drilled	–	Swordsmen	7	All, 2/3 or 1/2	
	Only from 700	Medium Foot	Protected	Average	Drilled	–	Heavy Weapon	8		
			Armoured					10	6–9 0–8	6–18
	Any date	Medium Foot	Protected	Average	Drilled	Bow	–	7	0 or 1/2	
	Only from 700	Medium Foot	Armoured	Average	Drilled	Bow	–	9		
	Any date	Light Foot	Unprotected	Average	Drilled	Bow	–	5	0 or 1/3	
	Only before 700	Medium Foot	Protected	Poor	Undrilled	–	Swordsmen	4	All, 2/3 or 1/2	
	Only from 700	Medium Foot	Protected	Poor	Undrilled	–	Heavy Weapon	5	8–10 0–18	
	Any date	Medium Foot	Protected	Poor	Undrilled	Bow	–	4	0 or 1/2	
	Any date	Light Foot	Unprotected	Poor	Undrilled	Bow	–	3	0 or 1/3	
Detached archers		Medium Foot	Protected	Average	Drilled	Bow	–	7	6–8 0–8	
		Unprotected						6		
		Medium Foot	Protected	Poor	Undrilled	Bow	–	4	6–8 0–18	6–18
		Unprotected						3		
		Light Foot	Unprotected	Poor	Undrilled	Bow	–	3	4–6	0–6

YAYOI JAPANESE

This list covers Japanese armies from c.500 BC to 275 AD, representing the Yayoi culture of Japan from its origins until the first use of mounded tombs and iron armour ushered in the start of a new era. The Yayoi were not united and even their most powerful rulers controlled only alliances of semi-independent communities. Chinese sources say that over 100 Japanese states existed.

TROOP NOTES

Warriors wore simple clothing and tattoos, and fought with spears, dagger-axes, swords, wooden bows with the lower limb shorter than the upper, and slings. We assume archers were in the majority, as in later periods, though some regions favoured the sling over the bow. Spears were 2–3 metres long and shields could be very large. Some wooden armour has been found. At first both bronze and iron weapons were used, iron being predominant before the end of the period. It is not clear if separate weapons were used in different bodies. The dagger-axe was probably not heavy enough to count as a Heavy Weapon as it was nearer a spear.

Yayoi priestess-queen and bodyguards, by Angus McBride. Taken from Elite 35: Early Samurai AD 200–1500.

YAYOI JAPANESE STARTER ARMY

Commander-in-Chief	1	Field Commander
Sub-commanders	2	2 x Troop Commander
Spearmen	5 BGs	Each comprising 8 bases of spearmen: Average, Protected, Undrilled Medium Foot – Offensive Spearmen
Archers	2 BGs	Each comprising 8 bases of archers: Average, Unprotected, Undrilled Medium Foot – Bow
Slingers	5 BGs	Each comprising 6 bases of slingers: Average, Unprotected, Undrilled Light Foot – Sling
Camp	1	Unfortified camp
Total	12 BGs	Camp, 86 foot bases, 3 commanders

BUILDING A CUSTOMISED LIST USING OUR ARMY POINTS

Choose an army based on the maxima and minima in the list below. The following special instructions apply to this army:

- Commanders should be depicted as archers.
- A Japanese allied commander's contingent must conform to the Yayoi Japanese allies list below, but the troops in the contingent are deducted from the minima and maxima in the main list.

YAYOI JAPANESE

Territory Types: Agricultural, Hilly, Woodlands

C-in-C	Inspired Commander/Field Commander/Troop Commander						80/50/35		1	
Sub-commanders	Field Commander/Troop Commander						50/35		0–2	
Japanese allied commanders	Field Commander/Troop Commander						40/25		0–3	
Troop name	**Troop Type**				**Capabilities**		Points per base	Bases per BG	Total bases	
	Type	Armour	Quality	Training	Shooting	Close Combat				
Core Troops										
Archers	Medium Foot	Unprotected	Average	Undrilled	Bow	–	5	6–8	0–128	32– 128
	Medium Foot	Unprotected	Poor	Undrilled	Bow	–	3	6–8	0–16	
Slingers	Light Foot	Unprotected	Average	Undrilled	Sling	–	4	6–8	0–72	
	Light Foot	Unprotected	Poor	Undrilled	Sling	–	2	6–8	0–16	
Dagger-axe men and/or swordsmen	Medium Foot	Protected	Average	Undrilled	–	Swordsmen	6	6–8	0–90	12–90
	Medium Foot	Protected	Poor	Undrilled	–	Swordsmen	4	6–8	0–16	
Spearmen	Medium Foot	Protected	Average	Undrilled	–	Offensive Spearmen	7	6–8	0–90	
	Medium Foot	Protected	Poor	Undrilled	–	Offensive Spearmen	5	6–8	0–16	

YAYOI JAPANESE ALLIES

Allied commander	Field Commander/Troop Commander						40/25		1	
Troop name	**Troop Type**				**Capabilities**		**Points per base**	**Bases per BG**	**Total bases**	
	Type	Armour	Quality	Training	Shooting	Close Combat				
Archers	Medium Foot	Unprotected	Average	Undrilled	Bow	–	5	6–8	0–32	8–32
	Medium Foot	Unprotected	Poor	Undrilled	Bow	–	3	6	0–6	
Slingers	Light Foot	Unprotected	Average	Undrilled	Sling	–	4	6–8	0–18	
	Light Foot	Unprotected	Poor	Undrilled	Sling	–	2	6	0–6	
Dagger-axe men and/or swordsmen	Medium Foot	Protected	Average	Undrilled	–	Swordsmen	6	6–8	0–24	6–24
	Medium Foot	Protected	Poor	Undrilled	–	Swordsmen	4	6	0–6	
Spearmen	Medium Foot	Protected	Average	Undrilled	–	Offensive Spearmen	7	6–8	0–24	
	Medium Foot	Protected	Poor	Undrilled	–	Offensive Spearmen	5	6	0–6	

EARLY HORSE NOMAD

This list covers eastern steppe-based horse riding nomads from the appearance of the Hu on the northern frontiers of China c.400 BC until the re-establishment of the armoured horse archer as the dominant cavalry form c.500 AD.

The Hu were supplanted as the main nomad enemy c.200 BC by the Xiongnu, who remained the main northern threat to the Chinese throughout the Han dynasties. They were later supplemented, and then superseded, by the various Xianbei and Wuhuan tribes many of whom also founded states in China proper, which are covered by the Northern Dynasties Chinese list.

Other tribes covered by this list include the Tuyuhun, Xi and Qidan, the last of which founded an imperial state in the 10th century which is covered by the Liao list, and the relatively poor tribes of Manchuria.

TROOP NOTES

The earliest Chinese cavalry were copied from their Hu neighbours and appear to have been almost exclusively skirmishing horse archers. Later nomads developed heavier cavalry and adopted armour, with leather armour and wooden shields recorded as being used by the Xiongnu in early

Manchurian Cavalry

Western Han times. This was no doubt itself replaced by metal armour as this became available.

Around 300 AD many nomad cavalry adopted, at least as an ideal, cataphract equipment and changed from being horse archers to cavalry who primarily charged to contact with the lance. This change appears to have started with the Xianbei tribes in Manchuria but quickly spread to others often through spoils of war – the Xiongnu are said to have obtained their first horse armour when they captured 5,000 sets after a battle with the Xianbei. It also appears to coincide with adoption of the stirrup. Although such armour appears widespread within China we assume that the tribes of the steppe were more restricted and that a large number had lesser armour and retained horse archer tactics as they would be unsuited to lancer behaviour. The date of the change to cataphract tactics is arbitrary and in reality would not have been a sudden event, however, the nature of army lists is such that a date had to be set.

The Manchurian tribes were rather backward until after the end of this period. What armour they used was made of leather or bone. We assume that, in the absence of adequate equipment to allow successful shock tactics, they remained wholly horse archers.

EARLY HORSE NOMAD STARTER ARMY (AFTER 300 AD)

Commander-in-Chief	1	Field Commander
Sub-commanders	2	2 x Troop Commander
Cataphracts	2 BGs	Each comprising 4 bases of cataphracts: Superior, Heavily Armoured, Undrilled Cataphracts – Lancers, Swordsmen
Other lancers	2 BGs	Each comprising 4 bases of other lancers: Superior, Armoured, Undrilled Cavalry – Lancers, Swordsmen
Horse archers	4 BGs	Each comprising 4 bases of horse archers: Average, Unprotected, Undrilled Light Horse – Bow, Swordsmen
Foot archers	1 BG	8 bases of foot archers: Poor, Unprotected, Undrilled Light Foot – Bow
Fortified camp	1	Fortified camp
Total	9 BGs	Fortified camp, 32 mounted bases, 8 foot bases, 3 commanders

BUILDING A CUSTOMISED LIST USING OUR ARMY POINTS

Choose an army based on the maxima and minima in the list below. The following special instructions apply to this army:

- Commanders should be depicted as best equipped cavalry.
- An Early Horse Nomad allied commander's contingent must conform to the Early Horse Nomad allies list below, but the troops in the contingent are deducted from the minima and maxima in the main list.

EARLY HORSE NOMAD

Territory Types: Manchurians – Woodlands, Steppes. Others – Steppes

C-in-C		Inspired Commander/Field Commander/Troop Commander						80/50/35	1	
Sub-commanders		Field Commander						50	0–2	
		Troop Commander						35	0–3	
Early Horse Nomad allied commander		Field Commander/Troop Commander						40/25	0–1	

Troop name		Troop Type				Capabilities		Points per base	Bases per BG	Total bases
		Type	Armour	Quality	Training	Shooting	Close Combat			
Core Troops										
Best equipped cavalry	Only before 200 BC	Cavalry	Protected	Superior	Undrilled	Bow	Swordsmen	14	4–6	0–8
	Any from 200 BC to 299 AD	Cavalry	Protected	Superior	Undrilled	Bow	Swordsmen	14	4–6	4–18
	Only non-Manchurians from 1 to 299 AD	Cavalry	Armoured	Superior	Undrilled	Bow	Swordsmen	18	4–6	
	Only Manchurians from 300 AD	Cavalry	Protected	Superior	Undrilled	Bow	Swordsmen	14	4–6	
	Only non-Manchurians from 300 AD	Cavalry	Armoured	Superior	Undrilled	–	Lancers, Swordsmen	16	4–6	
		Cataphracts	Heavily Armoured	Superior	Undrilled	–	Lancers, Swordsmen	18		
Other cavalry		Light Horse	Unprotected	Average	Undrilled	Bow	Swordsmen	10	4–6	16–84
		Cavalry	Unprotected	Average	Undrilled	Bow	Swordsmen	10	4–6	
			Protected					11		
Optional Troops										
Foot archers		Medium Foot	Unprotected	Average	Undrilled	Bow	–	5	6–8	0–12
				Poor				3		
		Light Foot	Unprotected	Average	Undrilled	Bow	–	5	6–8	
				Poor				3		
Camp followers or other levies		Mob	Unprotected	Poor	Undrilled	–	–	2	10–12	0–12
Foot nomad subjects	Only Hu before 200 BC	Medium Foot	Protected	Average	Undrilled	–	Impact Foot, Swordsmen	7	6–8	0–24
							Light Spear	5		
Fortified camp								24		0–1
Allies										
Chinese rebel allies (Only Xiongnu from 200 to 150 BC) – Warring States to Western Han Chinese										
Qiang allies (Only Xiongnu or Xianbei from 200 BC to 214 AD) – Qiang and Di										

EARLY HORSE NOMAD ALLIES

Allied commander		Field Commander/Troop Commander						40/25	1	
Troop name		Troop Type				Capabilities		Points per base	Bases per BG	Total bases
		Type	Armour	Quality	Training	Shooting	Close Combat			
Best equipped cavalry	Only before 200 BC	Cavalry	Protected	Superior	Undrilled	Bow	Swordsmen	14	4–6	0–4
	Any from 200 BC to 299 AD	Cavalry	Protected	Superior	Undrilled	Bow	Swordsmen	14	4–6	0–8
	Only non-Manchurians from 1 to 299 AD	Cavalry	Armoured	Superior	Undrilled	Bow	Swordsmen	18	4–6	
	Only Manchurians from 300 AD	Cavalry	Protected	Superior	Undrilled	Bow	Swordsmen	14	4–6	
	Only non-Manchurians from 300 AD	Cavalry	Armoured	Superior	Undrilled	–	Lancers, Swordsmen	16	4–6	
		Cataphracts	Heavily Armoured	Superior	Undrilled	–	Lancers, Swordsmen	18		
Other cavalry		Light Horse	Unprotected	Average	Undrilled	Bow	Swordsmen	10	4–6	8–24
		Cavalry	Unprotected	Average	Undrilled	Bow	Swordsmen	10	4–6	
			Protected					11		

KO CHOSON KOREAN

The first Korean king is traditionally credited as ruling from as early as 2333 BC, and his descendants reigned in Choson, the "Land of Morning Calm". The Ko Choson list begins with the introduction of iron weapons c.400 BC and includes the Weiman-Choson era from 200 BC as well.

King Kijan established a military organization for the Korean Army and made Ko Choson one of the dominant powers in Korea. Its main enemies included nomadic tribes from Manchuria and roving bands of exiles who had been followers of a general who had been defeated in an attempt to gain control of China. Rule by King Kijan's family would be replaced by Weiman who led a remnant of the Yen faction from China. The Weiman-Choson rule ended when the Han Empire conquered Korea in 108 BC and establish four main commanderies to rule the region.

This list covers Korean armies from 400 to 108 BC.

TROOP NOTES

Bladesmen are armed with swords, axes or axe-spears (crude halberds). In later times shields were not common among foot troops, therefore we assume that they were not used in these very early armies.

KO CHOSON KOREAN STARTER ARMY		
Commander-in-Chief	1	Field Commander
Sub-commanders	2	2 x Troop Commander
Noble chariotry	1 BG	4 bases of noble chariotry: Superior, Undrilled Heavy Chariots – Bow
Noble cavalry	2 BGs	Each comprising 4 bases of noble cavalry: Superior, Armoured, Undrilled Cavalry – Bow, Swordsmen
Horse archers	1 BG	4 bases of horse archers: Average, Unprotected, Undrilled Light Horse – Bow
Mercenary nomads	1 BG	4 bases of mercenary nomads: Average, Unprotected, Undrilled Light Horse – Bow, Swordsmen
"Spearmen" and archers	2 BGs	Each comprising 8 bases of "spearmen" and archers: 4 Average, Unprotected, Undrilled Medium Foot – Heavy Weapon, 4 Average, Unprotected, Undrilled Medium Foot – Bow
Bladesmen	1 BGs	6 bases of bladesmen: Average, Protected, Undrilled Medium Foot – Swordsmen
Skirmishers	2 BGs	Each comprising 6 bases of skirmishers: Average, Unprotected, Undrilled Light Foot – Bow
Camp	1	Unfortified camp
Total	10 BGs	Camp, 20 mounted bases, 34 foot bases, 3 commanders

BUILDING A CUSTOMISED LIST USING OUR ARMY POINTS

Choose an army based on the maxima and minima in the list below. The following special instructions apply to this army:

- Commanders should be depicted as noble chariotry or cavalry.
- The minimum marked * only applies from 200 BC.

KO CHOSON KOREAN

Territory Types: Agricultural, Mountains, Hilly, Woodlands

Troop name		Troop Type				Capabilities		Points per base	Bases per BG	Total bases	
		Type	Armour	Quality	Training	Shooting	Close Combat				
C-in-C		Inspired Commander/Field Commander/Troop Commander						80/50/35		1	
Sub-commanders		Field Commander						50		0–2	
		Troop Commander						35		0–3	
Core Troops											
Noble chariotry		Heavy Chariots	–	Superior	Undrilled	Bow	–	20	4–6	0–6	4–12
Noble cavalry		Cavalry	Protected	Superior	Undrilled	Bow	Swordsmen	14	4–6	*4–12	
			Armoured					18			
Horse archers		Light Horse	Unprotected	Average	Undrilled	Bow	–	8	4–6	4–12	
"Spearmen" and archers		Medium Foot	Protected	Average	Undrilled	–	Heavy Weapon	7	1/2	6–8	16–100
		Medium Foot	Protected	Average	Undrilled	Bow	–	6	1/2		
		Medium Foot	Unprotected	Average	Undrilled	–	Heavy Weapon	6	1/2	6–8	
		Medium Foot	Unprotected	Average	Undrilled	Bow	–	5	1/2		
		Medium Foot	Unprotected	Poor	Undrilled	–	Heavy Weapon	4	1/2	8–10	
		Medium Foot	Unprotected	Poor	Undrilled	Bow	–	3	1/2		
Skirmishers		Light Foot	Unprotected	Average	Undrilled	Bow	–	5	6–8	6–12	
Bladesmen		Medium Foot	Protected	Average	Undrilled	–	Swordsmen	6	6–8	6–24	
Optional Troops											
Mercenary nomads		Light Horse	Unprotected	Average	Undrilled	Bow	Swordsmen	10	4–6		0–8
		Cavalry	Unprotected	Average	Undrilled	Bow	Swordsmen	10	4–6		
			Protected					11			
Scouts		Light Foot	Unprotected	Poor	Undrilled	Javelins	Light Spear	2	6–8	0–8	
Crossbowmen	Only from 200 BC	Light Foot	Unprotected	Average	Undrilled	Crossbow	–	5	4–6	0–6	
		Medium Foot	Unprotected	Average	Undrilled	Crossbow	–	5	4–6		
Peasant levy		Mob	Unprotected	Poor	Undrilled	–	–	2	8–12	0–16	
Allies											
Manchurian nomad allies – Early Horse Nomad											

WARRING STATES TO WESTERN HAN CHINESE

This list covers Chinese armies of the last phase of the Warring States from the introduction of massed crossbow use c.350 BC until the completion of unification under Qin Shi Huang (Qín Shìhuángdi) (255–210 BC) in 221; then the subsequent Qin Dynasty (221–206 BC) and the Western Han (207 BC–23 AD), including the reign of the usurper Wang Mang (9–23 AD). The Qin are said to have originated from a branch of the Yi tribes in modern Gansu province, and were established there as vassals by the Zhou.

Warfare continued to be endemic in the period until the unification of China under the first emperor. After that the concept of a unified realm ruled by an emperor favoured by the gods, the so called "Mandate of Heaven" was generally accepted and considered the natural state of things. However, this philosophy did not

Qin Commander

prevent the Qin dynasty being itself overthrown in 206 in a series of civil wars out of which the Han dynasty founded by Liu Bang (known as emperor Gaozu) emerged to rule and expand the empire for the next four centuries. The Han is divided into two periods, the Western Han from 207 BC–23 AD and the Eastern Han from 23–220 AD.

The main enemy of the Western Han dynasty were the nomadic Xiongnu who rose to dominate the inner Asian steppe around the same time that the Han dynasty was founded.

Crossbowmen

Initially the nomads had the upper hand until a series of campaigns, sometimes by entirely mounted Han forces, coupled with civil war within the Xiongnu confederacy (encouraged by the Chinese), broke their power. Following this Chinese power was extended west into the Tarim basin of central Asia which also served as a source of excellent horse stock for the Chinese cavalry – the so called "heavenly horses".

Towards the end of the 1st century BC the Han state suffered economic and social problems which led an aristocrat, Wang Mang, to believe that heaven had withdrawn its mandate from the dynasty, so justifying him in usurping power and declaring his own Xin dynasty. However, this did not outlast his death in 23 AD and in the following civil war the Han dynasty was restored.

TROOP NOTES

Qin and contemporary forces are illustrated by the figures of the terracotta warriors guarding the tomb of Qin Shi Huang at Lintong near Xian. Forces continued to include four horse chariots, but cavalry became increasingly important. Chariots are not always mentioned as part of armies in the period of civil wars following the death of the first emperor and probably ceased to be used some time during the 2nd century BC.

The Qin Imperial Guard, by Angus McBride. Taken from Men-at-Arms 218: Ancient Chinese Armies 1500–200 BC.

Dagger-axes (ge) were increasingly fitted with pi spearheads, and began to be replaced with iron halberds (ji) in the heads of which both components were combined. Long and short spears (mao and yan) and bronze straight swords (qian) continued in a subordinate role. Weapons were often mixed together for mutual support although separate specialist bodies were also used at times. Crossbows (nu) became the dominant missile weapon of Chinese infantry, and some cavalry adopted them also. Large stand-mounted crossbows appear in this period.

How Chinese cavalry were equipped is difficult to determine with any precision. Towards the end of the 4th century the Zhao state in northern China adopted Hu costume and increased the cavalry component of its army. This is traditionally stated to have been in 307 BC. Some cavalry seem to have used composite bows and imitated the light cavalry tactics of the Xiongnu, who became the principal external foe of the Chinese Imperial dynasties. Armour, crossbows, ji halberds and swords are also mentioned, with dismounted cavalry using swords and halberds. There are a number of depictions and models of cavalry armed only with ji which we regard as having equivalent effect on horseback to Light Spear, Swordsmen capabilities. One account has mounted crossbowmen dismounting to fight with swords and halberds which indicates that some troops were double armed. In line with Field of Glory grading policy we assume their primary role was that of shooters and so classify them as Crossbow, Swordsmen when mounted.

"Taigong's Six Secret teachings", from the later Warring States period, states: "When infantry engage in battle with chariots and cavalry, they must rely on hills and mounds, ravines and defiles." It makes the following recommendation for when such terrain is not available: "Order our officers and troops to set up the chevaux-de-frise and wooden caltrops, arraying the oxen and horses by units of five in their midst, and have them establish a four-sided martial assault formation. When you see the enemy's chariots and cavalry are about to advance, our men should evenly spread out the caltrops and dig ditches around the rear, making them five feet deep and wide." On this basis we feel that Medium Foot is undoubtedly the correct classification for Chinese infantry of this period, even though it may require rebasing of existing armies. We treat the above defences as Portable Defences.

Qin infantry are described in the Warring States period as "savage soldiers ... who will rush against the enemy helmetless and barefoot brandishing their halberds" and who "snatch off all protective clothes and race bareheaded after the foe". They are described as more fierce than soldiers of the eastern states, however, it was possible to use their eagerness for combat against them. On this basis we allow the better Qin infantry to be regraded as Undrilled and some to be Impact Foot to represent this, but they can no longer be Armoured.

Wei was conquered by Qin in 225 BC, Zhao and Yan in 222 BC. Zhongshan was destroyed by Zhao in 296 BC Therefore troops available only to those states cannot be used after those dates.

WARRING STATES CHINESE STARTER ARMY (ZHAO BEFORE 222 BC)		
Commander-in-Chief	1	Field Commander
Sub-commanders	2	2 x Troop Commander
Chariots	2 BGs	Each comprising 4 bases of chariots: Superior, Drilled Heavy Chariots – Crossbow
Horse archers	2 BGs	Each comprising 4 bases of horse archers: Average, Unprotected, Drilled Light Horse – Bow
Mixed close combat foot and crossbowmen	2 BGs	Each comprising 8 bases of close combat foot and crossbowmen: 4 Average, Armoured, Drilled Medium Foot – Heavy Weapon, Portable Defences, 4 Average, Armoured, Drilled Medium Foot – Crossbow
Mixed conscript close combat foot and crossbowmen	1 BG	8 bases of conscript close combat foot and crossbowmen: 4 Poor, Protected, Undrilled Medium Foot – Heavy Weapon, 4 Poor, Protected, Undrilled Medium Foot – Crossbow
Skirmishing crossbowmen	1 BG	6 bases of skirmishing crossbowmen: Average, Unprotected, Drilled Light Foot – Crossbow
Camp	1	Unfortified camp
Total	8 BGs	Camp, 16 mounted bases, 30 foot bases, 3 commanders

BUILDING A CUSTOMISED LIST USING OUR ARMY POINTS

Choose an army based on the maxima and minima in the list below. The following special instructions apply to this army:

- Commanders should be depicted as chariots or, from 307 BC, cavalry.
- A Chinese allied commander's contingent must conform to the Warring States to Western Han Chinese allies list below, but the troops in the contingent are deducted from the minima and maxima in the main list.
- The army must include at least as many Medium Foot crossbowmen bases as "close combat foot" bases.
- Medium Foot "close combat foot" and crossbowmen must all be in separately deployed BGs or all in mixed BGs.
- Drilled Cavalry can always dismount as Average, Armoured, Protected or Unprotected (as mounted type), Drilled, Medium Foot - Heavy Weapon.
- Minima marked * only apply before 200 BC or if any infantry bases are fielded. If no infantry are used, twice the normal maxima of non-chariot mounted bases may be fielded.
- If wuqiujiu armed with iron clubs are used, only the minimum number of chariots can be used.

Cavalry

WARRING STATES TO WESTERN HAN CHINESE

Territory Types: Western Han – Agricultural, Developed, Hilly, Tropical. Others – Agricultural, Developed, Hilly.

C-in-C		Inspired Commander/Field Commander/Troop Commander			80/50/35		1	
Sub-commanders		Field Commander				50	0–2	
		Troop Commander				35	0–3	
Chinese allied commanders	Only before 221 BC or from 209 to 202 BC	Field Commander/Troop Commander				40/25	0–3	

Troop name		Troop Type				Capabilities		Points per base	Bases per BG	Total bases
		Type	Armour	Quality	Training	Shooting	Close Combat			
Core Troops										
Chariots, *che*	Only before 209 BC	Heavy Chariots	–	Superior	Drilled	Crossbow	–	21	4–6	4–8
				Average				17		
	Only from 209 to 100 BC	Heavy Chariots	–	Average	Drilled	Crossbow	–	17	4–6	0–8
Cavalry		Cavalry	Armoured	Average	Drilled	Crossbow	Swordsmen	14	4–6	Before 209 BC 0–6, From 209 BC 4–12
			Protected					11		
			Unprotected					10		
		Cavalry	Armoured	Average	Drilled	–	Light Spear, Swordsmen	13	4–6	
			Protected					10		
			Unprotected					9		
Horse archers	Only Zhao or (from 200 BC) Han	Light Horse	Unprotected	Average	Drilled	Bow	–	8	4–6	0–12
	Others									0–6
Separately deployed close combat foot, *duanbing*		Medium Foot	Armoured	Average	Drilled	–	Heavy Weapon	10	6–8	*6–32
			Protected					8		
Mixed BGs of close combat foot and crossbowmen		Medium Foot	Armoured	Average	Drilled	–	Heavy Weapon	10	1/2 6–8	
			Protected					8		
		Medium Foot	Armoured	Average	Drilled	Crossbow	–	9	1/2	*6–32
			Protected					7		
Separately deployed crossbowmen, *nu*		Medium Foot	Protected	Average	Drilled	Crossbow	–	7	6–8	
Conscript close combat foot, *duanbing*		Medium Foot	Protected	Poor	Drilled	–	Heavy Weapon	6	8–10	0–32
					Undrilled			5		
Mixed BGs of conscript close combat foot and crossbowmen		Medium Foot	Protected	Poor	Drilled	–	Heavy Weapon	6	1/2 8–10	
					Undrilled			5		
		Medium Foot	Protected	Poor	Drilled	Crossbow	–	5	1/2	0 32
					Undrilled			4		
Conscript crossbowmen, *nu*		Medium Foot	Protected	Poor	Drilled	Crossbow	–	5	8–10	
					Undrilled			4		
Skirmishing crossbowmen, *nu*		Light Foot	Unprotected	Average	Drilled	Crossbow	–	5	6–8	0–12
Optional Troops										
Spearmen with long spears, *mao*		Medium Foot	Armoured	Average	Drilled	–	Offensive Spearmen	10	6–8	0–8
			Protected					8		
Spearmen with short spears, *yan*		Medium Foot	Armoured	Average	Drilled	–	Light Spear, Swordsmen	9	6–8	0–8
			Protected					7		
Swordsmen		Medium Foot	Armoured	Average	Drilled	–	Swordsmen	9	6–8	0–8
			Protected					7		
Wuqiujiu armed with iron clubs	Only Zhongshan	Medium Foot	Armoured	Superior	Drilled	–	Heavy Weapon	13	4–6	0–6
Convicts, prisoners of war		Mob	–	Poor	Undrilled	–	–	2	10–12	0–24
Large stand–mounted crossbows		Light Artillery	–	Average	Drilled	Light Artillery	–	17	2	0–4
Tribal allies	Only before 200 BC	Medium Foot	Protected	Average	Undrilled	–	Impact Foot, Swordsmen	7	6–8	0–16
	Only Qin, Wei or Yan from 300 BC	Light Horse	Unprotected	Average	Undrilled	Bow	Swordsmen	10	4–6	0–12
	Only Han from 200 BC	Cavalry	Protected	Average	Undrilled	Bow	Swordsmen	11	4–6	0–12
			Unprotected					10		
		Light Horse	Unprotected	Average	Undrilled	Bow	Swordsmen	10	4–6	
		Medium Foot	Protected	Average	Undrilled	–	Light Spear, Swordsmen	6	6–8	

Chevaux-de-frise, caltrops, placed spears, light carts and similar to cover half the bases of any non-tribal non-LF infantry BG	Portable Defences						3		Any
Carts, wagons and similar used as field defences	Field Fortifications						3		0–24
Fortified Camp							24		0–1
Special Campaigns									
Only Qin before 221 BC									
Replace all Average quality Medium Foot close combat foot and crossbowmen with	Separately deployed close combat foot, *duanbing*	Medium Foot	Protected / Unprotected	Average	Undrilled	—	Impact Foot, Swordsmen	7 / 6	6–8	6–32
	Mixed BGs of close combat foot and crossbowmen	Medium Foot	Protected / Unprotected	Average	Undrilled	—	Impact Foot, Swordsmen	7 / 6	1/2, 6–8	All/0
		Medium Foot	Protected / Unprotected	Average	Undrilled	Crossbow	—	6 / 5	1/2, 6–32	
	Separately deployed crossbowmen, *nu*	Medium Foot	Protected / Unprotected	Average	Undrilled	Crossbow	—	6 / 5	6–8	6–32

Western Han infantry, by Michael Perry. Taken from Men-at-Arms 284:
Imperial Chinese Armies (1): 200 BC–AD 589.

WARRING STATES TO WESTERN HAN CHINESE ALLIES

Allied commander		Field Commander/Troop Commander						40/25		1	
Troop name		Troop Type				Capabilities		Points per base	Bases per BG	Total bases	
		Type	Armour	Quality	Training	Shooting	Close Combat				
Chariots *che*	Before 209 BC	Heavy Chariots	–	Superior	Drilled	Crossbow	–	21	4	0–4	
				Average				17			
	From 209 BC to 100 BC	Heavy Chariots	–	Average	Drilled	Crossbow	–	17			
Cavalry		Cavalry	Armoured	Average	Drilled	Crossbow	Swordsmen	14	4–6	Before 209 BC 0–4, From 209 BC 4–6	
			Protected					11			
			Unprotected					10			
		Cavalry	Armoured	Average	Drilled	–	Light Spear, Swordsmen	13	4–6		
			Protected					10			
			Unprotected					9			
Horse archers	Zhao or from 200 BC Han	Light Horse	Unprotected	Average	Drilled	Bow	–	8	4–6	0–6	
	Others									0–4	
Separately deployed close combat foot, *duanbing*		Medium Foot	Armoured	Average	Drilled	–	Heavy Weapon	10	6–8	*6–18	
			Protected					8			
Mixed BGs of close combat foot and crossbowmen		Medium Foot	Armoured	Average	Drilled	–	Heavy Weapon	10	1/2	6–8	
			Protected					8			
		Medium Foot	Armoured	Average	Drilled	Crossbow	–	9	1/2	*6–18	
			Protected					7			
Separately deployed crossbowmen, *nu*		Medium Foot	Protected	Average	Drilled	Crossbow	–	7	6–8		
Conscript close combat foot, *duanbing*		Medium Foot	Protected	Poor	Drilled	–	Heavy Weapon	6	6–8	0–16	
					Undrilled			5			
Mixed BGs of Conscript close combat foot and crossbowmen		Medium Foot	Protected	Poor	Drilled	–	Heavy Weapon	6	1/2	6–8	
					Undrilled			5			
		Medium Foot	Protected	Poor	Drilled	Crossbow	–	5	1/2	0–16	
					Undrilled			4			
Conscript crossbowmen, *nu*		Medium Foot	Protected	Poor	Drilled	Crossbow	–	5	6–8		
					Undrilled			4			
Skirmishing crossbowmen, *nu*		Light Foot	Unprotected	Average	Drilled	Crossbow	–	5	6	0–6	

Han chariot, by Michael Perry. Taken from Men-at-Arms 284:
Imperial Chinese Armies (1): 200 BC–AD 589.

QIANG AND DI

The Qiang and Di were loosely allied groups of tribes from the north western borders of China who were a source of irritation to the various regimes in China, resulting in numerous retaliatory expeditions. The degree of the threat was such that under the Western Han one senior general proposed that, in order to reduce the cost of repeated actions against the Qiang, self supporting military colonies should be set up on the borders. However, this policy was not favoured by the Emperor and the colonies were not created. As well as fighting against the Chinese, they often supplied auxiliaries for Chinese campaigns, sometimes against other Qiang or Di tribes. It is possible that the Qiang were the ancestors of the later Tibetans, but this is uncertain. The largest Qiang and Di armies were alliances of many tribes.

Rather surprisingly, during the Northern Dynasties period a Di founded state, the Former Qin (351 AD–394 AD), actually managed to briefly unite the whole of the north in 376 AD. However, an ill-advised attempt to conquer

Levy Foot

the Eastern Jin, in the south, ended in disaster at the Battle of Fei River (383 AD), resulting in the rapid disintegration of the state into two successors.

This list covers Qiang and Di armies from their first appearance in Chinese accounts around 300 BC until their final rebellions against the Western Wei around 550 AD.

TROOP TYPES

There are few descriptions of Qiang and Di warriors. We know little other than that there were cavalry and infantry, that they were equipped with bows, spears, swords, short knives and armour, and that their cavalry appear to have been the best troops. Despite their often large numbers, Qiang and Di are described as being easily scattered. The only pictorial evidence thought to represent Qiang/Di close fighting foot shows most of them with sword and long shield, although some carry pole-arms. We treat them as having Light Spear, Swordsmen capability. Warrior battle groups rated as Armoured are those with a substantial proportion of metal-armoured men.

Although it is far from clear, we assume that the cavalry were heavily influenced by their nomad neighbours and so they are classified in the same way.

The Former Qin levied large numbers of Chinese infantry in the same way that some Northern Dynasties did, and some Chinese cavalry were also raised. The Chinese troops were of poor quality and it was their pitiful performance that lost the Fei River battle. The Qiang ruled Later Qin (384–417 AD) was a successor state to the Former Qin and it is likely they also used Chinese troops.

QIANG OR DI STARTER ARMY (AFTER 300 AD)		
Commander-in-Chief	1	Troop Commander
Sub-commanders	2	2 x Troop Commander
Cataphracts	2 BGs	Each comprising 4 bases of cataphracts: Superior, Heavily Armoured, Undrilled Cataphracts – Lancers, Swordsmen
Horse archers	4 BGs	Each comprising 4 bases of horse archers: Average, Unprotected, Undrilled Light Horse – Bow, Swordsmen
Warriors	3 BGs	Each comprising 6 bases of warriors: Average, Protected, Undrilled Medium Foot – Light Spear, Swordsmen
Foot archers	2 BGs	Each comprising 8 bases of foot archers: Average, Unprotected, Undrilled Light Foot – Bow
Camp	1	Unfortified camp
Total	11 BGs	Camp, 24 mounted bases, 34 foot bases, 3 commanders

BUILDING A CUSTOMISED LIST USING OUR ARMY POINTS

Choose an army based on the maxima and minima in the list below. The following special instructions apply to this army:

- Commanders should be depicted as cavalry.

- A Qiang or Di allied commander's contingent must conform to the Qiang and Di allies list below, but the troops in the contingent are deducted from the minima and maxima in the main list.
- The minimum marked * is reduced to 8 if troops marked ** are used.

QIANG AND DI

Territory Types: Former Qin or Later Qin – Agricultural, Developed, Hilly, Steppe. Others – Agricultural, Hilly, Mountains.

C-in-C		Inspired Commander/Field Commander/Troop Commander					80/50/35		1	
Sub-commanders		Field Commander					50		0–2	
		Troop Commander					35		0–2	
Qiang or Di allied commanders		Field Commander/Troop Commander					40/25		0–3	

Troop name		Troop Type				Capabilities		Points per base	Bases per BG	Total bases	
		Type	Armour	Quality	Training	Shooting	Close Combat				
Core Troops											
Cavalry	From 300 AD	Cataphracts	Heavily Armoured	Superior	Undrilled	–	Lancers, Swordsmen	18	4–6	0–8	6–24
		Cavalry	Armoured	Superior	Undrilled	–	Lancers, Swordsmen	16	4–6		
	Any date	Cavalry	Armoured	Superior	Undrilled	Bow	Swordsmen	18	4–6	6–24	
		Cavalry	Protected	Superior	Undrilled	Bow	Swordsmen	14	4–6		
		Cavalry	Protected	Average	Undrilled	Bow	Swordsmen	11	4–6	0–24	
			Unprotected					10			
		Light Horse	Unprotected	Average	Undrilled	Bow	Swordsmen	10	4–6		
Warriors		Medium Foot	Protected	Average	Undrilled	–	Light Spear, Swordsmen	6	6–10	*18–120	
		Medium Foot	Armoured	Average	Undrilled	–	Light Spear, Swordsmen	8	6–8	0–18	
Archers		Medium Foot	Unprotected	Average	Undrilled	Bow	–	5	6–8	6–24	
		Light Foot	Unprotected	Average	Undrilled	Bow	–	5	6–8		
Optional Troops											
Javelinmen		Light Foot	Unprotected	Average	Undrilled	Javelins	Light Spear	4	6–8	0–12	
Fortified camp								24		0–1	
Allies											
Chinese Rebel allies (Only from 184 AD to 214 AD) – Three Kingdoms to Southern Dynasties Chinese											
Xiongnu or Xianbei allies – Early Horse Nomads											
Special Campaigns											
Former Qin from 351 AD to 385 AD and Later Qin from 384 AD to 417 AD											
Levy foot with halberds, ji		Medium Foot	Protected	Poor	Undrilled	–	Heavy Weapon	5	8–10	**8–48	
Levy archers or crossbowmen		Medium Foot	Protected	Poor	Undrilled	Bow	–	4	6–8	0–16	**6–16
			Unprotected					3			
		Medium Foot	Protected	Poor	Undrilled	Crossbow	–	4	6–8	0–8	
			Unprotected					3			
Skirmishing archers		Light Foot	Unprotected	Poor	Undrilled	Bow	–	3	6–8	0–12	
Chinese cavalry		Cavalry	Armoured	Average	Undrilled		Lancers, Swordsmen	12	4–6	0–8	

QIANG AND DI ALLIES

Allied commander			Field Commander/Troop Commander				40/25		1	
Troop name		**Troop Type**				**Capabilities**		**Points per base**	**Bases per BG**	**Total bases**
		Type	Armour	Quality	Training	Shooting	Close Combat			
Cavalry	From 300 AD	Cataphracts	Heavily Armoured	Superior	Undrilled	—	Lancers, Swordsmen	18	4	0–4
		Cavalry	Armoured	Superior	Undrilled	—	Lancers, Swordsmen	16	4	
	Any date	Cavalry	Armoured	Superior	Undrilled	Bow	Swordsmen	18	4	0–12
		Cavalry	Protected	Superior	Undrilled	Bow	Swordsmen	14	4	
		Cavalry	Protected	Average	Undrilled	Bow	Swordsmen	11	4–6	0–12
			Unprotected					10		
		Light Horse	Unprotected	Average	Undrilled	Bow	Swordsmen	10	4–6	
Warriors		Medium Foot	Protected	Average	Undrilled	—	Light Spear, Swordsmen	6	6–10	8–40
		Medium Foot	Armoured	Average	Undrilled	—	Light Spear, Swordsmen	8	6–8	0–8
Archers		Medium Foot	Unprotected	Average	Undrilled	Bow	—	5	6–8	6–12
		Light Foot	Unprotected	Average	Undrilled	Bow	—	5	6–8	

THREE KINGDOMS KOREAN

This list covers Korean armies of the Three Kingdoms period.

SHILLA

Shilla evolved from a walled town called Saro, remaining a small city-state until the reign of King Naemul in 356 AD. He was credited as the ruler who first consolidated Shilla as a large confederated kingdom. This kingdom grew out of a confederation of twelve Chin-Han or Jinhan walled towns located south of the Han River in the eastern region of the peninsula.

By the 600s, Shilla controlled two-thirds of southern Korea and in an alliance with Tang China, destroyed the Koguryo dynasty. Next, in a remarkable feat of diplomatic fervour, Shilla was able to unite the defeated Paekche and Koguryo forces and prevent Tang China from colonising Korea again.

Shilla was initially disorganized and was dominated by Paekche and Koguryo. Through adept diplomacy and alliances, it was able to maintain a stalemate with the other Korean kingdoms. After 670 a period known as Unified Shilla existed. Unified Shilla fought numerous battles against Tang China, peasant revolts and disaffected nobles from the defeated regions of Koguryo and Paekche. Unified Shilla was eventually defeated by Koryo in 935.

The *Hwarang* were nobles' sons trained in military schools. We include them amongst the guard cavalry, regular cavalry or horse archers

The list covers Shilla armies from 57 BC to 935 AD.

KOGURYO

Koguryo was the strongest and richest of the original Korean kingdoms. As the most northerly of the kingdoms it had an extensive border with both China and Manchuria, and suffered numerous invasions by the dominant powers from those regions. It was able to hire numerous nomadic tribes as mercenaries or enlist entire tribes as allies. The use of entire nomadic tribes as

allies occurred mainly before 400 AD. Mercenaries were used throughout the era.

The successor state of Parhae was created in 698 by old Koguryo nobles with an infusion of Manchurian nobles from territory Koguryo previously controlled.

The successor state of Lesser Koguryo, also called Later Koguryo, was founded by exile nobles and supported by the Tang Chinese. This successor kingdom lasted from 698 until 733. An even later Neo-Koguryo was founded in 901 and became Koryo. Its armies can be found in the Koryo list.

The list covers Koguryo armies from 37 BC to 668 AD and Lesser Koguryo armies from 698 to 733.

PAEKCHE

Located in the south-western section of the peninsula, Paekche was formed by four distinct groups of people. These included the Puyo nobility who had migrated south from Buyeo, local tribes from Ma-Han, Chinese who remained after the downfall of the Han commanderies of Nang-rang and Dae-bang, and Japanese immigrants. Fifty-four small walled towns formed the core of the Paekche population. These towns were grouped together under the control of eight clans.

In the early years they often fought the commanderies and the Shilla, but their main enemy was Koguryo. Because of this, at different times they maintained alliances with both the Shilla and Japan. Paekche's height of power in the 300s AD was marked by an independent twenty year campaign in Japan. As late as 890, a Later-Paekche (Neo-Paekche) faction was formed by Paekche families in southwest Korea but was soon crushed.

The list covers Paekche armies from 18 BC to 660 AD.

KAYA

The Kaya confederation was the smallest of the rival states during the Three Kingdoms era. The confederation was located in the extreme south of Korea, which allowed many of the inhabitants to easily emigrate to Japan when political situations were bad. This confederation of six Pyon-Han tribes formed the 14 walled towns of Bye-on-han. Smaller than the other city-states, they actually maintained good relations with the Japanese. Kaya was the poorest and weakest of Korean kingdoms and often acted as an alliance balance among the other kingdoms. There is some evidence that it was temporarily dominated by the Japanese for a short period of time.

Kaya had a very small warrior class with fewer full time foot soldiers. Noble families and their factions were dominant only in a particular town. They were allied at various times with the Paekche, Shilla and Japanese.

This list covers Kaya armies from 40 AD to 560 AD.

TROOP NOTES

Guards battle groups represent a combination of clan nobles and professional warriors loyal to a particular commander.

Korean heavy cavalry charged with lance. Although they carried bows, they did not make much use of them while mounted.

"Spearmen" used a mixture of conventional spears, halberds similar to the Chinese ji, and tridents. We classify the mixture as Heavy Weapon. They were shieldless but provincial "spearmen" and archers wore armour under their outer garments.

KOGURYO KOREAN STARTER ARMY (AFTER 300 AD)

Commander-in-Chief	1	Field Commander
Sub-commanders	2	2 x Troop Commander
Guard cavalry	2 BGs	Each comprising 4 bases of guard cavalry: Superior, Heavily Armoured, Drilled Cataphracts – Lancers, Swordsmen
Regular cavalry	1 BG	4 bases of regular cavalry: Average, Armoured, Drilled Cavalry – Lancers, Swordsmen
Nomad mercenary cavalry	2 BGs	Each comprising 4 bases of nomad mercenary cavalry: Average, Unprotected, Undrilled Light Horse – Bow, Swordsmen
Provincial "spearmen" and archers in mixed battle groups	2 BGs	Each comprising 8 bases of provincial "spearmen" and archers in mixed battle groups: 4 Average, Protected, Drilled Medium Foot – Heavy Weapon, 4 Average, Protected, Drilled Medium Foot – Bow
Levy "spearmen" and archers	1 BG	10 bases of levy "spearmen" and archers: 5 Poor, Unprotected, Undrilled Medium Foot – Heavy Weapon, 5 Poor, Unprotected, Undrilled Medium Foot – Bow
Levy skirmishing archers	1 BG	8 bases of levy skirmishing archers: Poor, Unprotected, Drilled Light Foot – Bow
Camp	1	Unfortified camp
Total	9 BGs	Camp, 20 mounted bases, 34 foot bases, 3 commanders

BUILDING A CUSTOMISED LIST USING OUR ARMY POINTS

Choose an army based on the maxima and minima in the list below. The following special instructions apply to this army:

- Commanders should be depicted as guard or nobles.
- Guard cavalry must all be classified the same.
- The number of battle groups of nobles and retainers must be equal.
- The total number of bases of provincial foot in the army cannot exceed the total number of bases of levy foot by more than 50%.
- Provincial mixed battle groups can be half "spearmen", half archers or half "spearmen", half crossbowmen.
- The total number of bases of provincial "spearmen" in the army cannot exceed the total number of provincial archers and crossbowmen.
- The total number of bases of provincial

Medium Foot crossbowmen in the army cannot exceed the number of bases of provincial Medium Foot archers.

- Apart from Kayan allied contingents in a Kayan army, only one allied contingent can be used.

ONLY SHILLA

- Before 400 AD minima marked * do not apply, and all mounted troops maxima are halved.
- Before 400 AD at least half the bases of foot in the army (excluding allies) must be Poor.

ONLY PAEKCHE

- Before 400 AD minima marked * do not apply, and all mounted troops maxima are halved.

ONLY KAYA

- Before 400 AD minima marked * do not apply, and all mounted troops maxima are halved.

- The army can include up to two Kayan allied contingents. These must conform to the Three Kingdoms allies list below, but the troops in the contingent are deducted from the minima and maxima in the main list.

THREE KINGDOMS KOREAN

Territory Types: Developed, Hilly, Woodlands. All except Koguryo: Mountains.

C-in-C		Inspired Commander/Field Commander/Troop Commander						80/50/35		1	
Sub-commanders		Field Commander						50		0–2	
		Troop Commander						35		0–3	
Troop name		**Troop Type**				**Capabilities**		**Points per base**	**Bases per BG**	**Total bases**	
		Type	Armour	Quality	Training	Shooting	Close Combat				
Core Troops											
Guard cavalry	Any date	Cavalry	Armoured	Superior	Drilled	–	Lance, Swordsmen	17	4–6	*4–12	
	Only Koguryo from 300 or others from 400	Cataphracts	Heavily Armoured	Superior	Drilled	–	Lance Swordsmen	20	4–6		
Horse archers		Light Horse	Unprotected	Average	Drilled	Bow	–	8	4–6	0–12	
Nobles		Cavalry	Armoured	Superior	Undrilled	–	Lancers, Swordsmen	16	4–6	0–8	
Retainers		Cavalry	Protected	Average	Undrilled	–	Light Spear, Swordsmen	9	4–6	0–12	*8–36
Regular cavalry	Only Shilla from 600 or Koguryo	Cavalry	Armoured	Superior	Drilled	–	Lancers, Swordsmen	17	4–6	0–6	
	Only Shilla or Koguryo	Cavalry	Armoured / Protected	Average	Drilled	–	Lancers, Swordsmen	13 / 10	4–6	*4–12	
Nomad mercenary cavalry	Only Shilla or Koguryo	Light Horse	Unprotected	Average	Undrilled	Bow	Swordsmen	10	4–6	0–8	
		Cavalry	Unprotected / Protected	Average	Undrilled	Bow	Swordsmen	10 / 11	4–6		
Paekche or Koguryo exiles	Only Shilla from 670	Cavalry	Armoured	Superior	Undrilled	–	Lancers, Swordsmen	16	4–6	0–8	
Separately deployed provincial "spearmen"		Medium Foot	Protected	Average	Drilled	–	Heavy Weapon	8	6–8	6–36	
Provincial "spearmen" in mixed battle groups		Medium Foot	Protected	Average	Drilled	–	Heavy Weapon	8	1/2		
Provincial archers in mixed battle groups		Medium Foot	Protected	Average	Drilled	Bow	–	7	1/2	6–8	
Provincial crossbowmen in mixed battle groups		Medium Foot	Protected	Average	Drilled	Crossbow	–	7			6–36
Separately deployed provincial archers		Medium Foot	Protected	Average	Drilled	Bow	–	7	6–8		
Separately deployed provincial crossbowmen		Medium Foot	Protected	Average	Drilled	Crossbow	–	7	6–8		
Levy "spearmen"		Medium Foot	Unprotected	Poor	Undrilled	–	Heavy Weapon	4	1/2	8–10	10–96
Levy archers		Medium Foot	Unprotected	Poor	Undrilled	Bow	–	3	1/2		
Optional Troops											
Provincial skirmishing archers		Light Foot	Unprotected	Average	Drilled	Bow	–	5	6–8	0–24	
Foot nomads	Only Koguryo	Light Foot	Unprotected	Average	Undrilled	Bow	–	5	6–8	0–8	
Levy skirmishing archers		Light Foot	Unprotected	Poor	Undrilled	Bow	–	3	6–8	0–8	
Field fortifications		Field Fortifications						3		0–24	

Allies
Only Shilla
Kaya allies (Only before 550) – Three Kingdoms Korean
Koguryo or Paekche allies (Only from 350 to 660) – Three Kingdoms Korean
Tang Chinese Allies (Only from 660 to 670) – Western Wei to Early Tang Chinese
Only Koguryo
Japanese Allies (Only from 660) – Kofun-Nara Japanese
Kaya, Paekche or Shilla allies (Only before 550) – Three Kingdoms Korean
Tang Chinese allies (Only from 700) – Western Wei to Early Tang Chinese
Manchurian Nomad allies (Only before 400) – Early Horse Nomad
Only Paekche
Kaya allies – Three Kingdoms Korean
Koguryo or Shilla Allies (Only from 375) – Three Kingdoms Korean
Japanese Allies (Only from 375) – Kofun-Nara Japanese
Only Kaya
Kaya allies – Three Kingdoms Korean (Up to 2 contingents)
Japanese Allies (Only from 375) – Kofun-Nara Japanese
Paekche allies – Three Kingdoms Korean
Shilla Allies (Only from 375) – Three Kingdoms Korean

THREE KINGDOMS KOREAN ALLIES

Allied commander		Field Commander/Troop Commander						40/25	1		
Troop name		**Troop Type**				**Capabilities**		Points per base	Bases per BG	Total bases	
		Type	Armour	Quality	Training	Shooting	Close Combat				
Guard cavalry	Any date	Cavalry	Armoured	Superior	Drilled	–	Lance, Swordsmen	17	4	0–4	*4– 12
	Only Koguryo from 300 or others from 400	Cataphracts	Heavily Armoured	Superior	Drilled	–	Lance Swordsmen	20	4		
Horse archers		Light Horse	Unprotected	Average	Drilled	Bow	Swordsmen	10	4	0–4	
Nobles		Cavalry	Armoured	Superior	Undrilled	–	Lancers, Swordsmen	16	4	0–4	
Retainers		Cavalry	Protected	Average	Undrilled	–	Light Spear, Swordsmen	9	4	0–4	
Regular cavalry	Only Shilla or Koguryo	Cavalry	Armoured	Average	Drilled	–	Lancers, Swordsmen	13	4	0–4	
			Protected					10			
Separately deployed provincial "spearmen"		Medium Foot	Protected	Average	Drilled	–	Heavy Weapon	8	6–8	6–12	
Provincial "spearmen" in mixed battle groups		Medium Foot	Protected	Average	Drilled	–	Heavy Weapon	8	1/2		
Provincial archers in mixed battle groups		Medium Foot	Protected	Average	Drilled	Bow	–	7	1/2	6–8	6–12
Provincial crossbowmen in mixed battle groups		Medium Foot	Protected	Average	Drilled	Crossbow	–	7			
Separately deployed provincial archers		Medium Foot	Protected	Average	Drilled	Bow	–	7	6–8		
Separately deployed provincial crossbowmen		Medium Foot	Protected	Average	Drilled	Crossbow	–	7	6–8		
Provincial skirmishing archers		Light Foot	Unprotected	Average	Drilled	Bow	–	5	6–8	0–8	
Levy "spearmen"		Medium Foot	Unprotected	Poor	Undrilled	–	Heavy Weapon	4	1/2	8– 10	0–24
Levy archers		Medium Foot	Unprotected	Poor	Undrilled	Bow	–	3	1/2		

EASTERN HAN CHINESE

This list covers Chinese armies following the re-establishment of the Han dynasty in the civil wars that followed the fall of Wang Mang in 23 AD. The Han is now conventionally called Eastern Han to distinguish it from the earlier Western Han. The names are based on the relative locations of the Imperial capital under the two regimes – first Chang'an and then the more eastern Luoyang.

Although the disruption at the end of the Western Han did not result in much loss of Chinese territory, the outlying portions of the empire such as the Gansu corridor and Tarim Basin were lost and it took the brilliant campaigns

Eastern Han Infantry, by Michael Perry. Taken from Men-at-Arms 284:
Imperial Chinese Armies (1): 200 BC–AD 589.

of Ban Zhao at the end of the 1st century to re-establish control. These pushed Chinese territory to the borders of the Kushan and Parthian empires with diplomatic and commercial contacts with both being established.

The western conquests proved to be the high point of the Eastern Han and subsequently the dynasty entered a slow decline. During the reign of the Emperor Ling (168–189) the Han state

Wuhuan guards

started to disintegrate with rebels and warlords holding real power, although the last Han Emperor was not deposed until 220. However, as the armies of the period following this collapse were different from those that went before, this list ends with the death of Emperor Ling.

TROOP NOTES

Cavalry continued to become more and more important during the period and was often the decisive arm, especially when fighting the elusive steppe nomads when once again wholly mounted armies were used. See the Troop Notes in the Warring States to Western Han Chinese list for an explanation of the Chinese Cavalry classifications.

The Chinese in this period started to conscript barbarian troops into units led by Chinese officers. These included Xiongnu and Wuhuan who would provide cavalry and this may have started the introduction of heavy horse archers into the Chinese army which was completed in the following period.

EASTERN HAN CHINESE STARTER ARMY		
Commander-in-Chief	1	Field Commander
Sub-commanders	2	2 x Troop Commander
Wuhuan guards	1 BG	4 bases of Wuhuan guards: Superior, Armoured, Drilled Cavalry – Bow, Swordsmen
Chinese cavalry	1 BG	4 bases of Chinese cavalry: Average, Armoured, Drilled Cavalry – Crossbow, Swordsmen
Chinese horse archers	2 BGs	Each comprising 4 bases of Chinese horse archers: Average, Unprotected, Drilled Light Horse – Bow
"The Footsoldiers" guard	1 BG	6 bases of "The Footsoldiers" guard: Superior, Armoured, Drilled Medium Foot – Heavy Weapon
Close combat foot	2 BGs	Each comprising 6 bases of close combat foot: Average, Armoured, Drilled Medium Foot – Heavy Weapon
Crossbowmen	2 BGs	Each comprising 6 bases of crossbowmen: Average, Protected, Drilled Medium Foot – Crossbow
Camp	1	Unfortified camp
Total	9 BGs	Camp, 16 mounted bases, 30 foot bases, 3 commanders

BUILDING A CUSTOMISED LIST USING OUR ARMY POINTS

Choose an army based on the maxima and minima in the list below. The following special instructions apply to this army:

Spearmen

- Commanders should be depicted as cavalry.
- Tribal ally foot cannot be used with any Tribal ally mounted.
- The army must include at least as many Medium Foot crossbowmen bases as "close combat foot" bases.
- Chinese Cavalry can always dismount as Average, Armoured or Protected (as mounted type), Drilled, Medium Foot – Heavy Weapon.
- The minimum marked * only applies if any infantry are used.

EASTERN HAN CHINESE									
Territory Types: Agricultural, Developed, Hilly, Tropical									
C-in-C	Inspired Commander/Field Commander/Troop Commander						80/50/35	1	
Sub-commanders	Field Commander						50	0–2	
	Troop Commander						35	0–3	
Troop name	Troop Type				Capabilities		Points per base	Bases per BG	Total bases
	Type	Armour	Quality	Training	Shooting	Close Combat			
Core Troops									
Chinese Cavalry	Cavalry	Armoured	Average	Drilled	Crossbow	Swordsmen	14	4–6	4–16
		Protected					11		
	Cavalry	Armoured	Average	Drilled	–	Light Spear, Swordsmen	13	4–6	
		Protected					10		
Chinese horse archers	Light Horse	Unprotected	Average	Drilled	Bow	–	8	4–6	0–16
Close combat foot armed mainly with halberds, ji	Medium Foot	Armoured	Average	Drilled	–	Heavy Weapon	10	6–8	0–32
		Protected					8		
Crossbowmen, nu	Medium Foot	Protected	Average	Drilled	Crossbow	–	7	6–8	0–32
Conscript close combat foot with halberds, ji	Medium Foot	Protected	Poor	Drilled	–	Heavy Weapon	6	6–8	0–32
				Undrilled			5		
Conscript crossbowmen, nu	Medium Foot	Protected	Poor	Drilled	Crossbow	–	5	6–8	0–32
				Undrilled			4		
Skirmishing crossbowmen, nu	Light Foot	Unprotected	Average	Drilled	Crossbow	–	5	6–8	0–12
Optional Troops									
Chang River regiment (*Changshui*) Wuhuan guards	Cavalry	Armoured	Superior	Drilled	Bow	Swordsmen	19	4	0–4
Elite cavalry (*yueji*) guards	Cavalry	Armoured	Superior	Drilled	Crossbow	Swordsmen	18	4	
Conscripted barbarian cavalry	Cavalry	Armoured	Average	Drilled	Bow	Swordsmen	15	4–6	0–8
		Protected					12		
"Archers Who Shoot at a Sound" (*shesheng*) guards	Medium Foot	Protected	Superior	Drilled	Crossbow	–	9	6	0–6
"The Footsoldiers" (*fubing*) guards	Medium Foot	Armoured	Superior	Drilled	–	Heavy Weapon	13	6	

*18–64 (applies to the combined Medium Foot core troops total)

Spearmen with long spears, *mao*	Medium Foot	Armoured	Average	Drilled	—	Offensive Spearmen	10	6–8	0–8
Spearmen with short spears, *yan*	Medium Foot	Armoured	Average	Drilled	—	Light Spear, Swordsmen	9	6–8	0–8
		Protected					7		
Swordsmen	Medium Foot	Armoured	Average	Drilled	—	Swordsmen	9	6–8	0–8
		Protected					7		
Convicts, prisoners of war	Mob	—	Poor	Undrilled	—	—	2	10–12	0–24
Bolt-shooters	Light Artillery	—	Average	Drilled	Light Artillery	—	17	2	0–4
Tribal allies	Medium Foot	Protected	Average	Undrilled	—	Impact Foot, Swordsmen	7	6–8	0–16
	Medium Foot	Protected	Average	Undrilled	—	Light Spear, Swordsmen	6	6–8	
	Cavalry	Protected	Average	Undrilled	Bow	Swordsmen	11	4–6	0–16
		Unprotected					10		
	Light Horse	Unprotected	Average	Undrilled	Bow	Swordsmen	10	4–6	
Carts, wagons and similar used as field defences	Field Fortifications						3		0–24
Fortified Camp							24		0–1

THREE KINGDOMS, WESTERN JIN AND SOUTHERN DYNASTIES CHINESE

This list covers Chinese armies from the effective collapse of the Eastern Han, through the following period of disunity until reunification by the Western Jin, and then the subsequent dynasties in the south of China following the fall of the Western Jin, until their final conquest by the Sui.

During the reign of the Emperor Ling (168–189) the Han state started to fall apart with rebels and warlords holding real power, although the last Han emperor Liu Xie was not deposed until 220. The subsequent period is known as the Three Kingdoms after the three major states that arose after the final fall of the Han – Wei (220–265), Shu Han (221–263) and Wu (229–280). Wei controlled the northern part of the Han state, Shu Han the western and Wu the south.

Before the establishment of the Three Kingdoms, armies covered by this list are those of the various regional warlords and the remnants of the central government forces. During this period

most warfare was concentrated in the north and north-west around the traditional heartlands of the Qin and Han dynasties. Warfare of the period has been romanticised by the great literary work "The Romance of the Three Kingdoms", however, as might be expected, the reality was somewhat more sordid and the registered population of China fell from approximately 50 million under the Eastern Han to 16 million under the Western Jin.

One development of the period was the military use of the wheelbarrow by the Shu Han chancellor Zhuge Liang.

Despite reunifying China, the Western Jin itself soon collapsed following another series of civil wars, known as the War of the Eight Princes (291–306), which so weakened the Western Jin that it could not repel invasions from nomadic peoples to the north, primarily the Xianbei. These soon started to set up their own states in northern China. However, the Jin managed to survive in

southern China thanks to the unsuitability of the terrain for the cavalry on which the northern armies heavily depended. They formed the Eastern Jin which was the first of a series of Southern Dynasties that ruled the south, and at times part of the north, until the Sui conquest of the last southern dynasty, Chen, in 589.

TROOP NOTES

Troop quality was very variable in this period with many troops being of poor quality. This was especially true of the Eastern Jin and other southern dynasties where the best troops were often those which had followed magnates from the north to escape the barbarian invasions or specially recruited troops such as the Northern Headquarters Troops.

Cavalry was now the dominant troop type although it was often in short supply, especially for southern states. Infantry had difficulty standing up to cavalry in the open and some southern armies were forced to rely on the use of wagons as fortifications and "fire bases" in a number of campaigns against northern cavalry based armies.

Crossbow use appears to have declined in this period with the bow having a revival.

At the start of the period, armies from the north-west had a reputation for being better quality and more used to war than other parts of China, probably because of continued fighting against barbarian invaders. They also used long spears as opposed to the more usual weapons.

"Dare to die" volunteer

SOUTHERN DYNASTIES CHINESE STARTER ARMY (AFTER 317 AD)		
Commander-in-Chief	1	Field Commander
Sub-commanders	2	2 x Troop Commander
Chinese heavy cavalry	2 BGs	4 bases of Chinese heavy cavalry: Superior, Heavily Armoured, Drilled Cataphracts – Lancers, Swordsmen
Chinese horse archers	1 BG	4 bases of Chinese horse archers: Average, Unprotected, Drilled Light Horse – Bow
Better quality close combat foot with halberds	2 BGs	Each comprising 8 bases of better quality close combat foot with halberds: Average, Protected, Drilled Medium Foot – Heavy Weapon
Other close combat foot with halberds	1 BG	10 bases of other close combat foot with halberds: Poor, Protected, Undrilled Medium Foot – Heavy Weapon
Better quality crossbowmen	1 BG	8 bases of better quality crossbowmen: Average, Protected, Drilled Medium Foot – Crossbow
Other crossbowmen	1 BG	6 bases of other crossbowmen: Poor, Protected, Undrilled Medium Foot – Crossbow
Skirmishing archers	1 BG	6 bases of skirmishing archers: Average, Unprotected, Drilled Light Foot – Bow
Camp	1	Unfortified camp
Total	9 BGs	Camp, 12 mounted bases, 46 foot bases, 3 commanders

Southern Dynasty troops, by Michael Perry. Taken from Men-at-Arms 284:
Imperial Chinese Armies (1): 200 BC–AD 589.

BUILDING A CUSTOMISED LIST USING OUR ARMY POINTS

Choose an army based on the maxima and minima in the list below. The following special instructions apply to this army:

- Commanders should be depicted as cavalry.
- A Chinese allied commander's contingent must conform to the Three Kingdoms, Western Jin and Southern Dynasties Chinese Allies list below, but the troops in the contingent are deducted from the minima and maxima in the main list.

45

THREE KINGDOMS, WESTERN JIN AND SOUTHERN DYNASTIES CHINESE

Territory Types: Western Jin – Agricultural, Developed, Hilly, Tropical. Wu, Southern Dynasties – Developed, Hilly, Tropical. Others – Agricultural, Developed, Hilly.

C-in-C		Inspired Commander/Field Commander/Troop Commander						80/50/35		1	
Sub-commanders		Field Commander						50		0–2	
		Troop Commander						35		0–3	
Chinese allied commanders		Field Commander/Troop Commander						40/25		0–2	

Troop name			Troop Type				Capabilities		Points per base	Bases per BG	Total bases	
			Type	Armour	Quality	Training	Shooting	Close Combat				
Core Troops												
Chinese heavy cavalry	Wu and Southern Dynasties	Any date	Cavalry	Armoured	Average	Drilled	Bow	Swordsmen	15	4–6	4–8	
					Superior				19			
		Only from 317	Cataphracts	Heavily Armoured	Average	Drilled	–	Lancers, Swordsmen	16	4–6		
					Superior				20			
	Other states & dynasties		Cavalry	Armoured	Average	Drilled	Bow	Swordsmen	15	4–6	4–12	
					Superior				19			
Chinese horse archers	Wu and Southern Dynasties		Light Horse	Unprotected	Average	Drilled	Bow	–	8	4–6	0–6	
	Other states & dynasties										4–12	
Better quality close combat foot armed mainly with halberds, ji			Medium Foot	Protected	Average	Drilled	–	Heavy Weapon	8	6–8	0–16	0–32
						Undrilled			7			
Better quality crossbowmen, nu			Medium Foot	Protected	Average	Drilled	Crossbow	–	7	6–8	0–12	
						Undrilled			6			
Better quality archers			Medium Foot	Protected	Average	Drilled	Bow	–	7	6–8	0–8	
						Undrilled			6			
Other close combat foot with halberds, ji			Medium Foot	Protected	Poor	Undrilled	–	Heavy Weapon	5	6–10	10–64	16–100
Other crossbowmen, nu			Medium Foot	Protected	Poor	Undrilled	Crossbow	–	4	6–8	6–48	
				Unprotected					3			
Other archers			Medium Foot	Protected	Poor	Undrilled	Bow	–	4	6–8	0–32	
				Unprotected					3			
Skirmishing crossbowmen, nu			Light Foot	Unprotected	Average	Undrilled	Crossbow	–	5	6–8	0–12	
Skirmishing archers			Light Foot	Unprotected	Average	Undrilled	Bow	–	5	6–8		
Optional Troops												
Spearmen with long spears, mao			Medium Foot	Protected	Average	Undrilled	–	Offensive Spearmen	7	6–8	0–8	
					Poor				5			
Spearmen with short spears, yun			Medium Foot	Protected	Average	Undrilled	–	Light Spear, Swordsmen	6	6–8		
					Poor				4			
"Dare to die" volunteers	"Double armour" troops		Medium Foot	Armoured	Average	Undrilled	–	Heavy Weapon	9	6–8	0–8	
	Others		Medium Foot	Protected	Average	Undrilled	–	Impact Foot, Swordsmen	7	6–8		
Swordsmen and archer units	Only Southern Dynasties from 420		Medium Foot	Protected	Average	Undrilled	–	Swordsmen	6	1/2 6–8	0–16	
			Medium Foot	Protected	Average	Undrilled	Bow	–	6	1/2		
			Medium Foot	Protected	Poor	Undrilled	–	Swordsmen	4	1/2 6–8		
			Medium Foot	Protected	Poor	Undrilled	Bow	–	4	1/2		
Bolt-shooters or light rope pulled stone-throwers			Light Artillery	–	Average	Drilled	Light Artillery	–	17	2	0–4	
Tribal auxiliaries	Any		Medium Foot	Protected	Average	Undrilled	–	Light Spear	5	6–8	0–16	0–16
	Any except Wu, Shu Han and Southern Dynasties		Cavalry	Protected	Average	Undrilled	Bow	Swordsmen	11	4–6	0–8	
				Unprotected					10			
			Light Horse	Unprotected	Average	Undrilled	Bow	Swordsmen	10	4–6		
	Only Wei, Shu Han, Western Jin and North-Western armies		Medium Foot	Protected	Average	Undrilled	–	Light Spear, Swordsmen	6	6–8	0–16	
	Only Wu, Shu Han or Southern Dynasties		Medium Foot	Protected	Average	Undrilled	–	Impact Foot, Swordsmen	7	6–8	0–16	

			Average	Undrilled	Crossbow		17	2–4	0–12
Carts and wagons manned by missile troops	Only Southern Dynasties	Battle Wagons	–	Poor	Undrilled	Crossbow	–	11		
Carts, wagons and similar used as field defences		Field Fortifications						3		0–24
Fortified Camp								24		0–1
Special Campaigns										
North–Western armies before 221										
Replace "close combat foot" with "long spear" armed infantry		Medium Foot	Protected	Average	Undrilled	–	Offensive Spearmen	7	6–8	All
Cannot use any troops restricted to named states other than "North–Western armies"										
Southern Dynasties (Liang) in 554										
Elephants		Elephants	–	Average	Undrilled	–	–	25	2	0–2
Allies										
Qiang or Di allies (only before 347, any but Wu) – Qiang and Di										
Xiongnu, Xianbei or Wuhuan allies (Only Wei or Western Jin) – Early Horse Nomad										

THREE KINGDOMS, WESTERN JIN AND SOUTHERN DYNASTIES CHINESE ALLIES

Allied commander			Field Commander/Troop Commander				40/25		1	
Troop name		**Troop Type**				**Capabilities**		**Points per base**	**Bases per BG**	**Total bases**
		Type	Armour	Quality	Training	Shooting	Close Combat			
Chinese heavy cavalry	Any date	Cavalry	Armoured	Average	Drilled	Bow	Swordsmen	15	4	0–4
				Superior				19		
	Only from 317	Cataphracts	Heavily Armoured	Average	Drilled	–	Lancers, Swordsmen	16	4	
				Superior				20		
Chinese horse archers		Light Horse	Unprotected	Average	Drilled	Bow	–	8	4	0–4
Better quality close combat foot armed mainly with halberds, ji		Medium Foot	Protected	Average	Drilled	–	Heavy Weapon	8	6–8	0–12
					Undrilled			7		
Better quality crossbowmen, nu		Medium Foot	Protected	Average	Drilled	Crossbow	–	7	6–8	0–8
					Undrilled			6		0–24
Better quality archers		Medium Foot	Protected	Average	Drilled	Bow	–	7	6–8	0–8
					Undrilled			6		
Other close combat foot with halberds, ji		Medium Foot	Protected	Poor	Undrilled	–	Heavy Weapon	5	6–8	0–16
Other crossbowmen, nu		Medium Foot	Protected	Poor	Undrilled	Crossbow	–	4	6–8	0–12
			Unprotected					3		8–24
Other archers		Medium Foot	Protected	Poor	Undrilled	Bow	–	4	6–8	0–8
			Unprotected					3		
Skirmishing crossbowmen, nu		Light Foot	Unprotected	Average	Undrilled	Crossbow	–	5	6–8	0–8
Skirmishing archers		Light Foot	Unprotected	Average	Undrilled	Bow	–	5	6–8	
Swordsmen and archer units	Only Southern Dynasties from 420	Medium Foot	Protected	Average	Undrilled	–	Swordsmen	6	1/2	6–8	0–8
		Medium Foot	Protected	Average	Undrilled	Bow		6	1/2		
		Medium Foot	Protected	Poor	Undrilled	–	Swordsmen	4	1/2	6–8	
		Medium Foot	Protected	Poor	Undrilled	Bow		4	1/2		

KOFUN-NARA JAPANESE

This list covers the Kofun period from 276 AD, through the *Taika* Great Reform edict of 646 which created the *ritsuriyo* army, a Chinese-style conscript army, until the removal of the capital to Heian in 794. This period saw great increases in the use of iron armour, the introduction of cavalry, the gradual consolidation of most of Japan under an Imperial dynasty based in the Yamato basin with the capital at Nara, and military interventions in Korea. Armies of 10–25,000 men were common in the early period, and may have risen to 100,000 by the end.

TROOP NOTES

The members and retainers of aristocratic clans called *uji* provided most of the troops, fighting as archers, some with iron *tanko* armour and large wooden *tate* shields, others as spearmen. The *yugei* "quiver-bearers" were a guards unit armed in the same style. The introduction of cavalry and lamellar *keiko* armour was probably inspired by changing military practices in Korea, and a large-scale immigration from the former Chinese commanderies in Korea in 408 may have contributed to the introduction of mounted archery. Cavalry are mentioned occasionally in the 5th century when there is even some evidence for Korean-style horse-armour, and became more common in the 6th.

Artillery is first mentioned in 618 when Koguryo presented some *o-yumi* bolt-shooters and stone-throwers captured from the Sui Chinese.

The Nara regime established a centralised administration and national militia army on the Chinese model, which was completed with the Taiho code of 702. A militia regiment *gundan* was created in each province, and provided drafts for the Jin battalions of expeditionary armies. Senior officers were local officials, junior officers commoners selected for 'skill with the bow and horse'. *Heishi* militiamen mostly fought as infantry with bow, long sword and dagger, and were issued with armour on campaign. Each squad of five had one pavise, and these were formed into a shield-wall, and some *heishi* fought with 3–4 metre spears, probably with the pavises in the front ranks, while others fought as cavalry.

Two men from each 50-man platoon used *o-yumi* stand-mounted crossbow-artillery, but whether they used one weapon between them or one each with assistance from others is unknown; so the proportion of *o-yumi* to infantry is uncertain, but could have been very high. The *o-yumi* was thought to be particularly effective against the Emishi.

Heishi could also be selected for service as *sakimori*, stationed in the south-west to protect against Chinese and Korean invasion, as *chinpei* in the north to fight the Emishi, or as guards in the capital.

Inspired Commander

Kofun empress-regent and troops, by Angus McBride. Taken from Elite 35: Early Samurai AD 200–1500.

KOFUN-NARA JAPANESE STARTER ARMY (AFTER 646)

Commander-in-Chief	1	Field Commander
Sub-commanders	2	2 x Troop Commander
Armoured horse archers	2 BGs	Each comprising 4 bases of armoured horse archers: Superior, Armoured, Undrilled Cavalry – Bow, Swordsmen
Emishi cavalry	1 BG	4 bases of Emishi cavalry: Superior, Armoured, Undrilled Cavalry – Bow, Swordsmen
Heishi, sakimori or chinpei	4 BGs	Each comprising 6 bases of heishi, sakimori or chinpei: 3 Average, Armoured, Drilled Medium Foot – Bow, Light Spear, 3 Average Armoured, Drilled Medium Foot – Bow
Levy or pacified Emishi foot archers	2 BGs	Each comprising 8 bases of levy or pacified Emishi foot archers: Poor, Unprotected, Undrilled Light Foot – Bow
Camp	1	Unfortified camp
Total	9 BGs	Camp, 12 mounted bases, 40 foot bases, 3 commanders

BUILDING A CUSTOMISED LIST USING OUR ARMY POINTS

Choose an army based on the maxima and minima in the list below. The following special instructions apply to this army:

- Commanders should be depicted as nobles.
- A Japanese allied commander's contingent must conform to the Kofun-Nara Japanese allies list below, but the troops in the contingent are deducted from the minima and maxima in the main list.

KOFUN-NARA JAPANESE

Territory Types: Agricultural, Developed, Hilly.

C-in-C		Inspired Commander/Field Commander/Troop Commander						80/50/35		1	
Sub-commanders		Field Commander						50		0–2	
		Troop Commander						35		0–3	
Japanese allied commanders	Only before 646	Field Commander/Troop Commander						40/25		0–2	

Troop name		Troop Type				Capabilities		Points per base	Bases per BG	Total bases
		Type	Armour	Quality	Training	Shooting	Close Combat			
Core Troops										
Nobles and retainers with bows behind standing shields	Only before 400	Medium Foot	Armoured	Superior	Undrilled	Bow	–	11	6–8	16–78
				Average				8		
Nobles and retainers with spears		Medium Foot	Protected	Superior	Undrilled	–	Offensive Spearmen	9	6–8	6–36
				Average				7		
Armoured horse archers	Only from 400	Cavalry	Armoured	Superior	Undrilled	Bow	Swordsman	18	4–6	4–8
Retainers with bows behind standing shields	Only from 400 to 645	Medium Foot	Armoured	Average	Undrilled	Bow	Light Spear	8	1/2 6–8	18–120
						Bow	–	8	1/2	
		Medium Foot	Armoured	Poor	Undrilled	Bow	Light Spear	6	1/2 6–8	
						Bow	–	6	1/2	
		Medium Foot	Protected	Average	Undrilled	Bow	Light Spear	6	1/2 6–8	
						Bow	–	6	1/2	
		Medium Foot	Protected	Poor	Undrilled	Bow	Light Spear	4	1/2 6–8	
						Bow	–	4	1/2	

Troop name		Type	Armour	Quality	Training	Shooting	Close Combat	Points per base	Bases per BG	Total bases
Heishi, sakimori or chinpei	Only from 646	Medium Foot	Armoured	Average	Drilled	Bow	Light Spear	9	1/2	6–8	18–96
						Bow	—	9	1/2		
		Medium Foot	Armoured	Poor	Drilled	Bow	Light Spear	7	1/2	6–8	
						Bow	—	7	1/2		
		Medium Foot	Protected	Average	Drilled	Bow	Light Spear	7	1/2	6–8	
						Bow	—	7	1/2		
		Medium Foot	Protected	Poor	Drilled	Bow	Light Spear	5	1/2	6–8	
						Bow	—	5	1/2		
Optional Troops											
Be or other levy archers, or pacified Emishi		Medium Foot	Unprotected	Poor	Undrilled	Bow	—	3		6–8	0–16
		Light Foot	Unprotected	Poor	Undrilled	Bow	—	3		6–8	
Yugei or other guard archers	Only from 500	Medium Foot	Armoured	Superior	Drilled	Bow	Swordsman	13		4	0–4
					Undrilled			12			
Emishi cavalry	Only from 646	Cavalry	Protected	Superior	Undrilled	Bow	Swordsmen	14		4	0–4
			Armoured					18			
Heishi sakimori or chinpei mounted archers	Only from 646	Cavalry	Protected	Average	Drilled	Bow	Swordsmen	12		4	0–4
Artillery oyumi	Only from 646	Light Artillery	—	Average	Drilled			17		2	0–2 per heishi, sakimoro or chinpei BG
Allies											
Kaya Korean allies (only before 562) – Three Kingdoms Korean											
Paekche Korean allies (only before 700) – Three Kingdoms Korean											

KOFUN-NARA JAPANESE ALLIES

Allied commander			Field Commander/Troop Commander					40/25		1	
Troop name		Troop Type				Capabilities		Points per base	Bases per BG	Total bases	
		Type	Armour	Quality	Training	Shooting	Close Combat				
Nobles and retainers with bows behind standing shields	Only before 400	Medium Foot	Armoured	Superior	Undrilled	Bow	—	11	6–8	6–18	
				Average				8			
Retainers with spears		Medium Foot	Protected	Superior	Undrilled	—	Offensive Speamen	9	6–8	0–8	
				Average				7			
Armoured horse archers	Only from 400	Cavalry	Armoured	Superior	Undrilled	Bow	Swordsman	18	4	0–4	
Retainers with bows behind standing shields	Only from 400 to 645	Medium Foot	Armoured	Average	Undrilled	Bow	Light Spear	8	1/2	6–8	6–24
						Bow	—	8	1/2		
		Medium Foot	Armoured	Poor	Undrilled	Bow	Light Spear	6	1/2	6–8	
						Bow	—	6	1/2		
		Medium Foot	Protected	Average	Undrilled	Bow	Light Spear	6	1/2	6–8	
						Bow	—	6	1/2		
		Medium Foot	Protected	Poor	Undrilled	Bow	Light Spear	4	1/2	6–8	
						Bow	—	4	1/2		
Heishi, sakimori or chinpei	Only from 646	Medium Foot	Armoured	Average	Drilled	Bow	Light Spear	9	1/2	6–8	6–24
						Bow	—	9	1/2		
		Medium Foot	Armoured	Poor	Drilled	Bow	Light Spear	7	1/2	6–8	
						Bow	—	7	1/2		
		Medium Foot	Protected	Average	Drilled	Bow	Light Spear	7	1/2	6–8	
						Bow	—	7	1/2		
		Medium Foot	Protected	Poor	Drilled	Bow	Light Spear	5	1/2	6–8	
						Bow	—	5	1/2		
Artillery oyumi	Only from 646	Light Artillery	—	Average	Drilled			17	2	0–2 per heishi, sakimoro or chinpei BG	

NORTHERN DYNASTIES CHINESE

This list covers Chinese armies from the foundation of the first barbarian ruled state in China in 304 – the Xiongnu ruled Han Zhao (304–329) – to the conquest of the Northern Qi (550–577) by the Northern Zhou. It does not, however, include the Western Wei and subsequent Northern Zhou regimes following the probable formation of a regular infantry system starting about 540 by the Western Wei state. Their armies and the later Sui dynasty that finally reunified all of China are included in the Western Wei to Early Tang Chinese list.

The period is often split into two parts, firstly the more chaotic Sixteen Kingdoms period from 304 to 439, during which time the north of China was only briefly united, and then the

Northern Dynasty archer and cavalryman, by Michael Perry. Taken from Men-at-Arms 284:
Imperial Chinese Armies (1): 200 BC–AD 589.

more stable Northern Dynasties period from the unification of north China in 439 by the Northern Wei (386–534) ruled by the Xianbei Tuoba clan. Despite its stability, the Northern Wei eventually split into two, the Eastern Wei (534–550) and Western Wei (534–556).

During the Sixteen Kingdoms period the northern dynasties often had the worst of the fighting with the southern dynasties – despite their apparent military superiority due to their large numbers of steppe-style cavalry. This was presumably because of the instability of the northern states. Following the unification by the Northern Wei the balance of power shifted sharply in favour of the north. From that time onwards the south was mostly on the defensive and its territorial extent was on the wane. Despite this, until the northern states developed an effective naval force, the south could not be conquered.

TROOP NOTES

The most important and effective part of Northern Dynasty armies were the cavalry provided by the ruling peoples of the Xianbei and, to a lesser extent, the Xiongnu. The foundation of the

Levy Crossbowmen

northern states coincided with the appearance of cataphract cavalry amongst the nomads, which itself may have been linked to the widespread adoption of the stirrup around the same time. Whether full cataphract equipment was ever universal is open to question and so the cavalry of these armies has the option to be either Heavily Armoured or Armoured.

At the same time that cataphract equipment became popular, heavy cavalry tactics appear to have become based around a decisive charge with the lance as opposed to initial shooting with bows prior to a charge. However, the Xianbei ruling the former Yan (337–370) state on one occasion in 352 used a large formation of armoured horse archers in conjunction with other bodies of lancer cavalry.

Although they were de-tribalised, the ruling nomadic peoples maintained, to a great degree, their traditional lifestyle whilst dominating north China. On this basis the majority of the cavalry is classified as Undrilled. However, a lesser number of Drilled cavalry are allowed to represent the guard troops based around the Imperial capital following the formation of the Northern Wei, whose Tuoba rulers often followed a policy of sinicisation.

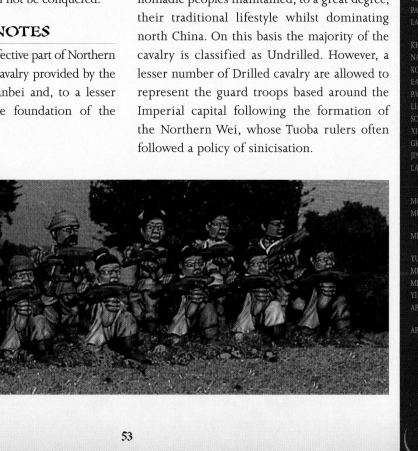

Occasionally auxiliaries were hired from the steppe to augment the cavalry forces. By the end of this period they would once again include armoured horse archers.

Infantry, although often raised in large numbers from amongst the Han Chinese subject people, was uniformly of a poor quality. One Xianbei leader stated "The troops under your command are Han. I fear they will be of no assistance." However, the northern states are recorded as fielding close formation Chinese spearmen, presumably developed as a way for the infantry to stand up to the otherwise dominant cavalry. Crossbow use appears to have been on an even smaller scale than the previous period.

"Pug nosed" archers are based on armoured archers with specific facial features, models of which have been found in tombs of the period. It is speculated that they represent troops of a better quality than the normal Chinese levies.

The continued existence of "Dare to die" or similar troops is speculative.

NORTHERN DYNASTIES CHINESE STARTER ARMY		
Commander-in-Chief	1	Field Commander
Sub-commanders	2	2 x Troop Commander
Heavy cavalry	1 BG	6 bases of heavy cavalry: Superior, Heavily Armoured, Undrilled Cataphracts – Lancers, Swordsmen
Heavy cavalry	2 BGs	Each comprising 4 bases of heavy cavalry: Superior, Armoured, Undrilled Cavalry – Lancers, Swordsmen
Light horse archers	1 BG	4 bases of light horse archers: Average, Unprotected, Undrilled Light Horse – Bow
Steppe auxiliaries	2 BGs	Each comprising 4 bases of steppe auxiliaries: Average, Unprotected, Undrilled Light Horse – Bow, Swordsmen
Levy foot with halberds	2 BGs	Each comprising 10 bases of levy foot with halberds: Poor, Protected, Undrilled Medium Foot – Heavy Weapon
Skirmishing archers	1 BG	8 bases of skirmishing archers: Poor, Unprotected, Undrilled Light Foot – Bow
Camp	1	Unfortified camp
Total	9 BGs	Camp, 26 mounted bases, 28 foot bases, 3 commanders

BUILDING A CUSTOMISED LIST USING OUR ARMY POINTS

Choose an army based on the maxima and minima in the list below. The following special instructions apply to this army:

- Commanders should be depicted as heavy or guard cavalry.

- The minimum marked * only applies if any non-allied infantry are used.
- A Chinese allied commander's contingent must conform to the Northern Dynasties Chinese allies list below, but the troops in the contingent are deducted from the minima and maxima in the main list.

NORTHERN DYNASTIES CHINESE

Territory Types: Agricultural, Developed, Hilly, Steppes

C-in-C	Inspired Commander/Field Commander/Troop Commander						80/50/35	1	
Sub-commanders	Field Commander						50	0–2	
	Troop Commander						35	0–3	
Chinese allied commander	Field Commander/Troop Commander						40/25	0–1	

Troop name	Troop Type				Capabilities		Points per base	Bases per BG	Total bases
	Type	Armour	Quality	Training	Shooting	Close Combat			
Core Troops									
Heavy cavalry	Cavalry	Armoured	Superior	Undrilled	–	Lancers, Swordsmen	16	4–6	8–36
			Average	Undrilled			12		
	Cataphracts	Heavily Armoured	Superior	Undrilled	–	Lancers, Swordsmen	18	4–6	
			Average				14		
Light horse archers	Light Horse	Unprotected	Average	Undrilled	Bow	–	8	4–6	0–12
Levy foot with halberds, ji	Medium Foot	Protected	Poor	Undrilled	–	Heavy Weapon	5	8–10	0–32 *16–48
Levy spearmen	Heavy Foot	Protected	Poor	Undrilled	–	Defensive Spearmen	4	8–10	0–48
Levy archers or crossbowmen	Medium Foot	Protected	Poor	Undrilled	Bow	–	4	6–8	0–16 0–16
		Unprotected					3		
	Medium Foot	Protected	Poor	Undrilled	Crossbow	–	4	6–8	0–8
		Unprotected					3		
Skirmishing archers	Light Foot	Unprotected	Poor	Undrilled	Bow	–	3	6–8	0–12
Optional Troops									
Guard cavalry	Only from 439	Cataphracts	Heavily Armoured	Superior	Drilled	–	Lancers, Swordsmen	20	4–6	0–8
		Cavalry	Armoured	Superior	Drilled	–	Lancers, Swordsmen	17	4–6	
Steppe auxiliaries	Only from 500	Cavalry	Armoured	Superior	Undrilled	Bow	Swordsmen	18	4–6	0–8
	Any date	Light Horse	Unprotected	Average	Undrilled	Bow	Swordsmen	10	4–6	
		Cavalry	Unprotected	Average	Undrilled	Bow	Swordsmen	10	4–6	
			Protected					11		
"Dare to die" volunteers or similar	"Double armour" troops	Medium Foot	Armoured	Average	Undrilled	–	Heavy Weapon	9	6–8	0–8
	Others	Medium Foot	Protected	Average	Undrilled	–	Impact Foot, Swordsmen	7	6–8	
"Pug–nosed" archers	Medium Foot	Protected	Average	Undrilled	Bow	–	6	6–8	0–12
Bolt-shooters or light rope pulled stone-throwers	Light Artillery	–	Average	Drilled	Light Artillery	–	17	2	0–4
Qiang or similar auxiliaries	Medium Foot	Protected	Average	Undrilled	–	Light Spear, Swordsmen	6	6–8	0–12
Fortified Camp							24		0–1
Allies									
Qiang or Di allies (Only Han Zhao and Former Zhao) – Qiang and Di									
Nomad allies – Early Horse Nomad (before 500) or Later Horse Nomad (from 500)									
Special Campaigns									
Only Former Yan in 352									
Armoured horse archers	Cavalry	Armoured	Superior	Undrilled	Bow	Swordsmen	18	4–6	8–18
			Average				14		

NORTHERN DYNASTIES CHINESE ALLIES

Allied commander	Field Commander/Troop Commander						40/25		1	
Troop name	**Troop Type**				**Capabilities**		**Points per base**	**Bases per BG**	**Total bases**	
	Type	Armour	Quality	Training	Shooting	Close Combat				
Heavy cavalry	Cavalry	Armoured	Superior	Undrilled	–	Lancers, Swordsmen	16	4–6	6–18	
			Average				12			
	Cataphracts	Heavily Armoured	Superior	Undrilled	–	Lancers, Swordsmen	18	4–6		
			Average				14			
Light horse archers	Light Horse	Unprotected	Average	Undrilled	Bow	–	8	4	0–4	
Levy foot with halberds, ji	Medium Foot	Protected	Poor	Undrilled	–	Heavy Weapon	5	8–10	0–16	*8–24
Levy spearmen	Heavy Foot	Protected	Poor	Undrilled	–	Defensive Spearmen	4	8–10	0–24	
Levy archers or crossbowmen	Medium Foot	Protected	Poor	Undrilled	Bow	–	4	6–8	0–8	
		Unprotected					3			
	Medium Foot	Protected	Poor	Undrilled	Crossbow	–	4	6–8		
		Unprotected					3			

LATER HINDU NORTH INDIAN

This list covers Hindu North Indian armies from the fall of the Gupta Empire in the mid-5th century AD until 1500. It does not cover the 5th and 6th century Kidarite and Hephthalite kingdoms, which have their own lists in Field of Glory Companion 5: *Legions Triumphant*.

The era following the fall of the Gupta Empire was a period of chaos, especially in the northern region of the sub-continent. For a brief period, the Vardhan Empire under Harsa provided some stability for most of the region. However, the fall of the Vardhan Empire resulted in more division

Bladesmen

of territory into a multitude of smaller city-states who were all vying for power.

Some consolidation occurred under the Rajputs and others, but many of these small countries would fall to incursions from the northwest. The effect of the Muslim invasions upon Indian culture would become permanent as the centuries passed.

VARDHAN (570–647)

Of the Vardhan kings, Harsha (606–647) is the best known as he expanded his rule over territories that stretched from Nepal in the north to the Narmada River in the south, up to Assam in the east and Malwa in the west. One of Harsha's strongest allies was Kamrupa in Assam. However, this extended realm did not survive Harsha's death in 647 and rapidly collapsed.

RAJPUTS

Rajasthan, located in the north-western region of India, was able to remain unchanged and was not dominated to any great extent by the early Indian empires. The Rajput clans flourished during the turmoil which followed the collapse of the Gupta Empire and Rajput ruled kingdoms start to appear from the middle of the 7th century. There are traditionally said to be 36 clans of the Rajputs including the Pratiharas, the Pariharas of Marwar, the Rathor clan of Pali-Jaipur, the Sisodias of Udaipur-Chittorgarh, the Kachhwahas of Jaipur, the Bhattis of Jaisalmer, the Solanki-Chalukya and the Chauhans of the Agnikula clan.

All Rajputs claimed to be descended from the *Kshatriya* class, the traditional military order of the Vedic people. The Rajputs were chronically unable to unite, and as they bore the brunt of the Muslim invasions of India, they tended to suffer greatly despite many acts of great heroism. When facing defeat the men would often ride to battle to die whilst the women would commit mass suicide, ritually throwing themselves onto funeral pyres. Despite repeated defeats, especially at the hands of the Ghaznavids, Ghurids and the Delhi Sultanate, they proved very resilient, re-establishing their kingdoms when they had the chance, and some kingdoms were still in existence to meet the Moghul invasion of the early 16th century. The Bhattis of Jaisalmer were unusual in that they lived in a remote citadel city in the Thar desert of the north west and occasionally used camels in warfare.

HINDU INDIAN CITY-STATES (500–1300)

In addition to the various Rajput kingdoms a number of other Hindu city-states existed through the period following the Guptas. These rose and fell in prominence over time and were eventually brought under the rule of the Delhi Sultanate. Some of the more powerful city-states covered in this list include:

Valabhi near Bhavnagar in Gujarat lasted until 770. The Ganga-Orissa dynasty came to power in about 1000 and lasted until the 1300s in eastern India just south of Bengal.

The Solanki-Chalukya was a Rajput dominated dynasty from Gujarat which lasted from the 942 until 1243.

The Palas expanded far beyond the normal extent of a city-state and created an extensive north Indian empire from 760 until the 1100s. It was finally conquered by the Sena Dynasty based in Bengal. The Sena domination of the Bengal region lasted from 1070 until 1230.

TROOP NOTES

Hindu military organization was based on traditional and often sacred sources. The bow appears to have been the chief infantry weapon. A smaller curved bow became popular in the later part of the medieval era. A wide variety of bladed weapons were also in use.

Rajput warriors were mainly horsemen. They were dressed in saffron robes. They were armed with spears, swords, bows and shields. They were supplemented in their armies by the usual foot warriors.

Elephant

RAJPUT STARTER ARMY

Commander-in-Chief	1	Troop Commander
Sub-commanders	2	2 x Troop Commander
Elephants	2 BGs	Each comprising 2 Elephants: Average, Undrilled Elephants
Cavalry	2 BGs	Each comprising 4 bases of cavalry: Superior, Armoured, Undrilled Cavalry – Lancers, Swordsmen
Cavalry	2 BGs	Each comprising 4 bases of cavalry: Superior, Protected, Undrilled Cavalry – Lancers, Swordsmen
Light cavalry	1 BG	4 bases of light cavalry: Average, Unprotected, Undrilled Light Horse – Javelins, Light Spear
Archers	2 BGs	Each comprising 8 bases of archers: Average, Unprotected, Undrilled Medium Foot – Bow
Bladesmen	1 BG	6 bases of bladesmen: Average, Unprotected, Undrilled Medium Foot – Swordsmen
Hill tribe skirmishers	1 BG	6 bases of hill tribe skirmishers: Average, Unprotected, Undrilled Light Foot – Bow
Camp	1	Unfortified camp
Total	11 BGs	Camp, 24 mounted bases, 28 foot bases, 3 commanders

BUILDING A CUSTOMISED LIST USING OUR ARMY POINTS

Choose an army based on the maxima and minima in the list below. The following special instructions apply to this army:

- Commanders should be depicted on elephants or as cavalry.
- An army must represent a specific state, at a specific date during the period of existence of that state.

LATER HINDU NORTH INDIAN

Territory Types: Bhatti Rajputs – Desert, Developed. Others – Agricultural, Hilly, Woodlands.

C-in-C		Inspired Commander/Field Commander/Troop Commander						80/50/35		1
Sub-commanders		Field Commander						50		0–2
		Troop Commander						35		0–3
Troop name		**Troop Type**				**Capabilities**		**Points per base**	**Bases per BG**	**Total bases**
		Type	Armour	Quality	Training	Shooting	Close Combat			
Core Troops										
Elephants		Elephants	–	Average	Undrilled	–	–	25	2	2–8
Cavalry	Only Rajputs	Cavalry	Armoured	Superior	Undrilled	–	Lancers, Swordsmen	16	4–6	0–20
		Cavalry	Protected	Superior	Undrilled	–	Lancers, Swordsmen	12	4–6	4–24
				Average				9		
	Only others	Cavalry	Armoured	Superior	Undrilled	–	Lancers, Swordsmen	16	4	0–4
		Cavalry	Armoured	Average	Undrilled	–	Lancers, Swordsmen	12	4–6	0–18
		Cavalry	Protected	Average	Undrilled	–	Lancers, Swordsmen	9	4–6	4–24
Archers		Medium Foot	Unprotected	Average	Undrilled	Bow	–	5	6–8	12–64
Bladesmen		Medium Foot	Unprotected	Average	Undrilled	–	Swordsmen	5	6–8	6–18
Peasants		Mob	Unprotected	Poor	Undrilled	–	–	2	10–12	0–24

Optional Troops										
Light cavalry		Light Horse	Unprotected	Average	Undrilled	Bow	—	8	4–6	
		Light Horse	Unprotected	Average	Undrilled	Javelins	Light Spear	7	4–6	0–6
Camelry	Only Bhatti Rajputs	Camelry	Protected	Average	Undrilled	—	Light Spear	9	4–6	
Javelinmen		Light Foot	Unprotected	Average	Undrilled	Javelins	Light Spear	4	6–8	0–24	0–24
Spearmen		Medium Foot	Protected	Average	Undrilled	—	Light Spear, Swordsmen	6	6–8	0–16
Forest or hill tribe skirmishers		Light Foot	Unprotected	Average	Undrilled	Bow	—	5	4–6	0–6
Kashmiri slingers		Light Foot	Unprotected	Average	Undrilled	Sling	—	4	4–6	
Allies										
Only Vardhan										
North Indian city-state allies – Later Hindu North Indian (Up to 2 contingents)										
Pandya–Tamil allies – Later Hindu South Indian										
Only Rajputs										
Rajput allies – Later Hindu North Indian (Up to 2 contingents)										
Only Others										
North Indian city-state allies – Later Hindu North Indian (Up to 2 contingents)										
Pandya–Tamil allies – Later Hindu South Indian										
Rajput allies – Later Hindu North Indian										

LATER HINDU NORTH INDIAN ALLIES

Allied commander		Field Commander/Troop Commander				40/25		1		
Troop name		**Troop Type**				**Capabilities**		**Points per base**	**Bases per BG**	**Total bases**
		Type	Armour	Quality	Training	Shooting	Close Combat			
Elephants		Elephants	—	Average	Undrilled	—	—	25	2	2
Cavalry	Only Rajputs	Cavalry	Armoured	Superior	Undrilled	—	Lancers, Swordsmen	16	4–6	0–8	4–8
		Cavalry	Protected	Superior	Undrilled	—	Lancers, Swordsmen	12	4–6	0–8
				Average				9		
	Only others	Cavalry	Armoured	Average	Undrilled	—	Lancers, Swordsmen	12	4–6	0–6
		Cavalry	Protected	Average	Undrilled	—	Lancers, Swordsmen	9	4–6	0–8
Archers		Medium Foot	Unprotected	Average	Undrilled	Bow	—	5	6–8	6–18
Bladesmen		Medium Foot	Unprotected	Average	Undrilled	—	Swordsmen	5	4–6	4–6
Javelinmen		Light Foot	Unprotected	Average	Undrilled	Javelins	Light Spear	4	6–8	0–8	0–8
Spearmen		Medium Foot	Protected	Average	Undrilled	—	Light Spear, Swordsmen	6	4–6	0–6
Peasants		Mob	Unprotected	Poor	Undrilled	—	—	2	6	0–6

LATER HINDU SOUTH INDIAN

This list covers Hindu South Indian armies from the mid-5th century AD until 1500. These are armies from the areas of India from the Deccan southwards, and also Sri Lanka, where it was difficult to raise horses and so infantry and elephants dominated the battlefield.

States include city-states of varying size and importance, the Pandyas, Pallavas, Hoysalas, Cholas Vijayanagar and the Sinhalese states in what is now Sri Lanka.

Elephant

CITY-STATES

Chalukya dominated the Deccan area of central and southern India. The Chalukyas established different dynasties based in different areas and periods of time. These Dynasties were the Early, Eastern and Western. The Early or Badami Chalukyas held power in northern Karnataka from 543 until 753. The Eastern Chalukya dynasty established power in Vengi in 624 and lasted until 1075. The Western or Kalyani Chalukyas' power lasted from 973 until 1189.

PANDYAS

The Pandyas were a Tamil kingdom in the south of India who enjoyed two major periods of power. Firstly from the mid-6th century until the mid-9th, when they were eclipsed by the rising Chola kingdom, and then from the mid-13th century as Chola waned until they were again eclipsed by the rise of the south Indian super-power of Vijayanagar.

PALLAVA KINGDOM

The Pallavas were another Tamil kingdom of South India. More minor than the Pandyas, they nevertheless ruled a significant area at the start of this period.

HOYSALA EMPIRE

The Hoysala Empire ruled in the Karnataka region of southern India from about 1100 to 1342 when they were absorbed by Vijayanagar. They were powerful enough to stand up to the Chola Empire and were allied with them on occasion, often against their great rivals the Pandyas, although they were usually the junior party in these alliances.

CHOLA EMPIRE

The Chola Empire dominated South India, and at times parts of Sri Lanka, from 985 to 1246. They had previously been a powerful state in the earlier Sangam age (roughly 300 BC to 300 AD), but had then declined, allowing others to dominate the area and them. They were restored to greatness in the reign of Rajaraja the Great (985–1014) and at its greatest extent their empire reached as far north as Bengal and the base of the Himalayas. They also held overseas territory in Indonesia, but their hold there was tenuous, and without direct intervention these lands fell away rapidly. Eventually their power was broken by the re-emergence of the Pandyas and they ultimately became a small part of the Vijayanagar Empire.

VIJAYANAGAR

The Vijayanagara Empire dominated the Deccan from 1336 until approximately 1660, with the last century being a period of weakened influence. It was founded by Harihara or Hakka, and his brother Bukka Raya. Its capital city was Vijayanagara, which they founded in 1336. For two centuries, the Vijayanagar Empire dominated all of southern India. The empire also acted as the main opponent to blunt the advances of the five main Muslim Sultanates from the north and fought a series of wars with the Bahmani Sultanate for control of the Deccan. The Empire reached its peak during the rule of Krishna Deva Raya in the early 16th century.

TROOP NOTES

Hindu military organization was based on traditional and often sacred sources. The bow appears to have been the chief infantry weapon. A smaller curved bow became popular in the later part of the medieval era. A wide variety of bladed weapons were also in use.

Southern Indian armies were always short of horses, often having to import them at vast cost only for them to die quickly due to the climate. This was compensated to some extent by the larger number of elephants available, but their armies remained infantry based for the most part. Vijayanagar was the partial exception, bringing in Muslim mercenary cavalry and also training some of its own cavalry in Muslim tactics.

The Chola Empire retained an effective and well-trained standing army which was expanded at times of war with short term soldiers.

Muslim Cavalry

LATER HINDU SOUTH INDIAN STARTER ARMY			
Commander-in-Chief	1	Troop Commander	
Sub-commanders	2	2 x Troop Commander	
Elephants	4 BGs	Each comprising 2 Elephants: Average, Undrilled Elephants	
Cavalry	2 BGs	Each comprising 4 bases of cavalry: Average, Protected, Undrilled Cavalry – Lancers, Swordsmen	
Archers	2 BGs	Each comprising 8 bases of archers: Average, Unprotected, Undrilled Medium Foot – Bow	
Bladesmen	1 BG	6 bases of bladesmen: Average, Unprotected, Undrilled Medium Foot – Swordsmen	
Spearmen	1 BG	8 bases of spearmen: Average, Protected, Undrilled Medium Foot – Light Spear, Swordsmen	
Javelinmen	2 BGs	Each comprising 8 bases of javelinmen: Average, Unprotected, Undrilled Light Foot – Javelins, Light Spear	
Camp	1	Unfortified camp	
Total	12 BGs	Camp, 16 mounted bases, 46 foot bases, 3 commanders	

BUILDING A CUSTOMISED LIST USING OUR ARMY POINTS

Choose an army based on the maxima and minima in the list below. The following special instructions apply to this army:

- Commanders should be depicted on elephants or as cavalry.
- An army must represent a specific state, at a specific date during the period of existence of that state.

LATER HINDU SOUTH INDIAN

Territory Types: Agricultural, Hilly, Tropical.

C-in-C		Inspired Commander/Field Commander/Troop Commander						80/50/35	1	
Sub-commanders		Field Commander						50	0–2	
		Troop Commander						35	0–3	
Troop name		Troop Type				Capabilities		Points per base	Bases per BG	Total bases
		Type	Armour	Quality	Training	Shooting	Close Combat			
Core Troops										
Elephants		Elephants	–	Average	Undrilled	–	–	25	2	4–12
Cavalry		Cavalry	Protected	Average	Undrilled	–	Lancers, Swordsmen	9	4–6	0–8
Archers	Any	Medium Foot	Unprotected	Average	Undrilled	Bow	–	5	6–8	0–100	16–100
	Only Chola Empire from 985 to 1246	Medium Foot	Unprotected	Average	Drilled	Bow	–	6	6–8	12–24
Sinhalese militia	Only Sinhalese	Medium Foot	Unprotected	Poor	Undrilled	Bow	–	3	8–10	16–60
Bladesmen	Any	Medium Foot	Unprotected	Average	Undrilled	–	Swordsmen	5	6–8	0–40	6–40
	Only Chola Empire from 985 to 1246	Medium Foot	Unprotected	Average	Drilled	–	Swordsmen	6	6–8	6–18
Peasants		Mob	Unprotected	Poor	Undrilled	–	–	2	8–12	0–20
Optional Troops										
Light cavalry	Only Vijayanagar	Light Horse	Unprotected	Average	Undrilled	Bow	–	8	4–6	0–6
		Light Horse	Unprotected	Average	Undrilled	Javelins	Light Spear	7	4–6	
Chariots	Only before 900	Light Chariots	–	Average	Undrilled	Bow	–	13	4	0–4
		Heavy Chariots	–	Average	Undrilled	Bow	–	16	4	
Javelinmen		Light Foot	Unprotected	Average	Undrilled	Javelins	Light Spear	4	6–8	0–24	0–24
Spearmen		Medium Foot	Protected	Average	Undrilled	–	Light Spear, Swordsmen	6	6–8	0–16
Forest or hill tribe skirmishers		Light Foot	Unprotected	Average	Undrilled	Bow	–	5	4–6	0–6
Muslim trained or mercenary horse	Only Vijayanagar from 1400	Cavalry	Armoured	Superior	Drilled	Bow	Swordsmen	19	4–6	0–8
				Average				15		
Rocket troops	Only Vijayanagar	Light Artillery	–	Average	Undrilled	Light Artillery	–	15	2	0–8
Bombards	Only Vijayanagar from 1470	Heavy Artillery	–	Average	Undrilled	Heavy Artillery	–	20	2	0–2
Allies										
Only Chola Empire										
Hoysala allies – Later Hindu South Indian										
Only Others										
North Indian city-state allies (Any except Sinhalese or Vijayanagar) – Later Hindu North Indian										
Pandya–Tamil allies – Later Hindu South Indian										
Rajput allies (Any except Sinhalese or Vijayanagar) – Later Hindu North Indian										

LATER HINDU SOUTH INDIAN ALLIES

Allied commander		Field Commander/Troop Commander					40/25		1	
Troop name		**Troop Type**				**Capabilities**		**Points per base**	**Bases per BG**	**Total bases**
		Type	Armour	Quality	Training	Shooting	Close Combat			
Elephants		Elephants	–	Average	Undrilled	–	–	25	2	2–4
Cavalry		Cavalry	Protected	Average	Undrilled	–	Lancers, Swordsmen	9	4	0–4
Archers	Any	Medium Foot	Unprotected	Average	Undrilled	Bow	–	5	6–8	0–32	6–32
	Only Chola Empire from 985 to 1246	Medium Foot	Unprotected	Average	Drilled	Bow	–	6	6–8	6–8
Sinhalese militia	Only Sinhalese	Medium Foot	Unprotected	Poor	Undrilled	Bow	–	3	8–10	6–30
Bladesmen	Any,	Medium Foot	Unprotected	Average	Undrilled	–	Swordsmen	5	6–8	0–12	4–12
	Only Chola Empire from 985 to 1246	Medium Foot	Unprotected	Average	Drilled	–	Swordsmen	6	4–6	4–6
Javelinmen		Light Foot	Unprotected	Average	Undrilled	Javelins	Light Spear	4	6–8	0–8	0–8
Spearmen		Medium Foot	Protected	Average	Undrilled	–	Light Spear, Swordsmen	6	4–6	0–6
Peasants		Mob	Unprotected	Poor	Undrilled	–	–	2	6	0–6

CENTRAL ASIAN CITY-STATES

This list covers the armies of the city-states of central Asia, mainly in Khwarazm and the Tarim basin around the Taklamakan desert, from the end of Kushan dominance around 500 AD until the final independent Tarim basin cities were absorbed into Turkish realms around 1000. The western Sogdian cities of Khwarazm had fallen to the Arabs by the end of the 8th century.

Whilst most of the cities in the area could only field armies of the order of 2,000 heavy cavalry plus auxiliaries there were exceptions such as Kucha, which could on occasion field forces of around

Field Commander

50,000 men. Local Turkish allies were often available, but they were also usually available for their enemies as well.

These are the cities that the Tang expeditionary forces of the 630s and 640s faced as they attempted to exert Chinese control over central Asia. With the numbers of men that the Tang could put into the field most cities submitted voluntarily and the Tang allowed their rulers to remain in power as vassals.

TROOP NOTES

The noble cavalry were usually armed with lances and bows and are usually depicted as charging with their lances in stereotypical heroic style. However, it is possible that steppe-style warfare was common in some areas and/or periods and so we allow either a charging lancer or steppe-style horse archer interpretation, but all must be classified the same.

CENTRAL ASIAN CITY-STATES STARTER ARMY		
Commander-in-Chief	1	Field Commander
Sub-commanders	2	2 x Troop Commander
Noble cavalry	5 BGs	Each comprising 4 bases of noble cavalry: Superior, Armoured, Undrilled Cavalry – Lancers, Swordsmen
Horse archers	3 BGs	Each comprising 4 bases of horse archers: Average, Unprotected, Undrilled Light Horse – Bow
Foot archers	2 BGs	Each comprising 6 bases of foot archers: Average, Unprotected, Undrilled Light Foot – Bow
Camp	1	Unfortified camp
Total	9 BGs	Camp, 32 mounted bases, 12 foot bases, 3 commanders

BUILDING A CUSTOMISED LIST USING OUR ARMY POINTS

Choose an army based on the maxima and minima in the list below. The following special instructions apply to this army:

- Commanders should be depicted as Noble cavalry.
- Noble cavalry must be either all Lancers, Swordsmen or all Bow, Swordsmen.

CENTRAL ASIAN CITY-STATES									
Territory Types: Agricultural, Steppe									
C-in-C	Inspired Commander/Field Commander/Troop Commander						80/50/35	1	
Sub-commanders	Field Commander						50	0–2	
	Troop Commander						35	0–3	
Troop name	Troop Type				Capabilities		Points per base	Bases per BG	Total bases
	Type	Armour	Quality	Training	Shooting	Close Combat			
Core Troops									
Noble cavalry	Cavalry	Armoured	Superior	Undrilled	–	Lancers, Swordsmen	16	4–6	8–48
			Average				12		
	Cavalry	Armoured	Superior	Undrilled	Bow	Swordsmen	18	4–6	
			Average				14		
Horse archers	Light Horse	Unprotected	Average	Undrilled	Bow	–	8	4–6	4–16
	Light Horse	Unprotected	Average	Undrilled	Bow	Swordsmen	10	4–6	
	Cavalry	Unprotected	Average	Undrilled	Bow	Swordsmen	10	4–6	
		Protected					11		
Foot archers	Medium Foot	Unprotected	Average	Undrilled	Bow	–	5	6–8	6–36
	Light Foot	Unprotected	Average	Undrilled	Bow	–	5	6–8	
Optional Troops									
City militia spearmen	Heavy Foot	Protected	Poor	Undrilled	–	Defensive Spearmen	4	8–10	0–24
	Mob	Unprotected	Poor	Undrilled	–	–	2	10–12	
Artillery	Light Artillery	–	Average	Drilled	Light Artillery	–	17	2	0–2
Allies									
Turkish allies – Later Horse Nomads or Western Turkish – see Field of Glory Companion 7: *Decline and Fall: Byzantium at War*									
Special Campaigns									
Only Sogdia before 700									
Persian exiles	Cavalry	Armoured	Superior	Undrilled	Bow	Swordsmen	18	4–6	0–6
			Average				14		

CENTRAL ASIAN CITY-STATES ALLIES

Allied commander	Field Commander/Troop Commander						50/35		1
Troop name	**Troop Type**				**Capabilities**		**Points per base**	**Bases per BG**	**Total bases**
	Type	Armour	Quality	Training	Shooting	Close Combat			
Noble cavalry	Cavalry	Armoured	Superior	Undrilled	–	Lancers, Swordsmen	16	4–6	8–16
			Average				12		
	Cavalry	Armoured	Superior	Undrilled	Bow	Swordsmen	18	4–6	
			Average				14		
Horse archers	Light Horse	Unprotected	Average	Undrilled	Bow	–	8	4–6	4–8
	Light Horse	Unprotected	Average	Undrilled	Bow	Swordsmen	10	4–6	
	Cavalry	Unprotected	Average	Undrilled	Bow	Swordsmen	10	4–6	
		Protected					11		
Foot archers	Medium Foot	Unprotected	Average	Undrilled	Bow	–	5	6–8	6–18
	Light Foot	Unprotected	Average	Undrilled	Bow	–	5	6–8	

WESTERN WEI TO EARLY TANG CHINESE

This list covers Chinese armies from the 540s AD when the Western Wei (535–556) in the north of China, and the following Northern Zhou (557–581), started to develop a standing army that included infantry, until the collapse of the military system of the Tang in the aftermath of the rebellion started by An Lushan (755–763).

During this period China was once again united under the Sui dynasty (581–618) and this unification survived the bout of civil wars that caused its fall in the wake of a series of disastrous invasions of Korea. Under the Tang (from 618 on) China again conquered large tracts of land to the west, the so called Gansu Corridor and the Turfan basin bringing them into contact with the Arab caliphate, which was itself expanding into the area at the time. This led, in 751, to the only recorded clash between an Arab army and a Chinese army in this period at the Talas River, in which the Tang army was defeated due to the defection of their local allies.

The initial attempt to create an effective infantry force by the Western Wei involved the adoption of local warlords into the military hierarchy along with their troops, which were called *xiang bing*. The Sui also used this method during their invasions of Korea, although their troops were called *xiaoguo*. Around 550, a more substantial force called the Twenty-four Armies appeared, under the command of 12 senior generals, who were tied closely to the emperor. This process also marked the re-establishment of a more direct imperial control over the military, leading to a reduction in the likelihood of a rebellion. By Tang times the system had solidified into the *fubing* militia system where troops were organised into regiments which rotated guard duty at the capital with provincial postings, and were collected together as needed for campaigns. This system worked well for short term campaigns, but by the end of the 7th century longer term campaigns became more usual and the *fubing* regiments came to be made up of professional career soldiers. Unfortunately, at the same time military commands on the borders became more permanent and larger, placing large numbers of troops under the command of a single general for extended periods of time. This, coupled with a decline in the troops around the capital, made the circumstances for a rebellion more favourable and ultimately led to An Lushan's great uprising.

TROOP NOTES

Cavalry remained the premier arm of the army, although now effective infantry was also a recognised part, both being recruited under the fubing system. Initially the cavalry followed the cataphract pattern of the preceding three centuries, but increasing Turkish influence led to a lightening of equipment in imitation of current steppe style and an increase in the importance of mounted archery. There are occasional Tang references to mounted crossbowmen.

Sui Heavy Cavalry

The equipment of Tang *fubing* infantry is not clear. There is the implication that all troops should be armed with bows, but the split of the infantry into two types – *bubing*, "marching troops", and *bushe*, "foot shooters" – indicates that in practice there may have been a distinction between those equipped for close combat and those equipped for shooting. Whilst both bows and crossbows were used, the former appear to have been more common, so formations that may have used both mixed together are classified as having Bow capability.

Tang training manuals describe tactics based on "companies" (dui) of 50 men deployed in loose formation shooting with bows and crossbows followed by an attack by spearmen and the missile men, who are also equipped with swords and expected to take part in the close combat on pain of death. The loose formation and charges by relatively small groups in succession suggests that neither Heavy Foot nor Spearmen classification would be correct, therefore, we feel that Medium Foot Light Spear, Swordsmen and Bow, Swordsmen in mixed battle groups best represents these troops.

EARLY TANG CHINESE STARTER ARMY		
Commander-in-Chief	1	Field Commander
Sub-commanders	2	2 x Troop Commander
Heavy cavalry	3 BGs	Each comprising 4 bases of heavy cavalry: Superior, Armoured, Drilled Cavalry – Bow, Swordsmen
Chinese light horse archers	1 BG	4 bases of Chinese light horse archers: Average, Unprotected, Drilled Light Horse – Bow
Tribal auxiliaries	1 BG	4 bases of tribal auxiliaries: Average, Unprotected, Undrilled Light Horse – Bow, Swordsmen
Fubing infantry	2 BGs	Each comprising 6 bases of fubing infantry: 3 Average, Protected, Drilled Medium Foot – Light Spear, Swordsmen, 3 Average, Protected, Drilled Medium Foot – Bow, Swordsmen
Crossbowmen	1 BG	6 bases of crossbowmen: 6 Average, Protected, Drilled Medium Foot – Crossbow, Swordsmen
Skirmishers	1 BG	8 bases of skirmishers: Average, Unprotected, Drilled Light Foot – Bow
Camp	1	Unfortified camp
Total	9 BGs	Camp, 20 mounted bases, 26 foot bases, 3 commanders

BUILDING A CUSTOMISED LIST USING OUR ARMY POINTS

Choose an army based on the maxima and minima in the list below. The following special instructions apply to this army:

- Commanders should be depicted as heavy or guard cavalry
- The minimum marked * does not apply to Yang Guang's Korean campaigns 613 to 614, nor to Tang armies or contingents, but if any such troops are used at least the minimum number must be fielded.

Crossbowman

WESTERN WEI TO EARLY TANG CHINESE

Territory Types: Sui and Early Tang – Agricultural, Developed, Hilly, Tropical. Others – Agricultural, Developed, Hilly

C-in-C		Inspired Commander/Field Commander/Troop Commander						80/50/35		1	
Sub-commanders		Field Commander						50		0–2	
		Troop Commander						35		0–3	
Troop name		Troop Type				Capabilities		Points per base	Bases per BG	Total bases	
		Type	Armour	Quality	Training	Shooting	Close Combat				
Core Troops											
Heavy cavalry	Western Wei, Northern Zhou and Sui	Cataphracts	Heavily Armoured	Superior	Drilled	—	Lancers, Swordsmen	20	4–6	6–16	
				Average				16			
		Cavalry	Armoured	Superior	Drilled	—	Lancers, Swordsmen	17	4–6		
				Average				13			
	Tang	Cataphracts	Heavily Armoured	Superior	Drilled	—	Lancers, Swordsmen	20	4–6	0–6	12–30
				Average				16			
		Cavalry	Armoured	Superior	Drilled	Bow	Swordsmen	19	4–6	12–30	
				Average				15			
		Cavalry	Armoured	Average	Drilled	Crossbow	Swordsmen	14	4–6	0–6	
Chinese light horse archers		Light Horse	Unprotected	Average	Drilled	Bow	—	8	4–6	0–8	
Xiang bing, fubing, xiaoguo or other professional infantry		Medium Foot	Protected	Average	Drilled	—	Light Spear, Swordsmen	7	1/2	6–8	*12–80
		Medium Foot	Protected	Average	Drilled	Bow	Swordsmen	8	1/2		
Optional Troops											
Tribal auxiliaries	Only Western Wei or Northern Zhou	Medium Foot	Protected	Average	Undrilled	—	Light Spear, Swordsmen	6	6–8	0–12	
	Any before 630	Light Horse	Unprotected	Average	Undrilled	Bow	Swordsmen	10	4–6	0–6	
		Cavalry	Unprotected	Average	Undrilled	Bow	Swordsmen	10	4–6		
			Protected					11			
	Only Tang from 630	Cavalry	Armoured	Superior	Undrilled	Bow	Swordsmen	18	4	0–4	0–16
		Cavalry	Protected	Average	Undrilled	Bow	Swordsmen	11	4–6	0–16	
			Unprotected					10			
		Light Horse	Unprotected	Average	Undrilled	Bow	Swordsmen	10	4–6		
Anti-cavalry squads		Heavy Foot	Protected	Average	Undrilled	—	Swordsmen	6	4–8	0–8	
					Drilled			7			
		Heavy Foot	Protected	Average	Undrilled	—	Heavy Weapon	7			
					Drilled			8			
Crossbowmen		Medium Foot	Protected	Average	Drilled	Crossbow	Swordsmen	8	6–8	0–8	
Skirmishers		Light Foot	Unprotected	Average	Drilled	Bow	—	5	6–8	0–8	
Fortified Camp								24		0–1	

Allies									
Rouran, Turkish or Uighur allies – Later Horse Nomads (Tang may use 2 contingents)									
Qarluq, Turgesh or similar western Turk allies (Only Tang after 650) – Western Turkish – see Field of Glory Companion 7: *Decline and Fall: Byzantium at War*									
Khotan, Turfan or similar allies (Only Tang after 630) – Central Asian city-states									
Shilla Korean allies (Only Tang 660 to 668) – Three Kingdoms Korean									
Special Campaigns									
Yang Guang's Korean campaigns 613 to 614									
Demoralised and/or hastily raised fubing	Medium Foot	Protected	Poor	Drilled	–	Light Spear, Swordsmen	5	1/2	8–10	24–80
	Medium Foot	Protected	Poor	Drilled	Bow	Swordsmen	6	1/2		
Li Shimin's Tang armies from 617 to 626									
Black clothed and armoured guard	Cataphracts	Heavily Armoured	Elite	Drilled	–	Lancers, Swordsmen	23		2	0–2
	Cavalry	Armoured	Elite	Drilled	–	Lancers, Swordsmen	20			
	Cavalry	Armoured	Elite	Drilled	Bow	Swordsmen	22			
C-in-C must be an Inspired Commander									

WESTERN WEI TO EARLY TANG CHINESE ALLIES

Allied commander		Field Commander/Troop Commander						40/25		1	
Troop name		Troop Type				Capabilities		Points per base	Bases per BG	Total bases	
		Type	Armour	Quality	Training	Shooting	Close Combat				
Heavy cavalry	Western Wei, Northern Zhou and Sui	Cataphracts	Heavily Armoured	Superior	Drilled	–	Lancers, Swordsmen	20	4–6	4–8	
				Average				16			
		Cavalry	Armoured	Superior	Drilled	–	Lancers, Swordsmen	17	4–6		
				Average				13			
	Tang	Cavalry	Armoured	Superior	Drilled	Bow	Swordsmen	18	4–6	6–16	
				Average				14			
Chinese light horse archers		Light Horse	Unprotected	Average	Drilled	Bow	–	8	4	0–4	
Xiang bing, fubing, xiaoguo or other professional infantry		Medium Foot	Protected	Average	Drilled	–	Light Spear, Swordsmen	7	1/2	6–8	*6–24
		Medium Foot	Protected	Average	Drilled	Bow	Swordsmen	8	1/2		

LATER HORSE NOMAD

This list covers eastern steppe-based nomads from the re-emergence of the armoured horse archer as the dominant troop type around 500 AD until the end of the period covered by our rules. The western nomads, who were similar to their eastern cousins, are covered by the Western Turkish list in Field of Glory Companion 7: *Decline and Fall*, and the Seljuq Turks and related peoples in Field of Glory Companion 4: *Swords and Scimitars*.

The list covers, amongst others, the Rouran, eastern Turkish khaganate, Uighur, Shatuo, pre-Liao Qidan and Qarakhanids, as well as more minor steppe tribes. It also covers eastern steppe-based Mongol armies before and after the Mongol conquest period – before 1218 and from 1266 to 1500. The Mongols of the conquest period are covered by the Mongol Conquest list in this book. China-based states formed by nomads such as the Shatuo, Qidan and Mongols

are covered by their own lists in this book. The Golden Horde is covered by the Tatar list in Field of Glory Companion 6: *Eternal Empire*, the Ilkhanids by the Ilkhanid Mongol list in Field of Glory Companion 4: *Swords and Scimitars* and the Mongol invasion of Europe by the Mongol Invasion list in Field of Glory Companion 10: *Oath of Fealty*.

The period saw a series of nomad powers exert control over the inner Asian steppe area, dominating weaker tribes until their power faded and the previously subject tribes revolted and broke the power of the dominant peoples. This cycle was repeated a number of times until the rise of the Mongols made them the dominant power, a position they held even after the breakup of the universal Mongol khanate, after which dominance remained with the strongest of the Mongol peoples.

After the collapse of their steppe empire (c.744–840) to the Kyrgyz, the Uighurs moved westward and established control over some of the central Asian cities in and around the Tarim basin – based around Ganzhou and Turfan. These could call upon settled militia infantry as well as their Uighur tribesmen. The resulting Uighur kingdoms were not aggressive and at times were willing to be vassals and allies of more powerful nations, such as the Qara-Khitai and Mongols, and were thus able to maintain some degree of independence until they were finally absorbed by the Mongols in the early 14th century.

Uighurs, by Angus McBride. Taken from Elite 30: Attila and the Nomad Hordes.

TROOP NOTES

Armoured cavalry were now more important than ever, with some being described as "Iron Cavalry" by the Chinese, who said that these were even better equipped than their own cavalry. However, in general, leather was the most common form of horse armour and levels of protection did not quite reach the degree they had previously when cataphracts were used. On this basis we classify the best cavalry as armoured. There was a return to more mobile tactics.

The Manchurian tribes were relatively backward. At the time of the Sui dynasty, what armour they used was still made of leather or bone.

Under Muslim influence the Qarakhanids are reported to have maintained a small body of *ghilman* as professional soldiers.

Cavalryman

LATER HORSE NOMAD STARTER ARMY		
Commander-in-Chief	1	Field Commander
Sub-commanders	2	2 x Troop Commander
Best equipped cavalry	4 BGs	Each comprising 4 bases of best equipped cavalry: Superior, Armoured, Undrilled Cavalry – Bow, Swordsmen
Other cavalry	4 BGs	Each comprising 4 bases of other cavalry: Average, Unprotected, Undrilled Light Horse – Bow, Swordsmen
Foot archers	1 BG	6 bases of foot archers: Average, Unprotected, Undrilled Light Foot – Bow
Camp	1	Unfortified camp
Total	9 BGs	Camp, 32 mounted bases, 6 foot bases, 3 commanders

BUILDING A CUSTOMISED LIST USING OUR ARMY POINTS

Choose an army based on the maxima and minima in the list below. The following special instructions apply to this army:

• Commanders should be depicted as best equipped cavalry.

• A Later Horse Nomad allied commander's contingent must conform to the Late Horse Nomad allies list below, but the troops in the contingent are deducted from the minima and maxima in the main list.

• The minimum marked * only applies if any foot are used.

LATER HORSE NOMAD

Territory Types: Uighurs from 856 to 1335, Qarakhanids, Chagatai Mongols – Agricultural, Steppes. Manchurians – Woodlands, Steppes. Others – Steppes.

C-in-C		Inspired Commander/Field Commander/Troop Commander						80/50/35	1	
Sub-commanders		Field Commander						50	0–2	
		Troop Commander						35	0–3	
Later Horse Nomad allied commander		Field Commander/Troop Commander						40/35	0–1	
Troop name		**Troop Type**				**Capabilities**		**Points per base**	**Bases per BG**	**Total bases**
		Type	Armour	Quality	Training	Shooting	Close Combat			
Core Troops										
Best equipped cavalry	Only Manchurians before 650	Cavalry	Protected	Superior	Undrilled	Bow	Swordsmen	14	4–6	4–18
	Only Mongols before 1218 or Manchurians from 650	Cavalry	Armoured	Superior	Undrilled	Bow	Swordsmen	18	4–6	4–18
	Only Mongols from 1266	Cavalry	Armoured	Superior	Drilled	Bow	Swordsmen	19	4–6	6–30
					Undrilled			18		
	Others	Cavalry	Armoured	Superior	Undrilled	Bow	Swordsmen	18	4–6	6–30
Other cavalry	Any	Light Horse	Unprotected	Average	Undrilled	Bow	Swordsmen	10	4–6	12–84
		Cavalry	Unprotected	Average	Undrilled	Bow	Swordsmen	10	4–6	
			Protected					11		
	Only Mongols from 1266	Light Horse	Unprotected	Average	Drilled	Bow	Swordsmen	10	4–6	
				Superior				12		
		Cavalry	Unprotected	Average	Drilled	Bow	Swordsmen	11	4–6	
			Unprotected	Superior				13		
			Protected	Average				12		
			Protected	Superior				15		
Optional Troops										
Ghilman	Only Qarakhanids from 999 to 1211	Cavalry	Armoured	Superior	Drilled	Bow	Swordsmen	19	4–6	0–6
Foot archers		Medium Foot	Unprotected	Average	Undrilled	Bow	–	5	6–8	0–12
				Poor				3		
		Light Foot	Unprotected	Average	Undrilled	Bow	–	5	6–8	
				Poor				3		
Militia Spearmen	Only Uighur from 856 to 1335	Heavy Foot	Protected	Poor	Undrilled	–	Defensive Spearmen	4	8–10	16–48
Militia archers		Medium Foot	Unprotected	Poor	Undrilled	Bow	–	3	8–10	0–24
Camp followers or other levies		Mob	Unprotected	Poor	Undrilled	–	–	2	10–12	0–12
Fortified camp								24		0–1
Allies										
Tibetan allies (Only Uighurs from 1014 to 1028)										
Qara Khitai allies (Only Qarakhanids from 1128 to 1207 or Kuchlug-Naiman from 1211 to 1218) – Liao										
Special Campaigns										
Eastern Turks in 597										
Sui allies – Western Wei to Early Tang										
Eastern Turks in 628										
Tang allies – Western Wei to Early Tang										

LATER HORSE NOMAD ALLIES

Allied commander		Field Commander/Troop Commander						40/35		1
Troop name		**Troop Type**				**Capabilities**		**Points per base**	**Bases per BG**	**Total bases**
		Type	Armour	Quality	Training	Shooting	Close Combat			
Best equipped cavalry	Only Manchurians before 650	Cavalry	Protected	Superior	Undrilled	Bow	Swordsmen	14	4–6	0–6
	Only Mongols before 1218 or Manchurians from 650	Cavalry	Armoured	Superior	Undrilled	Bow	Swordsmen	18	4–6	0–6
	Only Mongols from 1266	Cavalry	Armoured	Superior	Drilled	Bow	Swordsmen	19	4–6	4–12
					Undrilled			18		
	Others	Cavalry	Armoured	Superior	Undrilled	Bow	Swordsmen	18	4–6	4–12
Ghilman	Only Qarakhanids from 999 to 1211	Cavalry	Armoured	Superior	Drilled	Bow	Swordsmen	19	4	0–4
Other cavalry	Any	Light Horse	Unprotected	Average	Undrilled	Bow	Swordsmen	10	4–6	4–24
		Cavalry	Unprotected	Average	Undrilled	Bow	Swordsmen	10	4–6	
			Protected					11		
	Only Mongols from 1266	Light Horse	Unprotected	Average	Drilled	Bow	Swordsmen	10	4–6	
				Superior				12		
		Cavalry	Unprotected	Average	Drilled	Bow	Swordsmen	11	4–6	
			Unprotected	Superior				13		
			Protected	Average				12		
			Protected	Superior				15		
Foot archers	Only Shatuo	Medium Foot	Unprotected	Average	Undrilled	Bow	–	5	4–6	0–6
				Poor				3		
		Light Foot	Unprotected	Average	Undrilled	Bow	–	5	4–6	
				Poor				3		
Militia Spearmen	Only Uighur from 856 to 1335	Heavy Foot	Protected	Poor	Undrilled	–	Defensive Spearmen	4	8–10	*8–16
Militia archers		Medium Foot	Unprotected	Poor	Undrilled	Bow	–	3	8–10	0–8

TIBETAN

This list covers Tibetan armies from the early 7th century AD when the various Tibetan states were unified into an empire by Songtsän Gampo of the Yarlung dynasty. This empire fell apart in the mid-9th century, but the successor states continued to have some military influence in the region until c.1065 despite continual in-fighting.

Until the collapse of the empire, the Tibetans were a serious danger to the Tang Chinese and even managed to capture the capital of Chang'an on one occasion in 763, briefly setting up an ineffectual puppet regime. Wars between the two continued, sometimes using allied states such as Nanzhao, until 821 when a peace treaty was

Commander and Cataphracts

signed. This was mostly adhered to – partly because both states were no longer in any position to undertake major offensives due to internal problems.

In addition to fighting China, Tibet also intervened in central Asia and India, although to little lasting effect.

TROOP NOTES

Tibetan cavalry were noted for their very complete armour for both man and horse. When fighting dismounted on foot they used long spears.

One army in India mainly consisted of allied Nepalese cavalry, thus multiple Nepalese allies are allowed.

TIBETAN STARTER ARMY (BEFORE 851)		
Commander-in-Chief	1	Field Commander
Sub-commanders	2	2 x Troop Commander
Cataphracts	4 BGs	Each comprising 4 bases of cataphracts: Superior, Heavily Armoured, Drilled Cataphracts – Lancers, Swordsmen
Nomad mercenaries	1 BG	4 bases of nomad mercenaries: Average, Unprotected, Undrilled Light Horse – Bow, Swordsmen
Spearmen	1 BG	6 bases of spearmen: Average, Protected, Drilled Heavy Foot – Defensive Spearmen
Archers	1 BG	6 bases of archers: Average, Protected, Drilled Medium Foot – Bow
Tribesmen	1 BG	6 bases of tribesmen: Average, Unprotected, Undrilled Light Foot – Bow
Camp	1	Unfortified camp
Total	8 BGs	Camp, 20 mounted bases, 18 foot bases, 3 commanders

BUILDING A CUSTOMISED LIST USING OUR ARMY POINTS

Choose an army based on the maxima and minima in the list below. The following special instructions apply to this army:

- Commanders should be depicted as cataphracts.
- Other than 2 Nepalese allied contingents only 1 ally can be fielded.
- Cataphracts can always dismount as Heavy Foot, Heavily Armoured, Superior, Drilled, Offensive Spearmen.
- A Tibetan allied commander's contingent must conform to the Tibetan allies list below, but the troops in the contingent are

deducted from the minima and maxima in the main list.

- From 851 only one sub-commander can be fielded.

Spearmen

TIBETAN

Territory Types: Hilly, Developed, Mountains

C-in-C	Inspired Commander/Field Commander/Troop Commander						80/50/35	1	
Sub-commanders	Field Commander						50	0–2	
	Troop Commander						35	0–3	
Tibetan allied commanders	Field Commander/Troop Commander						40/25	0–2	

Troop name	Troop Type				Capabilities		Points per base	Bases per BG	Total bases
	Type	Armour	Quality	Training	Shooting	Close Combat			
Core Troops									
Cataphracts	Cataphracts	Heavily Armoured	Superior	Drilled	–	Lancers, Swordsmen	20	4–6	8–48
Optional Troops									
Spearmen	Heavy Foot	Protected	Average	Drilled	–	Defensive Spearmen	7	6–8	0–8
		Armoured					9		
Archers	Medium Foot	Protected	Average	Drilled	Bow	–	7	6–8	0–8
Tribesmen	Light Foot	Unprotected	Average	Undrilled	Bow	–	5	6–8	0–8
Nomad mercenaries	Only before 851	Cavalry	Armoured	Superior	Undrilled	Bow	Swordsmen	18	4–6	0–6
		Light Horse	Unprotected	Average	Undrilled	Bow	Swordsmen	10		
		Cavalry	Unprotected	Average	Undrilled	Bow	Swordsmen	10		
			Protected					11		
Fortified camp							24		1
Allies									
Nepalese allies (Only before 704) (Up to 2 contingents)									
Eastern Turkish and other nomad allies – Later Horse Nomad (not Uighur)									
Western Turkish allies – see Field of Glory Companion 7: *Decline and Fall: Byzantium at War*									
Khotanese allies (Only before 851) – Central Asian city-states									
Nanzhao allies (Only from 754 to 793)									
Special Campaigns									
Only from 795 to 801									
Abbasid cavalry	Cavalry	Armoured	Superior	Drilled	–	Lancers, Swordsmen	17	4–6	4–8
				Undrilled			16		
	Cavalry	Armoured	Average	Drilled	–	Lancers, Swordsmen	13	4–6	
				Undrilled			12		
Abbasid spearmen and archers	Heavy Foot	Protected	Average	Undrilled	–	Defensive Spearmen	6	2/3	6–9	0–9
	Light Foot	Unprotected	Average	Undrilled	Bow	–	5	1/3		
	Heavy Foot	Protected	Poor	Undrilled	–	Defensive Spearmen	4	2/3	6–9	
	Light Foot	Unprotected	Poor	Undrilled	Bow	–	3	1/3		

TIBETAN ALLIES

Allied commander	Field Commander/Troop Commander						50/35	1	

Troop name	Troop Type				Capabilities		Points per base	Bases per BG	Total bases
	Type	Armour	Quality	Training	Shooting	Close Combat			
Cataphracts	Cataphracts	Heavily Armoured	Superior	Drilled	–	Lancers, Swordsmen	20	4–6	4–12

NEPALESE ALLIES

Allied commander	Field Commander/Troop Commander						50/35	1	

Troop name	Troop Type				Capabilities		Points per base	Bases per BG	Total bases
	Type	Armour	Quality	Training	Shooting	Close Combat			
Cavalry	Cavalry	Armoured	Average	Undrilled	Bow	Swordsmen	14	4–6	8–18
		Protected					11		
Foot archers	Light Foot	Unprotected	Average	Undrilled	Bow	–	5	6	0–6

PARHAE KOREAN

Parhae was a multi-ethnic state created by old Koguryo nobles and Manchurian nobles from old Koguryo lands located in the Manchurian holdings of the original kingdom. It extended far north and south of the Yalu and Tumen rivers and maintained five capitals. Though supported by the Chinese Tang Dynasty, Parhae's semi-independent status resulted in several conflicts with Tang China, other nomadic northern tribes and Korean Shilla.

Ex-Koguryo nobles often inter-married with the nomads and controlled key towns or resources in the region.

The list covers the armies of Parhae from 698 to 926 AD.

TROOP NOTES

Korean regular cavalry and provincials are remnants of the Korean professional soldier class that have sworn loyalty to the Manchurians. Korean nobles, retainers and levy foot are troops loyal to a specific Koguryo high ranking noble.

"Spearmen" used a mixture of conventional spears, halberds and tridents. We classify the mixture as Heavy Weapon. They remained shieldless.

PARHAE KOREAN STARTER ARMY		
Commander-in-Chief	1	Field Commander
Sub-commanders	2	2 x Troop Commander
Manchurian nobles	2 BGs	Each comprising 4 bases of Manchurian nobles: Superior, Armoured, Undrilled Cavalry – Bow, Swordsmen
Regular cavalry	1 BG	4 bases of regular cavalry: Average, Protected, Drilled Cavalry – Lancers, Swordsmen
Other nomad cavalry	2 BGs	Each comprising 4 bases of other nomad cavalry: Average, Unprotected, Undrilled Light Horse – Bow, Swordsmen
Provincial "spearmen" and archers in mixed battle groups	2 BGs	Each comprising 8 bases of provincial "spearmen" and archers in mixed battle groups: 4 Average, Protected, Drilled Medium Foot – Heavy Weapon, 4 Average, Protected, Drilled Medium Foot – Bow
Levy "spearmen" and archers	1 BG	10 bases of levy "spearmen" and archers: 5 Poor, Unprotected, Undrilled Medium Foot – Heavy Weapon, 5 Poor, Unprotected, Undrilled Medium Foot – Bow
Levy skirmishing archers	1 BG	8 bases of levy skirmishing archers: Poor, Unprotected, Drilled Light Foot – Bow
Foot nomads	1 BG	6 bases of foot nomads: Average, Unprotected, Undrilled Light Foot – Bow
Camp	1	Unfortified camp
Total	10 BGs	Camp, 20 mounted bases, 40 foot bases, 3 commanders

BUILDING A CUSTOMISED LIST USING OUR ARMY POINTS

Choose an army based on the maxima and minima in the list below. The following special instructions apply to this army:

- Commanders should be depicted as nobles.
- The minima marked * apply if any Koguryo nobles or retainers are used.
- The total number of bases of provincial foot in the army cannot exceed the total number of bases of levy foot by more than 50%.

- Provincial mixed battle groups can be half "spearmen", half archers or half "spearmen", half crossbowmen.
- The total number of bases of provincial "spearmen" in the army cannot exceed the total number of provincial archers and crossbowmen.
- The total number of bases of provincial Medium Foot crossbowmen in the army cannot exceed the number of bases of provincial Medium Foot archers.
- Only one allied contingent can be used.

PARHAE KOREAN

Territory Types: Developed, Hilly, Woodlands

C-in-C	Inspired Commander/Field Commander/Troop Commander						80/50/35	1			
Sub-commanders	Field Commander						50	0–2			
	Troop Commander						35	0–3			
Troop name	**Troop Type**				**Capabilities**		**Points per base**	**Bases per BG**		**Total bases**	
	Type	Armour	Quality	Training	Shooting	Close Combat					
Core Troops											
Manchurian nobles	Cavalry	Armoured	Superior	Undrilled	Bow	Swordsmen	18	4–6		4–16	16–40
Other nomad cavalry	Light Horse	Unprotected	Average	Undrilled	Bow	Swordsmen	10	4–6		8–24	
	Cavalry	Unprotected	Average	Undrilled	Bow	Swordsmen	10	4–6			
		Protected					11				
Korean regular cavalry	Cavalry	Armoured	Average	Drilled	–	Lancers, Swordsmen	13	4–6		4–8	
		Protected					10				
Koguryo nobles	Cavalry	Armoured	Superior	Undrilled	–	Lancers, Swordsmen	16	4–6		*4	
Koguryo retainers	Cavalry	Protected	Average	Undrilled	–	Light Spear, Swordsmen	9	4–6		*4–6	
Korean mounted scouts	Light Horse	Unprotected	Average	Undrilled	Bow	–	8	4		0–4	
Levy "spearmen"	Medium Foot	Unprotected	Poor	Undrilled	–	Heavy Weapon	4	1/2	8–10	10–72	
Levy archers	Medium Foot	Unprotected	Poor	Undrilled	Bow	–	3	1/2			
Optional Troops											
Separately deployed provincial "spearmen"	Medium Foot	Protected	Average	Drilled	–	Heavy Weapon	8	6–8		0–18	
Provincial "spearmen" in mixed battle groups	Medium Foot	Protected	Average	Drilled	–	Heavy Weapon	8	1/2	6–8		
Provincial archers in mixed battle groups	Medium Foot	Protected	Average	Drilled	Bow	–	7	1/2		0–18	
Provincial crossbowmen in mixed battle groups	Medium Foot	Protected	Average	Drilled	Crossbow	–	7				
Separately deployed provincial archers	Medium Foot	Protected	Average	Drilled	Bow	–	7	6–8			
Separately deployed provincial crossbowmen	Medium Foot	Protected	Average	Drilled	Crossbow	–	7	6–8			
Provincial skirmishing archers	Light Foot	Unprotected	Average	Drilled	Bow	–	5	6–8		0–8	
Foot nomads	Light Foot	Unprotected	Average	Undrilled	Bow	–	5	6–8		0–8	
Levy skirmishing archers	Light Foot	Unprotected	Average	Undrilled	Bow	–	3	6–8		0–8	
Field fortifications	Field Fortifications						3			0–24	
Allies											
Tang Chinese allies (Only before 750) – Western Wei to Early Tang Chinese											
Manchurian Nomad allies – Later Horse Nomad											

LATE TANG TO FIVE DYNASTIES CHINESE

From 755 to 763 the Tang Empire was rocked by a major rebellion started by An Lushan, one of the powerful military governors (*jiedushi*) of the northern provinces. Around the same time, a number of major raids by the Tibetans also destabilised the regime and caused further disruption, leading to a loss of power by the central authorities and, as a result, more power accruing to the army commanders.

The Tang dynasty was ended in 907 when Zhu Wen deposed the last emperor and founded his own Later Liang dynasty. By this stage China was already effectively fragmented between a large number of squabbling generals, many of whom now claimed to be head of state. The central government had ceased to have an effective army since the rebellion of Huang Chao (875–884).

Commander

This subsequent period is known as the "Five Dynasties" period as traditionally the Chinese have only recognised the dynasties based in the north, of which there were five major ones, as legitimate, whilst the southern states, along with the Northern Han, are described as the "Ten Kingdoms".

The Five Dynasties were the Later Liang (907–923), Later Tang (923–936), Later Jin (936–947), Later Han (947–951) and Later Zhou (951–960). Note that the Later Tang was a Shatuo-ruled dynasty and is not the same as the Late Tang, which is the latter part of the Tang dynasty and not a separate dynasty in itself.

The Ten Kingdoms were the Wu (902–937), Wuyue (907–978), Min (909–945), Chu (927–951), Southern Han (917–971), Former Shu (907–925), Later Shu (935–965), Jingnan (924–963), Southern Tang (937–976) and Northern Han (951–979). Apart from the Northern Han all of these were based in the south of China.

One major result of the disruption was a loss of many of the better horse rearing grounds and thus a decline in the number, and often quality, of the cavalry available to the Chinese. On occasion this was offset by provision of large numbers of good cavalry by allied nomads such as the Uighur and Shatuo Turks. As was usual in Chinese military history, the northern states retained larger numbers of effective cavalry as they held the remaining breeding grounds. This was also helped by the fact that some of them were ruled by emperors descended from the Shatuo Turks, who had settled in Hedong province (in modern Shanxi), and whose leaders governed there from 883.

Tang official and elite troops, by Michael Perry. Taken from Men-at-Arms 295: Imperial Chinese Armies (2): 590–1260 AD.

This list covers Late Tang armies from the start of the An Lushan rebellion to 907, Shatuo-ruled Hedong from 883 to 907, Five Dynasties armies until the fall of the Later Zhou in 960, and Ten Kingdoms armies until the final conquest by the Song of the Southern Tang in 976 and the Northern Han kingdom in 979. Note that the Shatuo-ruled Kingdom of Jin (908–923), which formed the basis of the Later Tang, is treated as a Five Dynasties army.

Possibly the most important event of the period occurred in 936, when Shi Jiangtang, the Shatuo founder of the Later Jin dynasty, ceded a portion of Chinese territory to the Qidan empire in return for military support. This territory, known as the Sixteen Prefectures, including modern Beijing, was strategically important as it provided control of access to the north east China plain across the mountain passes of the region. The recovery of this territory became an obsession for subsequent Chinese dynasties, particularly the Song, who made a number of dubious strategic decisions based on the desire to recover this land, contributing to their loss of the whole of the north to the Jin.

TROOP NOTES

It is unclear how much of the Early Tang military system survived in the chaos that followed the rebellion of An Lushan, especially with respect to the infantry. Armies were often hurriedly raised and their quality was variable, especially in the north of China where warfare was almost continuous through the period. We assume that in such circumstances sophisticated formations are likely to be replaced by more basic ones, and thus shooters and close combat troops are less likely to have been in mixed formations. However, we allow for a number of mixed formations to remain for the better troops, as they were the usual deployment in the following Song period, which suggests continuity.

The succeeding Song used crossbows as their main missile weapon for the foot and it is likely that the changeover from bows took place at some time during the period covered by this list. However, as it is impossible to say when this change took place we allow missile troops the choice of bow or crossbow but this choice must apply to all the battle groups in the army.

Southern Auxilaries

SHATUO STARTER ARMY (IN HEDONG BEFORE 908)		
Commander-in-Chief	1	Field Commander
Sub-commanders	2	2 x Troop Commander
Good cavalry	3 BGs	Each comprising 4 bases of good cavalry: Superior, Armoured, Undrilled Cavalry – Bow, Swordsmen
Shatuo tribesmen	3 BGs	Each comprising 4 bases of Shatuo tribesmen: Average, Unprotected, Undrilled Light Horse – Bow, Swordsmen
Regular infantry	2 BGs	Each comprising 8 bases of regular infantry: 4 Average, Protected, Drilled Medium Foot – Light Spear, Swordsmen, 4 Average, Protected, Drilled Medium Foot – Bow
Skirmishers	1 BG	6 bases of skirmishers: Average, Unprotected, Undrilled Light Foot – Bow
Camp	1	Unfortified camp
Total	9 BGs	Camp, 24 mounted bases, 22 foot bases, 3 commanders

BUILDING A CUSTOMISED LIST USING OUR ARMY POINTS

Choose an army based on the maxima and minima in the list below. The following special instructions apply to this army:

- Commanders should be depicted as guard cavalry.
- A Chinese allied commander's contingent must conform to the Late Tang to Five Dynasties Chinese Allies list below, but the troops in the contingent are deducted from the minima and maxima in the main list.

- Where there is a choice of Bow or Crossbow capability for troops, this represents alternative possibilities of their historical armament. All such troops must be classed the same other than southern auxiliaries.
- The minima marked * only apply if more than one battle group of militia are used.
- Nanzhao or Liao allies cannot be used with any non-Chinese allied contingent.
- Southern auxiliaries cannot be used with Uighur or Shatuo Turk allies.

LATE TANG TO FIVE DYNASTIES CHINESE									
Territory Types: Late Tang – Agricultural, Developed, Hilly, Tropical. Shatuo in Hedong, Five Dynasties, Northern Han – Agricultural, Developed, Hilly. Others – Developed, Hilly, Tropical.									
C-in-C		Inspired Commander/Field Commander/Troop Commander					80/50/35	1	
Sub-commanders		Field Commander					50	0–2	
		Troop Commander					35	0–3	
Chinese allied commander		Field Commander/Troop Commander					40/25	0–1	
Troop name		Troop Type				Capabilities		Points per base	Bases per BG	Total bases
		Type	Armour	Quality	Training	Shooting	Close Combat			
Core Troops										
Guard and similar good cavalry	Only Shatuo in Hedong before 908	Cavalry	Armoured	Superior	Undrilled	Bow	Swordsmen	18	4–6	4–16
	Only Five Dynasties and Northern Han	Cavalry	Armoured	Superior	Drilled	Bow	Swordsmen	19	4–6	
	Others	Cavalry	Armoured	Superior	Drilled	Bow	Swordsmen	19	4	0–4

Chinese cavalry		Cavalry	Armoured	Average	Drilled	Bow	Swordsmen	15	4–6	0–8
			Protected					12		
Chinese light horse archers		Light Horse	Unprotected	Average	Drilled	Bow	–	8	4	0–4
Shatuo tribesmen	Only Shatuo in Hedong before 908	Light Horse	Unprotected	Average	Undrilled	Bow	Swordsmen	10	4–6	8–24
		Cavalry	Protected	Average	Undrilled	Bow	Swordsmen	11	4–6	
			Unprotected					10		
Regular infantry	Only Late Tang and Ten Kingdoms (excluding Northern Han)	Medium Foot	Protected	Average	Drilled	–	Light Spear, Swordsmen	7	1/2	6–8	12–64
		Medium Foot	Protected	Average	Drilled	Bow or Crossbow	–	7	1/2	
	Others	Medium Foot	Protected	Average	Drilled	–	Light Spear, Swordsmen	7	1/2	6–8	6–32
		Medium Foot	Protected	Average	Drilled	Bow or Crossbow	–	7	1/2	

Optional Troops										
Steppe light cavalry	Only Late Tang, Five Dynasties and Northern Han	Light Horse	Unprotected	Average	Undrilled	Bow	Swordsmen	10	4	0–4
		Cavalry	Unprotected	Average	Undrilled	Bow	Swordsmen	10	4	
			Protected					11		
Anti-cavalry squads		Heavy Foot	Protected	Average	Undrilled	–	Heavy Weapon	7	4–8	0–8
					Drilled			8		
Militia spearmen		Medium Foot	Protected	Poor	Undrilled	–	Light Spear, Swordsmen	4	8–10	*8–56
Militia missile foot		Medium Foot	Protected	Poor	Undrilled	Bow or Crossbow	–	4	6–8	*6–40
			Unprotected					3		
Skirmishers		Light Foot	Unprotected	Average	Undrilled	Bow or Crossbow	–	5	6–8	0–8
				Poor				3		
Elephants	Only Southern Han	Elephants	–	Average	Undrilled	–	–	25	2	0–2
Southern auxiliaries	Only Late Tang and Ten Kingdoms, excluding Northern Han	Medium Foot	Protected	Average	Undrilled	–	Light Spear	5	6–8	0–16
		Medium Foot	Protected	Average	Undrilled	–	Impact Foot, Swordsmen	7	6–8	
		Medium Foot	Protected	Average	Undrilled	–	Light Spear, Swordsmen	6	6–8	
		Light Foot	Unprotected	Average	Undrilled	Bow or Crossbow	–	5	6–8	0–8
Light stone-throwers or heavy crossbow artillery		Light Artillery	–	Average	Drilled	Light Artillery	–	17	2	0–4
Heavy stone-throwers		Heavy Artillery	–	Average	Drilled	Heavy Artillery	–	25	2	0–2
Palisades or similar fortifications		Field Fortifications						3		0–24
Fortified Camp								24		0–1

Allies										
Uighur or Shatuo Turk (before 883) allies (Only Late Tang) – Later Horse Nomads (Up to 2 contingents)										
Nanzhao allies (Only Late Tang) – Nanzhao										
Tibetan allies (Only Late Tang) – Tibetan										
Liao allies (Only Later Jin and Northern Han) – Liao										

Special Campaigns										
Fang Guan in 756										
Ox drawn "chariots"		Battle Wagons	–	Poor	Undrilled	–	–	8	4	8–12

LATE TANG TO FIVE DYNASTIES CHINESE ALLIES

Allied commander		Field Commander/Troop Commander						40/25		1
Troop name		**Troop Type**				**Capabilities**		**Points per base**	**Bases per BG**	**Total bases**
		Type	Armour	Quality	Training	Shooting	Close Combat			
Guard and similar good cavalry	Only Five Dynasties and Northern Han	Cavalry	Armoured	Superior	Drilled	Bow	Swordsmen	19	4–6	4–6
Chinese cavalry		Cavalry	Armoured	Average	Drilled	Bow	Swordsmen	15	4	0–4
			Protected					12		
Regular infantry	Only Late Tang and Ten Kingdoms (excluding Northern Han)	Medium Foot	Protected	Average	Drilled	–	Light Spear, Swordsmen	7	1/2	6–8 6–24
		Medium Foot	Protected	Average	Drilled	Bow or Crossbow	–	7	1/2	
	Others	Medium Foot	Protected	Average	Drilled	–	Light Spear, Swordsmen	7	1/2	6–8 6–12
		Medium Foot	Protected	Average	Drilled	Bow or Crossbow	–	7	1/2	
Militia spearmen		Medium Foot	Protected	Poor	Undrilled	–	Light Spear, Swordsmen	4	8–10	*8–16
Militia missile foot		Medium Foot	Protected	Poor	Undrilled	Bow or Crossbow	–	4	6–8	*6–12
			Unprotected					3		

KHMER OR CHAMPA

This list covers Khmer armies from 802 to 1473 AD and Champa armies from 600 to 1500 AD.

KHMER

Khmer, which was also called the Kambuja Kingdom, was centred in Cambodia with its capital being Angkor from 802–1432. The Khmer expanded their power by establishing a number of vassal states. The peak of Khmer power is regarded by many as being in the 1100s, when it extended from northern Thailand in the west to the northern Tokin area of Vietnam in the east.

Civil wars dominated the 1200s and 1300s which weakened the Khmer state. In 1373 a long war with the Thais began which lasted until 1473 when the new capital at Phnom Penh was sacked by the Thais.

CHAMPA

Originally Champa had been a commandery of the Han Chinese Empire situated in Vietnam near Hue. The commanding general established his own kingdom while the Han Empire was in decline. Initially, regional warlords gave nominal allegiance to Hue in exchange for military help against rival tribes. Champa was heavily influenced by the Malayans which caused an Indianised culture to develop. Eventually the Cham people were united in 400 AD by a very aggressive king named Bhadravarman.

The Champa attacked the Tonkin area and further north into China proper. In 446 the Chinese launched an invasion of Champa in response to these raids and conquered it. The Chinese held power for a hundred years until a Champa revolt removed them.

Beginning in the 900s, wars were fought with the Dai Viet of Tonkin. By 1000 the Dai Viet had conquered Quang Nam followed swiftly by the fall of Binh Dinh in 1069. The weakened Champa was able to halt the Dai Viet advance but was unable to prevent invasion by the Khmer in 1145 and 1190. The Khmer controlled it until 1220.

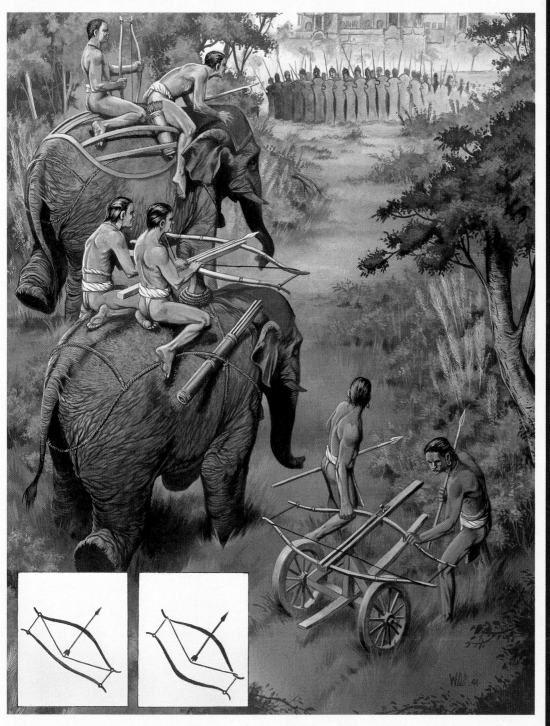

Champa artillery, by Wayne Reynolds. Taken from New Vanguard 43: Siege Weapons of the Fat East (1): AD 612–1300.

Though technically a vassal of the Khmer, Champa allied with the Vietnamese Tran to fend off Mongol invasions in 1284 and 1287. The Tran alliance was short-lived and the Tran invaded the south in 1312 to eliminate the Champa threat. Tran control over the Champa land only lasted until 1326 when a revolt with Chinese support freed the conquered people. The Champa resurgence was spurred by General Che Bong Nga. The Champa were able to regain most of their lost land. They even sacked Hanoi in 1371. Another Tran campaign in 1390 resulted in a second conquest of the Champa by the Tran. By the mid-1400s the Champa were no longer capable of mounting a 'Champa' operation.

TROOP NOTES

Ethnic infantry represent either Khmer or Champa troops with long shields and/or wearing some type of protective armour. Conscript foot represent local levies with limited training, round shield and no body armour. Subject troops are impressed troops from controlled areas with little motivation to fight.

Skirmishers cover a wide range of light troops expected to both scout and secure jungle flanks near the battlefield. They can be armed with javelins, blowguns, poisonous darts and even a few Champa 'fire oil' throwers.

Bolt-shooters can either be on wheeled carriages or mounted on elephants. Khmer and Champa elephant-mounted bolt-shooters are clearly shown in action in Khmer reliefs. As it seems unlikely that they were used for close-combat assault purposes, they are treated as normal Light Artillery in all respects and do not count as elephants for any purpose.

CHAMPA STARTER ARMY (AFTER 1170)		
Commander-in-Chief	1	Field Commander
Sub-commanders	2	2 x Troop Commander
Elephants	4 BGs	Each comprising 2 bases of elephants: Average, Undrilled Elephants
Cavalry	1 BG	4 bases of cavalry: Average, Unprotected, Drilled Cavalry – Crossbow
Cavalry	1 BG	4 bases of cavalry: Average, Unprotected, Drilled Light Horse – Bow
Spearmen	2 BGs	Each comprising 8 bases of spearmen: Average, Protected, Drilled Medium Foot – Light Spear
Conscript spearmen	1 BG	8 bases of conscript spearmen: Average, Unprotected, Undrilled Medium Foot – Light Spear
Archers	1 BG	6 bases of archers: Average, Unprotected, Drilled Light Foot – Bow
Skirmishers	1 BG	6 bases of skirmishers: Average, Unprotected, Undrilled Light Foot – Javelins, Light Spear
Bolt-shooters	1 BG	2 bases of bolt-shooters: Average, Undrilled Light Artillery – Light Artillery
Camp	1	Unfortified camp
Total	12 BGs	Camp, 16 mounted bases, 38 foot bases, 3 commanders

BUILDING A CUSTOMISED LIST USING OUR ARMY POINTS

Choose an army based on the maxima and minima in the list below. The following special instructions apply to this army:

- Khmer commanders should be depicted on elephants or in chariots or as Khmer cavalry.
- Champa commanders should be depicted on elephants.

KHMER OR CHAMPA

Territory Types: Tropical, Agricultural, Hilly

C-in-C		Inspired Commander/Field Commander/Troop Commander					80/50/35	1		
Sub-commanders		Field Commander					50	0–2		
		Troop Commander					35	0–3		
Troop name		Troop Type				Capabilities		Points per base	Bases per BG	Total bases
		Type	Armour	Quality	Training	Shooting	Close Combat			
Core Troops										
Khmer cavalry	Only Khmer	Cavalry	Protected	Average	Drilled	–	Light Spear	8	4	0–4	0–6
		Cavalry	Unprotected	Average	Drilled	–	Light Spear	7	4–6	0–6
Champa cavalry	Only Champa at any date	Light Horse	Unprotected	Average	Drilled	Bow	–	8	4	0–4	0–8
	Only Champa before 1170	Cavalry	Unprotected	Average	Drilled	–	Light Spear	7	4–6	0–6
	Only Champa from 1170	Cavalry	Unprotected	Average	Drilled	Crossbow	–	8	4–6	0–6
Elephants		Elephants	–	Average	Undrilled	–	–	25	2	4–12
Archers		Medium Foot	Protected	Average	Drilled	Bow	–	7	6–8	6–16
		Light Foot	Unprotected	Average	Drilled	Bow	–	5	6–8
Spearmen		Medium Foot	Protected	Average	Drilled	–	Light Spear	6	6–8	8–36
Conscript spearmen		Medium Foot	Unprotected	Average	Undrilled	–	Light Spear	4	8–10	8–80
Optional Troops										
Khmer chariots	Only Khmer before 1100	Light Chariots	–	Average	Undrilled	–	Light Spear	11	4	0–4
Subject cavalry		Cavalry	Unprotected	Poor	Undrilled	–	Light Spear	4	4–6	0–4
Crossbowmen		Light Foot	Unprotected	Average	Drilled	Crossbow	–	5	4–6	0–6
Skirmishers		Light Foot	Unprotected	Average	Undrilled	Javelins	Light Spear	4	6–8	0–8
Subject spearmen		Medium Foot	Unprotected	Poor	Undrilled	–	Light Spear	2	8–10	0–24	0–24
		Light Foot	Unprotected	Poor	Undrilled	Javelins	Light Spear	2	6–8	0–12
Subject archers		Medium Foot	Unprotected	Poor	Undrilled	Bow	–	3	6–8	0–8
		Light Foot	Unprotected	Poor	Undrilled	Bow	–	3		
Peasants		Mob	–	–	–	–	–	2	10–12	0–20
Bolt-shooters	Only from 1100	Light Artillery	–	Average	Undrillled	Light Artillery	–	15	2	0–4
Stone-throwers	Only from 1280	Heavy Artillery	–	Average	Undrilled	Heavy Artillery	–	20	2	0–2
Allies										
Only Khmer										
Champa allies – Khmer or Champa										
Thai allies (Only from 1300)										
Only Champa										
Chinese allies (Only from 1320 to 1370) – Yuan Chinese										
Khmer allies – Khmer or Champa										
Viet allies (Only from 1284 to 1287) – see Field of Glory Companion 13: *The Lost Scrolls*										

KHMER OR CHAMPA ALLIES

Allied commander		\multicolumn{4}{c	}{Field Commander/Troop Commander}			40/25	1	
Troop name		\multicolumn{4}{c	}{Troop Type}	\multicolumn{2}{c	}{Capabilities}	Points per base	Bases per BG	Total bases
		Type	Armour	Quality	Training	Shooting	Close Combat			
Khmer cavalry	Only Khmer	Cavalry	Protected	Average	Drilled	–	Light Spear	8	4	0–4
		Cavalry	Unprotected	Average	Drilled	–	Light Spear	7	4	
Champa cavalry	Only Champa at any date	Light Horse	Unprotected	Average	Drilled	Bow	–	8	4	0–4
	Only Champa before 1170	Cavalry	Unprotected	Average	Drilled	–	Light Spear	7	4	
	Only Champa from 1170	Cavalry	Unprotected	Average	Drilled	Crossbow	–	8	4	
Elephants		Elephants	–	Average	Undrilled	–	–	25	2	2–4
Archers		Medium Foot	Protected	Average	Drilled	Bow	–	7	4–6	4–6
		Light Foot	Unprotected	Average	Drilled	Bow	–	5	4–6	
Spearmen		Medium Foot	Protected	Average	Drilled	–	Light Spear	6	6–8	6–12
Conscript spearmen		Medium Foot	Unprotected	Average	Undrilled	–	Light Spear	4	8–10	0–20
Skirmishers		Light Foot	Unprotected	Average	Undrilled	Javelins	Light Spear	4	4	0–4

Khmer and Cham war canoes, by Wayne Reynolds. Taken from New Vanguard 61: Fighting Ships of the Far East (1): China and Southeast Asia 202 BC–AD 1419.

THAI ALLIES

- The commander should be depicted on an elephant.

THAI ALLIES									
Allied commander	Field Commander/Troop Commander						40/25		1
Troop name	Troop Type				Capabilities		Points per base	Bases per BG	Total bases
	Type	Armour	Quality	Training	Shooting	Close Combat			
Elephants	Elephants	–	Average	Undrilled	–	–	25	2	0–2
Cavalry	Cavalry	Protected	Average	Undrilled	–	Light Spear	7	4	0–4
		Unprotected					6		
Warriors	Medium Foot	Protected	Average	Undrilled	–	Light Spear	5	6–8	8–24
	Medium Foot	Protected	Average	Undrilled	–	Light Spear, Swordsmen	6	6–8	

NANZHAO

This list covers the Nanzhao kingdom, centered around Yunnan in modern China, from 738 to 937 AD and thereafter the subsequent Dali kingdom until 1253 when it was destroyed by the Mongols. From 902 to 937 the kingdom had several different names, however we treat them all as Nanzhao.

Originally under the domination of Tang China, Nanzhao rebelled in 750 as the Tang dynasty went into decline, and successfully defended itself against Tang attempts to regain control. Following this the two states actually co-operated on occasion, hence the alliances allowed in the two lists.

TROOP NOTES

Fupai guards are depicted as wearing leather armour, carrying long spears and the front ranks, at least, also carrying large shields. The majority of infantry, however, are shown as

Wangxiezi Tribal Cavalry

unarmoured, with no shields and armed with a smaller spear and swords.

Cavalry are reported to be armed with spears and bows, or later, spears and crossbows, and were possibly the most important part of Nanzhao armies. We assume that as Nanzhao was heavily influenced by the Chinese that they would operate in a manner close to that of the Chinese and so they are classified as either Bow, Swordsmen or Crossbow, Swordsmen.

NANZHAO STARTER ARMY (AFTER 795)		
Commander-in-Chief	1	Field Commander
Sub-commanders	2	2 x Troop Commander
Heavy cavalry	1 BG	4 bases of cavalry: Superior, Armoured, Drilled Cavalry – Crossbow, Swordsmen
Heavy cavalry	2 BGs	Each comprising 4 bases of cavalry: Superior, Protected, Drilled Cavalry – Crossbow, Swordsmen
Wangxiezi tribal cavalry	1 BG	4 bases of Wangxiezi tribal cavalry: Average, Unprotected, Undrilled Light Horse – Bow
Fupai guards	2 BGs	Each comprising 6 bases of fupai guards: 6 Superior, Protected, Drilled Medium Foot – Offensive Spearmen
Spearmen	2 BGs	Each comprising 6 bases of spearmen: Average, Unprotected, Drilled Medium Foot – Light Spear, Swordsmen
Tribal infantry	1 BG	6 bases of tribal infantry: Average, Protected, Undrilled Medium Foot – Impact Foot, Swordsmen
Archers	1 BG	6 bases of archers: Average, Unprotected, Drilled Light Foot – Bow
Camp	1	Unfortified camp
Total	10 BGs	Camp, 16 mounted bases, 36 foot bases, 3 commanders

BUILDING A CUSTOMISED LIST USING OUR ARMY POINTS

Choose an army based on the maxima and minima in the list below. The following special instructions apply to this army:

- Commanders should be depicted as heavy cavalry.

- Only one of the minima marked * applies. If one troop type so marked is taken then the other need not be.

- Only one of the minima marked ** applies. If one troop type so marked is taken then the other need not be.

- The minimum marked *** only applies if any tribal foot are used.

NANZHAO

Territory Types: Agricultural, Hilly, Woodlands

C-in-C		Inspired Commander/Field Commander/Troop Commander				80/50/35		1	
Sub-commanders		Field Commander				50/35		0–2	
		Troop Commander						0–3	

Troop name		Troop Type				Capabilities		Points per base	Bases per BG	Total bases
		Type	Armour	Quality	Training	Shooting	Close Combat			
Core Troops										
Heavy cavalry	Any date	Cavalry	Protected	Superior	Drilled	Bow	Swordsmen	15	4–6	*4–12
			Armoured					19		0–8
	From 795	Cavalry	Protected	Superior	Drilled	Crossbow	Swordsmen	14	4–6	*4–12
			Armoured					18		0–8
Fupai guards		Medium Foot	Protected	Superior	Drilled	–	Offensive Spearmen	10	6–8	6–16
Spearmen		Medium Foot	Unprotected	Average	Drilled	–	Light Spear, Swordsmen	6	6–10	12–48
Archers		Medium Foot	Unprotected	Average	Drilled	Bow	–	6	6–8	**6–12
			Protected					7		
		Light Foot	Unprotected	Average	Drilled	Bow	–	5		
Crossbowmen	Before 795	Medium Foot	Unprotected	Average	Drilled	Crossbow	–	6	4–6	0–6
			Protected					7		
	From 795	Medium Foot	Protected	Average	Drilled	Crossbow	–	7	6–8	**6–16
Optional Troops										
Cavalry Scouts		Light Horse	Unprotected	Average	Drilled	Bow	–	8	4	0–4
Wangxiezi tribal cavalry		Light Horse	Unprotected	Average	Undrilled	Bow	–	8	4	
			Unprotected	Average	Undrilled	Javelins	Light Spear	7		
Other tribal cavalry		Cavalry	Protected	Average	Undrilled	Bow	Swordsmen	11	4	0–4
Elephants		Elephants	–	Average	Undrilled	–	–	25	2	0–2
Tribal infantry		Medium Foot	Protected	Average	Undrilled	–	Impact Foot, Swordsmen	7	6–8	***6–16
		Medium Foot	Protected	Average	Undrilled	–	Light Spear	5	6–8	
Tribal skirmishers		Light Foot	Unprotected	Average	Undrilled	Bow	–	5	6–8	0–8
Fortified Camp								24		0–1
Allies										

Proto-Thai allies (Only from 1181) – Thai

Pyu Burmese allies (Only from 760 to 902)

Tang Chinese allies (Only from 728 to 740) – Western Wei to Early Tang

Tibetan allies (Only from 754 to 793)

Vietnamese rebel allies (Only from 860 to 866) – see Field of Glory Companion 13: *The Lost Scrolls*

NANZHAO ALLIES

Allied commander			Field Commander/Troop Commander				40/25	1	
Troop name		**Troop Type**				**Capabilities**		**Points per base**	**Bases per BG**	**Total bases**

Troop name		Type	Armour	Quality	Training	Shooting	Close Combat	Points per base	Bases per BG	Total bases	
Heavy cavalry	Any date	Cavalry	Protected	Superior	Drilled	Bow	Swordsmen	15	4–6	0–6	4–8
			Armoured					19		0–4	
	From 795	Cavalry	Protected	Superior	Drilled	Crossbow	Swordsmen	14	4–6	0–6	
			Armoured					18		0–4	
Fupai guards		Medium Foot	Protected	Superior	Drilled	–	Offensive Spearmen	10	6–8	6–8	
Spearmen		Medium Foot	Unprotected	Average	Drilled	–	Light Spear, Swordsmen	6	8–10	8–24	
Archers		Medium Foot	Unprotected	Average	Drilled	Bow	–	6	4–6	0–6	0–12
			Protected					7			
		Light Foot	Unprotected	Average	Drilled	Bow	–	5			
Crossbowmen	From 795	Medium Foot	Protected	Average	Drilled	Crossbow	–	7	6–8	0–8	
Tribal infantry		Medium Foot	Protected	Average	Undrilled	–	Impact Foot, Swordsmen	7	6–8	0–8	
		Medium Foot	Protected	Average	Undrilled	–	Light Spear	5	6–8		

PYU BURMESE ALLIES

- The commander should be depicted as cavalry.

PYU BURMESE ALLIES

Allied commander			Field Commander/Troop Commander				40/25	1	
Troop name		**Troop Type**				**Capabilities**		**Points per base**	**Bases per BG**	**Total bases**

Troop name	Type	Armour	Quality	Training	Shooting	Close Combat	Points per base	Bases per BG	Total bases
Cavalry	Cavalry	Protected	Average	Undrilled	–	Light Spear	7	4	0–4
Archers	Medium Foot	Protected	Average	Undrilled	Bow	–	6	6–8	6–18
		Unprotected					5		
	Light Foot	Unprotected	Average	Undrilled	Bow	–	5	6–8	
Spearmen	Medium Foot	Protected	Average	Undrilled	–	Light Spear	5	6–8	6–24

KORYO KOREAN

The Koryo dynasty has also been referred to as 'Neo-Koguryo' due to its centre of power being in northern Korea, and the family background of its rulers. After 770 AD, Korea was turbulent with peasant revolts and civil wars between the important families and their private armies. The Koryo leaders replaced the ruling Shilla factions by 918 with a Unification War that was conducted against other families until 935. Their dynasty lasted until 1392 when an internal revolt by General Yi overthrew the Koryo rulers.

The Koryo Dynasty resisted Mongol attacks for a number of years. Eventually, the Koryo were overwhelmed and became reluctant allies during the Mongol led invasions of Japan.

Japanese pirates surrendering to Korean forces, Tsushima 1389, by Richard Hook. Taken from *Warrior 125: Pirate of the Far East: 811–1639*.

This list covers Koryo Korean armies from 770 to 1392 AD.

TROOP NOTES

"Spearmen" used a mixture of conventional spears, halberds and tridents. We classify the mixture as Heavy Weapon.

The Koryo during their long reign developed several Guard units called the *Toryong* which were loyal to the ruling family rather than independent nobles or regional governors. The *To-bang* were a unit of "spearmen". The *Tae-gak* were a crossbow regiment. The *Singi* were heavily armoured mounted lancers. *To-bang* and *Tae-gak* guard units wore leather or metal hauberks under their choggi. *Kwang-gun* troops were from a new professional soldier class that had replaced the older regional military settlers and professionals that had comprised the Provincial troops.

The *Py-lom-u-ban* was a special force formed to fight Jurchen and Liao armies after 1100. The *Singi-gun* were the cavalry and the *Sinbugun* were the *Kwang-gun* infantry armed with shields and long spears with curved points. A third group in the force was called the *Hang-ma-gun* and consisted of Buddhist monks armed with javelins and shields.

KORYO KOREAN STARTER ARMY (AFTER 1100)		
Commander-in-Chief	1	Field Commander
Sub-commanders	2	2 x Troop Commander
Singi guard	2 BGs	Each comprising 4 bases of Singi guard: Superior, Heavily Armoured, Drilled Cataphracts – Lancers, Swordsmen
Singi-gun cavalry	1 BG	4 bases of Singi-gun cavalry: Superior, Armoured, Drilled Cavalry – Lancers, Swordsmen
Military school trainees	1 BG	4 bases of military school trainees: Average, Unprotected, Drilled Light Horse – Bow
To-bang guard	1 BG	6 bases of To-bang guard: Superior, Protected, Drilled Medium Foot – Heavy Weapon
Kwang-gun "spearmen" and archers in mixed battle groups	2 BGs	Each comprising 6 bases of Kwang-gun "spearmen" and archers in mixed battle groups: 3 Average, Protected, Drilled Medium Foot – Heavy Weapon, 3 Average, Protected, Drilled Medium Foot – Bow
Levy "spearmen" and archers	1 BG	10 bases of levy "spearmen" and archers: 5 Poor, Unprotected, Undrilled Medium Foot – Heavy Weapon, 5 Poor, Unprotected, Undrilled Medium Foot – Bow
Foot nomads	1 BG	6 bases of foot nomads: Average, Unprotected, Undrilled Light Foot – Bow
Camp	1	Unfortified camp
Total	9 BGs	Camp, 16 mounted bases, 34 foot bases, 3 commanders

BUILDING A CUSTOMISED LIST USING OUR ARMY POINTS

Choose an army based on the maxima and minima in the list below. The following special instructions apply to this army:

- Commanders should be depicted as *Singi* guard.
- The total number of bases of *Kwang-gun* spearmen in the army cannot exceed the total number of *Kwang-gun* archers and crossbowmen.

- The total number of bases of Medium Foot crossbowmen in the army cannot exceed the number of bases of Medium Foot archers.

- The minimum marked * applies if any troops so marked are used.

Korean trebuchet, by Wayne Reynolds. Taken from New Vanguard 43: Siege Weapons of the Far East (1): AD 612–1300.

KORYO KOREAN

Territory Types: Developed, Mountains, Hilly, Woodlands

C-in-C		Inspired Commander/Field Commander/Troop Commander					80/50/35	1	
Sub-commanders		Field Commander					50	0–2	
		Troop Commander					35	0–3	
Troop name		**Troop Type**				**Capabilities**	**Points per base**	**Bases per BG**	**Total bases**
		Type	Armour	Quality	Training	Shooting	Close Combat		
Core Troops									
Singi Guard		Cataphracts	Heavily Armoured	Superior	Drilled	–	Lancers, Swordsmen	20	4–6	4–12
		Cavalry	Armoured	Superior	Drilled	–	Lancers, Swordsmen	17	4–6	
Military school trainees		Light Horse	Unprotected	Average	Drilled	Bow	–	8	4–6	0–8
Kwang-gun cavalry		Cavalry	Armoured	Average	Drilled	–	Lancers, Swordsmen	13	4–6	4–18	8–40
Nomad nobles	Only before 1100	Cavalry	Armoured	Average	Undrilled	Bow	Swordsmen	18	4–6	0–6
Other nomad cavalry	Only before 1100	Light Horse	Unprotected	Average	Undrilled	Bow	Swordsmen	10	4–6	0–8
		Cavalry	Unprotected	Average	Undrilled	Bow	Swordsmen	10	4–6	
			Protected					11		
To-bang guard		Medium Foot	Protected	Superior	Drilled	–	Heavy Weapon	10	6–8	0–8
Tae-gak guard		Medium Foot	Protected	Superior	Drilled	Crossbow	–	9	6–8	0–8
Separately deployed Kwang-gun "spearmen"		Medium Foot	Protected	Average	Drilled	–	Heavy Weapon	8	6–8	6–24
Kwang-gun "spearmen" in mixed battle groups		Medium Foot	Protected	Average	Drilled	–	Heavy Weapon	8	1/2	
Kwang-gun archers in mixed battle groups		Medium Foot	Protected	Average	Drilled	Bow	–	7	1/2	6–8	6–24
Kwang-gun crossbowmen in mixed battle groups		Medium Foot	Protected	Average	Drilled	Crossbow	–	7		
Separately deployed Kwang-gun archers		Medium Foot	Protected	Average	Drilled	Bow	–	7	6–8	
Separately deployed Kwang-gun crossbowmen		Medium Foot	Protected	Average	Drilled	Crossbow	–	7	6–8	
Levy "spearmen"		Medium Foot	Unprotected	Poor	Undrilled	–	Heavy Weapon	4	1/2	8–10	10–56
Levy archers		Medium Foot	Unprotected	Poor	Undrilled	Bow	–	3	1/2	
Optional Troops									
Kwang-gun skirmishing archers		Light Foot	Unprotected	Average	Drilled	Bow	–	5	6–8	0–8
Foot Nomads		Light Foot	Unprotected	Average	Undrilled	Bow	–	5	6–8	0–8
Levy skirmishing archers		Light Foot	Unprotected	Poor	Undrilled	Bow	–	3	6–8	0–8
Handgunners	Only from 1375	Light Foot	Unprotected	Average	Drilled	Firearms	–	4	4	0–4
Peasants		Mob	Unprotected	Poor	Undrilled	–	–	2	10–12	0–12
Upgrade Kwang-gun cavalry to Singi-gun	Only from 1100	Cavalry	Armoured	Superior	Drilled	–	Lancers, Swordsmen	17	4–6	*4–12
Hang-ma-gun		Light Foot	Protected	Average	Drilled	Javelins	Light Spear	5	6–8	*0–8
Field fortifications		Field Fortifications						3		0–24
Allies									
Chinese allies (Only from 1300) – Yuan Chinese										
Manchurian Nomad allies – Later Horse Nomad										

KORYO KOREAN ALLIES

Allied commander	Field Commander/Troop Commander						40/25	1	
Troop name	Troop Type				Capabilities		Points per base	Bases per BG	Total bases
	Type	Armour	Quality	Training	Shooting	Close Combat			
Singi Guard	Cataphracts	Heavily Armoured	Superior	Drilled	—	Lancers, Swordsmen	20	4	0–4 / 8–12
	Cavalry	Armoured	Superior	Drilled	—	Lancers, Swordsmen	17	4	
Military school trainees	Light Horse	Unprotected	Average	Drilled	Bow	—	8	4	0–4
Kwang-gun cavalry	Cavalry	Armoured	Average	Drilled	—	Lancers, Swordsmen	13	4	0–6
Separately deployed Kwang-gun "spearmen"	Medium Foot	Protected	Average	Drilled	—	Heavy Weapon	8	6–8	3–8
Kwang-gun "spearmen" in mixed battle groups	Medium Foot	Protected	Average	Drilled	—	Heavy Weapon	8	1/2	
Kwang-gun archers in mixed battle groups	Medium Foot	Protected	Average	Drilled	Bow	—	7	1/2	6–8
Kwang-gun crossbowmen in mixed battle groups	Medium Foot	Protected	Average	Drilled	Crossbow	—	7	1/2	3–8
Separately deployed Kwang-gun archers	Medium Foot	Protected	Average	Drilled	Bow	—	7	6–8	
Separately deployed Kwang-gun crossbowmen	Medium Foot	Protected	Average	Drilled	Crossbow	—	7	6–8	
Levy "spearmen"	Medium Foot	Unprotected	Poor	Undrilled	—	Heavy Weapon	4	1/2	6–10 / 6–16
Levy archers	Medium Foot	Unprotected	Poor	Undrilled	Bow	—	3	1/2	

EARLY HEIAN JAPANESE

This list covers Japanese armies from the start of the period when the capital was at Heian-kyo (Kyoto, 794–1185 AD) until the earliest possible date for the introduction of the naginata and latest plausible date for archers behind shield walls – c.1040.

TROOP NOTES

Armies were much smaller than in the preceding *ritsuryo* period, in the low thousands or even mere hundreds. They were led by powerful local warlords fighting either for the Imperial court or on their own behalf, and based around relatives and retainers fighting as mounted archers. These and the *kondei*, ('strong fellows'), established in 792, evolved into the *bushi* or *samurai*.

Although the provincial *heishi* militia had been abolished in most of the country in 792, they remained in existence in the northern provinces of Mutsu and Dewa, where they served at least as late as the Emishi rising of 878, and were even increased in numbers in 815.

Oyumi artillery remained an essential part of 9th-century armies but were rare later because it became increasingly difficult to find skilled men to maintain them.

Most of the troops were still infantry archers, either retainers or conscripts, fighting as archers behind shield-walls as in the earlier period, but less well-trained.

Mounted Bushi

In 940 a strong wind blew over a line of pavises leaving the archers behind unprotected. Other

Banrui

infantry, conscripted peasants called *nimbei sei* in the 9th century and *banrui* allies in the 10th, included men with spears and small shields but were very unreliable.

EARLY HEIAN JAPANESE STARTER ARMY (BEFORE 900)

Commander-in-Chief	1	Troop Commander
Sub-commanders	2	2 x Troop Commander
Kondei and bushi	3 BGs	Each comprising 4 bases of kondei and bushi: Superior, Armoured, Undrilled Cavalry – Bow, Swordsmen
Pacified Emish mounted archers	1 BG	4 bases of pacified Emishi mounted archers: Superior, Protected, Undrilled Cavalry – Bow, Swordsmen
Followers fighting behind standing shields	3 BGs	Each comprising 8 bases of followers fighting behind standing shields: Average, Armoured, Undrilled Medium Foot – Bow
Pacified Emishi foot archers	1 BG	6 bases of pacified Emishi foot archers: Average, Unprotected, Undrilled Light Foot – Bow
Camp	1	Unfortified camp
Total	8 BGs	Camp, 16 mounted bases, 30 foot bases, 3 commanders

BUILDING A CUSTOMISED LIST USING OUR ARMY POINTS

Choose an army based on the maxima and minima in the list below. The following special instructions apply to this army:

- Commanders should be depicted as *kondei / bushi*.
- A Japanese allied commander's contingent must conform to the Early Heian Japanese allies list below, but the troops in the contingent are deducted from the minima and maxima in the main list.

Samurai commanders, by Richard Hook. Taken from Elite 125: Samurai Commanders (1): 940–1576.

EARLY HEIAN JAPANESE

Territory Types: Agricultural, Developed, Hilly

C-in-C	Inspired Commander/Field Commander/Troop Commander						80/50/35	1	
Sub-commanders	Field Commander						50	0–2	
	Troop Commander						35	0–3	
Japanese allied commanders	Field Commander/Troop Commander						40/25	0–2	

Troop name	Troop Type				Capabilities		Points per base	Bases per BG	Total bases
	Type	Armour	Quality	Training	Shooting	Close Combat			
Core Troops									
Kondei and bushi mounted archers	Before 900	Cavalry	Armoured	Superior	Undrilled	Bow	Swordsmen	18	4–6	4–16
	From 900									6–24
Followers fighting behind standing shields		Medium Foot	Armoured	Average	Undrilled	Bow	–	8	6–8	24–120
			Armoured	Poor				6		
			Protected	Average				6		
			Protected	Poor				4		
Heishi militia	Only Mutsu or Dewa provinces before 900	Medium Foot	Armoured	Poor	Drilled	Bow	Light Spear	7	1/2 6–8	
						Bow	–	7	1/2	
		Medium Foot	Protected	Poor	Drilled	Bow	Light Spear	5	1/2 6–8	
						Bow	–	5	1/2	
Nimbei sei conscripts, banrui or similar		Medium Foot	Unprotected	Poor	Undrilled	–	Light Spear	2	6–8	0–12
Optional Troops									
Pacified Emishi foot archers	Only before 900	Medium Foot	Unprotected	Average	Undrilled	Bow	–	5	6–8	0–8
		Light Foot	Unprotected	Average	Undrilled	Bow	–	5	6–8	
Pacified Emishi mounted archers	Only before 900	Cavalry	Armoured	Superior	Undrilled	Bow	Swordsman	18	4	0–4
			Protected					14		
Artillery oyumi	Only before 900	Light Artillery	–	Average	Drilled	Light Artillery	–	17	2	0–6
	Only from 900									0–2

EARLY HEIAN JAPANESE ALLIES

Allied commander	Field Commander/Troop Commander						40/25	1	
Troop name	Troop Type				Capabilities		Points per base	Bases per BG	Total bases
	Type	Armour	Quality	Training	Shooting	Close Combat			
Kondei and bushi mounted archers		Cavalry	Armoured	Superior	Undrilled	Bow	Swordsmen	18	4–6	4–8
Followers fighting behind standing shields		Medium Foot	Armoured	Average	Undrilled	Bow	–	8	6–8	8–36
			Armoured	Poor				6		
			Protected	Average				6		
			Protected	Poor				4		
Heishi militia	Only Mutsu or Dewa provinces before 900	Medium Foot	Armoured	Poor	Drilled	Bow	Light Spear	7	1/2 6–8	
						Bow	–	7	1/2	
		Medium Foot	Protected	Poor	Drilled	Bow	Light Spear	5	1/2 6–8	
						Bow	–	5	1/2	

PAGAN BURMESE

The Burmese city of Pagan (Bagan) was first established in 849 AD at a strategic location on the banks of the Irrawaddy by ethnically Burman peoples migrating into the area. Throughout this period small city-states of Mon or Pyu people dotted the Burmese landscape.

In 1044 King Anawrahta seized the throne of Pagan and attacked both Mon and Shan towns in the region and came to rule over most of modern Burma (Myanmar). The Pagan Empire

was centred on the city of Pagan and was dominated by ethnically Burman people. Other main centres of Pagan power were the cities of Ava and Toungoo.

Pagan Burma fought many campaigns against non-Burman towns in Burma, invading Chinese expeditions, city-states in the eastern part of India, and the Mongols of Yuan China. The Mongol expedition which conquered Pagan contained a higher percentage of Mongol troops than earlier Yuan armies which had failed.

Thai allies were from Lanna-thai and Sukho-thai.

This list covers Pagan Burmese armies from 849 until 1287 when Khubilai Khan's Mongols sacked Pagan.

TROOP NOTES

Marco Polo describes Burmese elephants at the battle of Vochan (1272) as having castles on their backs capable of accommodating 12 or 16 crew. However, Jewish and Greek sources also (probably unreliably) describe elephants from more westerly states with huge crews, so we do not treat Burmese elephants differently from others.

Unshielded troops classified as Protected wear quilted cotton armour. Some crossbowmen, at least, seem to have been double armed with spear or halberd.

Levy craftsmen represent the large numbers of peasants who responded to the muster call with only hammers and other tools. Their primary task was to build a palisade for the army each night. During a battle they were placed in the centre to absorb enemy missile fire.

Mong troops represent troops contributed by non-Burman towns. Mong was the common term for the many small walled towns in Burma, not to be confused with the Mon, which were (and still are) a non-Burman ethnic group, as were (are) the Shan.

The Pagan rulers used Indian bodyguards between 1040 and 1100. King Narapatisithu (1173–1210) established the foot guards.

PAGAN BURMESE STARTER ARMY		
Commander-in-Chief	1	Troop Commander
Sub-commanders	2	2 x Troop Commander
Elephants	4 BGs	Each comprising 2 bases of elephants: Average, Undrilled Elephants
Cavalry	2 BGs	Each comprising 4 bases of cavalry: Average, Protected, Undrilled Cavalry – Light Spear
Burman spearmen	2 BGs	Each comprising 6 bases of Burman spearmen: Average, Protected, Undrilled Medium Foot – Light Spear
Mon warriors	2 BGs	Each comprising 8 bases of Mon warriors: Average, Protected, Undrilled Medium Foot – Impact Foot, Swordsmen
Burman archers	2 BGs	Each comprising 6 bases of Burman archers: Average, Unprotected, Drilled Light Foot – Bow
Camp	1	Unfortified camp
Total	12 BGs	Camp, 16 mounted bases, 40 foot bases, 3 commanders

BUILDING A CUSTOMISED LIST USING OUR ARMY POINTS

Choose an army based on the maxima and minima in the list below. The following special instructions apply to this army:

- Commanders should be depicted on elephants or as cavalry.

PAGAN BURMESE

Territory Types: Agricultural, Mountains, Hilly, Woodlands, Tropical

C-in-C		Inspired Commander/Field Commander/Troop Commander					80/50/35		1	
Sub-commanders		Field Commander					50		0–2	
		Troop Commander					35		0–3	

Troop name		Troop Type				Capabilities		Points per base	Bases per BG	Total bases
		Type	Armour	Quality	Training	Shooting	Close Combat			
Core Troops										
Elephants	Only from 1100	Elephants	–	Average	–	–	–	25	2	4–12
Burman archers	Any date	Light Foot	Unprotected	Average	Undrilled	Bow	–	5	6–8	12–60
		Medium Foot	Protected	Average	Undrilled	Bow	–	6	6–8	
			Unprotected					5		
	Only from 1173	Medium Foot	Protected	Average	Drilled	Bow	–	7	6–8	
			Unprotected					6		
Burman spearmen	Any date	Medium Foot	Protected	Average	Undrilled	–	Light Spear	5	6–8	12–100
	Only from 1173	Medium Foot	Protected	Average	Drilled	–	Light Spear	6	6–8	
Optional Troops										
Guard cavalry	Only before 1040 or from 1173	Cavalry	Protected	Average	Drilled	–	Light Spear	8	4	0–4 / 0–8
Other Burman cavalry		Cavalry	Protected	Average	Undrilled	–	Light Spear	7	4–6	0–8
Indian bodyguard	Only from 1040 to 1100	Medium Foot	Protected	Average	Drilled	–	Light Spear, Swordsmen	7	4–6	0–6
Guard foot	Only from 1173	Medium Foot	Protected	Average	Drilled	–	Swordsmen	7	4–6	0–6
Burman crossbowmen	Any date	Light Foot	Unprotected	Average	Undrilled	Crossbow	–	5	6–8	0–12
		Medium Foot	Protected	Average	Undrilled	Crossbow	–	6	6–8	
			Unprotected					5		
	Only from 1173	Medium Foot	Protected	Average	Drilled	Crossbow	–	7	6–8	
			Unprotected					6		
Burman crossbowmen or archers with spear or halberd	Any date	Medium Foot	Protected	Average	Undrilled	Crossbow or Bow	Light Spear	6	6–8	
			Unprotected					5		
	Only from 1173	Medium Foot	Protected	Average	Drilled	Crossbow or Bow	Light Spear	7		
			Unprotected					6		
Mong cavalry		Cavalry	Unprotected	Poor	Undrilled	–	Light Spear	4	4	0–4
Mong spearmen		Medium Foot	Unprotected	Poor	Undrilled	–	Light Spear	2	6–8	0–12
Mong archers		Medium Foot	Unprotected	Poor	Undrilled	Bow	–	3	6–8	0–12
Mon warriors		Medium Foot	Protected	Average	Undrilled	–	Impact Foot, Swordsmen	7	8–12	0–16 / 0–24
		Medium Foot	Protected	Poor	Undrilled	–	Swordsmen	4	8–12	
Shan spearmen		Medium Foot	Unprotected	Average	Undrilled	–	Impact Foot	5	8–12	0–16
		Medium Foot	Unprotected	Poor	Undrilled	–	Light Spear	2	8–12	
Levy craftsmen or other peasants		Mob	Unprotected	Poor	Undrilled	–	–	2	10–12	0–24
Bolt-shooters		Light Artillery	–	Average	Undrilled	Light Artillery	–	15	2	0–2
Stone-throwers		Light Artillery	–	Average	Undrilled	Light Artillery	–	15	2	
Fortified camp								24		0–1
Allies										
Thai allies (Only from 1240)										

LIAO

This list covers Qidan (Khitan) armies from 907 AD until the fall of their Liao dynasty to the Jurchen Jin dynasty in 1125, and then the successor Qara Khitai (Western Liao/Xi Liao) state until its fall in 1211.

Although the Qidan had been in existence for centuries it wasn't until Yelü Abaoji took control of the tribes that the period of Qidan greatness began. In 905 he led 70,000 cavalry into China to the assistance of the Shatuo in Hedong, who were emerging as the major power at the end of the Tang dynasty. In 907 he was elected Khagan (Great Khan) of the Qidan peoples and this marks the real start of the imperial history of the Qidan.

Although they did not formally adopt the dynastic name of Liao until 947, Abaoji had used it as an era name from 916.

Always interested in China, the Liao took advantage of the Later Jin need for military support to obtain a strategically important territorial foothold in China proper, the so called Sixteen Prefectures. This also gave them control of a Chinese population and they exploited this by raising numerous Chinese infantry for a number of campaigns, although their strength was always their Qidan cavalry. To cope with a dual population of steppe people and sedentary Han Chinese the Liao developed an innovative dual system with parallel offices and officials, one set for the Qidan and the other for the Han Chinese. This system was also used by later steppe rulers of China.

Although the situation with the Sixteen Prefectures meant that there was always the possibility of war with the Song Chinese, Liao military superiority meant that the Song were forced to accept a peace treaty in 1005 that saw them pay a large annual tribute to the Liao.

However, with one brief exception, the peace held for over a century, making it one of the most successful peace treaties in history.

In the early 12th century the Liao suffered rebellions from their Jurchen subjects in Manchuria. The Song, sensing a possibility to recapture the Sixteen Prefectures, allied with the Jurchen. Despite little Song help, the Jurchens were surprisingly successful, and by 1125 the Liao Empire had utterly collapsed. However, one member of the ruling clan, Yelü Dashi, took a remnant of the Liao westward and founded a successor state in central Asia which is known as the Qara Khitai - although they themselves officially carried on using the Liao dynastic name and so are also known as the Xi Liao (Western Liao). The Qara Khitai maintained their new state until 1211 when its rule was usurped by exiled Naimans under Kuchlug. It fell in turn to the Mongols in 1218.

The medieval term for China – Cathay – is derived from Khitan/Khitai.

TROOP NOTES

Liao and Qara Khitai armies were based around their formidable ordo heavy cavalry fighting in traditional steppe-style, although particularly well-equipped. The full list of equipment was: nine pieces of iron armour, saddle clothes, bridles, armour of leather and iron for the horses, four bows, four hundred arrows, a long and a short spear, a club (mace), a halberd, small banner, hammer, awl, knife and flint, a bucket for the horse, a peck of dried food, a grappling hook, a felt umbrella and two hundred feet of rope! However, some of the cavalry may have been less well-equipped, lacking horse armour in particular, and these are identified as "foragers".

Liao council of war, by Michael Perry. Taken from Men-at-Arms 295:
Imperial Chinese Armies (2): 590–1260 AD.

Whilst these still meet the *Field of Glory* "Armoured" classification they may have been less effective than the fully equipped troops and so we allow the option for Average quality. These troops can also represent the Chinese cavalry that were present in some Liao armies.

Ordo Forager

Chinese infantry came mainly from the "Sixteen Prefectures" taken over from the Chinese Later Jin dynasty in 936 and so we assume they would follow the organisation of Chinese infantry of that time and not follow changes subsequently made in China under the Song dynasty. Anti-cavalry squads represent Chinese infantry armed with a mixture of two-handed swords, axes, pole axes and shorter swords. One of the main roles of such troops in Song armies was to fight enemy cavalry. We assume they served the same function in Liao armies, hence we have classified them as Heavy Foot.

LIAO STARTER ARMY (BETWEEN 936 AND 1125)

Commander-in-Chief	1	Field Commander
Sub-commanders	2	2 x Troop Commander
Ordo cavalry	2 BGs	Each comprising 4 bases of Ordo cavalry: Superior, Armoured, Drilled Cavalry – Bow, Swordsmen
Ordo "foragers"	2 BGs	Each comprising 4 bases of Ordo "foragers": Average, Armoured, Drilled Cavalry – Bow, Swordsmen
Tribal cavalry	2 BGs	Each comprising 4 bases of tribal cavalry: Average, Unprotected, Undrilled Light Horse – Bow, Swordsmen
Chinese regular infantry	3 BGs	Each comprising 6 bases of Chinese regular infantry: 3 Average, Protected, Drilled Medium Foot – Light Spear, Swordsmen, 3 Average, Protected, Drilled Medium Foot – Bow
Camp	1	Unfortified camp
Total	9 BGs	Camp, 24 mounted bases, 18 foot bases, 3 commanders

BUILDING A CUSTOMISED LIST USING OUR ARMY POINTS

Choose an army based on the maxima and minima in the list below. The following special instructions apply to this army:

- Commanders should be depicted as ordo cavalry.
- There must be at least as many ordo cavalry battle groups as ordo "forager" battle groups.
- Only one allied contingent can be used.

LIAO

Territory Types: Only before 936 – Steppes. Only from 936 to 1125 – Agricultural, Developed, Hilly, Steppes.
Only from 1126 – Agricultural, Developed, Steppes

C-in-C		Inspired Commander/Field Commander/Troop Commander					80/50/35		1	
Sub-commanders		Field Commander					50		0–2	
		Troop Commander					35		0–3	

Troop name		Troop Type				Capabilities		Points per base	Bases per BG	Total bases	
		Type	Armour	Quality	Training	Shooting	Close Combat				
Core Troops											
Ordo cavalry		Cavalry	Armoured	Superior	Drilled	Bow	Swordsmen	19	4–6	4–24	12–48
Ordo "foragers"		Cavalry	Armoured	Superior	Drilled	Bow	Swordsmen	19	4–6	4–30	
Ordo "foragers" or Chinese cavalry		Cavalry	Armoured	Average	Drilled	Bow	Swordsmen	15	4–6		
Tribal cavalry		Light Horse	Unprotected	Average	Undrilled	Bow	Swordsmen	10	4–6	4–30	
		Cavalry	Unprotected	Average	Undrilled	Bow	Swordsmen	10	4–6		
			Protected					11			
		Cavalry	Armoured	Superior	Undrilled	Bow	Swordsmen	18	4–6	0–6	
Optional Troops											
Tribal infantry		Light Foot	Unprotected	Average	Undrilled	Bow	–	5	6–8	0–12	
				Poor				3			
		Medium Foot	Unprotected	Average	Undrilled	Bow	–	5	6–8		
				Poor				3			
Anti-cavalry squads	Only from 936 to 1125	Heavy Foot	Protected	Average	Undrilled	–	Heavy Weapon	7	4–8	0–8	
					Drilled			8			
Other Chinese regular infantry		Medium Foot	Protected	Average	Drilled	–	Light Spear, Swordsmen	7	1/2	6–8	0–24
		Medium Foot	Protected	Average	Drilled	Bow or Crossbow	–	7	1/2		
Chinese militia		Medium Foot	Protected	Poor	Undrilled	–	Light Spear, Swordsmen	4	8–10	0–16	0–30
		Medium Foot	Protected	Poor	Undrilled	Bow or Crossbow	–	4	8–10	0–24	
			Unprotected					3			
Chinese light stone-throwers or heavy crossbow artillery		Light Artillery	–	Average	Drilled	Light Artillery	–	17	2	0–2	
City militia	Only from 1130	Heavy Foot	Protected	Poor	Undrilled	–	Defensive Spearmen	4	8–10	0–16	
Fortified camp								24		0–1	
Allies											
Khwarazmian allies (Only from 1198 to 1207) – Khwarazmian – see Field of Glory Companion 4: Swords and Scimitars: The Crusades											
Northern Han allies (Only from 951 to 979) – Late Tang to Five Dynasties Chinese											
Qarakhanid allies (Only from 1128 to 1207) – Later Horse Nomads											
Uighur allies (Only from 1130 to 1208) – Later Horse Nomads											
Xi, Tatar or other steppe allies – Later Horse Nomads											
Special Campaigns											
Yelu Deguang in 947											
Sacrificial poor quality troops		Cavalry	Protected	Poor	Undrilled	Bow	Swordsmen	9	4–6	4–8	
Qara Khitai in 1210											
Elephants		Elephants	–	Average	Undrilled	–	–	25	2	2	

LIAO ALLIES

Allied commander		Field Commander/Troop Commander					50/35		1	
Troop name	Troop Type				Capabilities		Points per base	Bases per BG	Total bases	
	Type	Armour	Quality	Training	Shooting	Close Combat				
Ordo cavalry	Cavalry	Armoured	Superior	Drilled	Bow	Swordsmen	19	4–6	4–8	4–16
Ordo "foragers"	Cavalry	Armoured	Superior	Drilled	Bow	Swordsmen	19	4–6	0–8	
Ordo "foragers" or Chinese cavalry	Cavalry	Armoured	Average	Drilled	Bow	Swordsmen	15	4–6		
Tribal cavalry	Light Horse	Unprotected	Average	Undrilled	Bow	Swordsmen	10	4–6	0–8	
	Cavalry	Unprotected	Average	Undrilled	Bow	Swordsmen	10	4–6		
		Protected					11			

SONG CHINESE

In 960 AD Zhao Kuangyin engineered a coup against the Later Zhou and set up his own Song dynasty in their stead. Remarkably, although there was no real difference between the regimes, the Song did not just become the sixth dynasty but went on to once again unite most of China.

Initial Song wars were against other Chinese armies, and in this they were generally successful. However, following the overthrow of the Liao vassal state of Northern Han, the second Song Emperor decided to try and recapture the

Song Emperor

disputed Sixteen Prefectures ceded to the Liao by the Later Jin in 936. Unfortunately this overstretched an already weary Song army and it was heavily defeated, with the emperor fleeing the field in a mule cart. War continued until 1005 with the Song mainly on the defensive. In 1005 the Chanyuan Covenant was agreed which saw the Song pay a large annual indemnity of 200,000 bolts of silk and 100,000 ounces of silver to the Liao in exchange for peace, which lasted for over a century – although it had to be renegotiated once, to Song disadvantage, to prevent the Liao joining the Xi Xia in a war against the Song.

Eventually the rebellion of the Manchurian Jurchen against their Liao overlords gave the Song an opportunity to try and regain lost Chinese territory. However, this backfired as the Jurchen objected to handing over the Sixteen Prefectures to the Song on the not unreasonable grounds that the Song had not met their obligations under their alliance. A Song attempt to take territory by force was an abject failure and a rapid Jurchen counter-attack drove the Song from northern China to south of the Yangtze River. The Song imperial family was almost entirely wiped out by the Jurchen, but the one surviving prince managed to hold the remnants of the state together in the

south, and with the help of loyal generals, such as Yue Fei, held the Yangtze line. The subsequent state in the south is conventionally known as Southern Song and the former unified state as the Northern Song.

In a mirror of the situation with the Liao, the Song mostly managed to accept their militarily inferior position and so generally remained at peace with the Jurchens, who had now declared their own Jin dynasty. However, their ambition was to regain control of the whole of China and occasional, usually unsuccessful, campaigns were launched to regain territory. In the 13th century, as the Jin came under attack from the Mongols,

now unified by Genghis Khan, the Song attempted to reclaim lost territory whilst the Jin were thus preoccupied. As previously, they badly misjudged the situation and soon found themselves at war with the victorious Mongols.

Once again the fact that the south of China is poor territory for cavalry aided the Chinese and the Mongols made limited headway to start with. However, under Khubilai Khan, who as well as being Great Khan was also the first Yuan emperor, the Mongols finally created an effective riverine navy, and this, combined with an attack from the western part of China, eventually conquered the Southern Song in 1279. The last

Northern Song troops, by Michael Perry. Taken from Men-at-Arms 295: Imperial Chinese Armies (2): 590–1260 AD.

Song emperor, a 9-year old boy, was drowned after the final naval battle when a court official jumped into the sea with him.

This list covers both Northern and Southern Song armies, the former from 960 to 1127, and the latter from then until the end of the Yuan conquest in 1279.

TROOP NOTES

Infantry formations were made up of a single rank of close combat troops armed with a mix of spears, pole arms and swords, three ranks of crossbowmen and a single rank of archers. They were expected to put the enemy to flight by dense crossbow shooting. We feel that a classification as Medium Foot, half Light Spear, Crossbow, half Crossbow, best reproduces the historical effect.

From around 1067, under the influence of the reformer Wang Anshi, the close combat troops in the infantry were equipped with a larger proportion of large swords, axes and pole arms. This does not affect their classification when in mixed battle groups, but gives the option of classification as Heavy Weapon if the infantry are

Regular Infantry

deployed in separate bodies. It is possible that the proportion of close combat troops increased around this time as well.

A mid-11th century writer recommended that weapons should not be mixed in the same formation and that crossbowmen could stop a cavalry charge on their own. It is unclear if this advice was put into practice, however an account from Southern Song times suggests that some infantry could not cope with Jin cavalry which would be consistent with a unit with no missile power being attacked. Therefore, we allow battle groups of separate troops to be fielded but on an all or none basis.

"Companies of Archers" were a militia on the northern borders of the Northern Song. They were given the produce of vacant fields to support themselves and equip them with armour and a horse. They are described as being equal to their enemy in weapons, armour, saddlery and horses. As the enemy would mainly be the Liao it is probable that the account talks them up somewhat and so we only rate them as Protected at best.

The Southern Song general Yue Fei successfully used picked bodies of specially trained men allegedly armed with the *zhanmadao*, "horse chopping sword", against the Jin armies in campaigns between 1129 and 1141. As the *zhanmadao* is associated with heavy *mazhadao* swords and pole-axes, they are treated as Heavy Weapons. Their tactics may have been adopted by other similar troops in his army as halberds and crossbows were said to be the weapons the Jin most feared in Song armies.

NORTHERN SONG CHINESE STARTER ARMY

Commander-in-Chief	1	Field Commander
Sub-commanders	2	2 x Troop Commander
Guard cavalry	2 BGs	Each comprising 4 bases of guard cavalry: Superior, Armoured, Drilled Cavalry – Bow, Swordsmen
Other cavalry	2 BGs	Each comprising 4 bases of other cavalry: Average, Protected, Drilled Cavalry – Bow, Swordsmen
Regular infantry in mixed formations	3 BGs	Each comprising 8 bases of regular infantry in mixed formations: 4 Average, Protected, Drilled Medium Foot – Crossbow, Light Spear, 4 Average, Protected, Drilled Medium Foot – Crossbow
Skirmishers	1 BG	6 bases of skirmishers: Average, Unprotected, Drilled Light Foot – Bow
Southern auxiliaries	1 BG	6 bases of southern auxiliaries: Average, Unprotected, Undrilled Light Foot – Bow
Camp	1	Unfortified camp
Total	9 BGs	Camp, 16 mounted bases, 36 foot bases, 3 commanders

SOUTHERN SONG CHINESE STARTER ARMY

Commander-in-Chief	1	Field Commander (Yue Fei)
Sub-commanders	2	2 x Troop Commander
Guard cavalry	1 BG	4 bases of guard cavalry: Superior, Armoured, Drilled Cavalry – Bow, Swordsmen
Other cavalry	2 BGs	Each comprising 4 bases of other cavalry: Average, Protected, Drilled Cavalry – Bow, Swordsmen
Retrained close fighting infantry	3 BGs	Each comprising 8 bases of Chinese close fighting infantry: Average, Protected, Drilled Heavy Foot – Heavy Weapon
Crossbowmen	2 BGs	Each comprising 8 bases of crossbowmen: Average, Protected, Drilled Medium Foot – Crossbow
Camp	1	Unfortified camp
Total	8 BGs	Camp, 12 mounted bases, 40 foot bases, 3 commanders

BUILDING A CUSTOMISED LIST USING OUR ARMY POINTS

Choose an army based on the maxima and minima in the list below. The following special instructions apply to this army:

- Commanders should be depicted as guard cavalry.

- From 1050 only one set of troops with minima marked * can be used.
- The minima marked ** only apply if regular infantry in separate formations are used.
- "Companies of Archers" cannot be used with Southern Auxiliaries.

SONG CHINESE

Territory Types: Northern Song – Agricultural, Developed, Hilly, Tropical. Southern Song – Developed, Hilly, Tropical

C-in-C		Inspired Commander/Field Commander/Troop Commander					80/50/35	1	
Sub-commanders		Field Commander					50	0–2	
		Troop Commander					35	0–3	

Troop name		Troop Type				Capabilities		Points per base	Bases per BG	Total bases
		Type	Armour	Quality	Training	Shooting	Close Combat			
Core Troops										
Guard and similar good cavalry	Only Northern Song	Cavalry	Armoured	Superior	Drilled	Bow	Swordsmen	19	4–6	4–12
	Only Southern Song	Cavalry	Armoured	Superior	Drilled	Bow	Swordsmen	19	4	0–4
Other cavalry		Cavalry	Armoured	Average	Drilled	Bow	Swordsmen	15	4–6	4–8
			Protected					12		
		Cavalry	Armoured	Poor	Drilled	Bow	Swordsmen	12	4–6	
			Protected					10		
Regular infantry in mixed formations	Any date	Medium Foot	Protected	Average	Drilled	Crossbow	Light Spear	7	1/2	*18–64
		Medium Foot	Protected	Average	Drilled	Crossbow	–	7	1/2	
	Only from 1005	Medium Foot	Protected	Poor	Drilled	Crossbow	Light Spear	5	1/2	6–8
		Medium Foot	Protected	Poor	Drilled	Crossbow	–	5	1/2	
Regular infantry in separate formations	Only from 1050	Medium Foot	Protected	Average	Drilled	–	Heavy Weapon	8	6–8	**6–16
				Poor				6		
		Medium Foot	Protected	Average	Drilled	Crossbow	–	7	6–8	**12–40	*18–64
				Poor				5		
		Medium Foot	Protected	Average	Drilled	Bow	–	7	6–8	0–16
				Poor				5		
Optional Troops										
"Companies of Archers"	Only Northern Song	Cavalry	Protected	Average	Undrilled	Bow	Swordsmen	11	4	0–4
			Unprotected					10		
Crossbow guards	Only Southern Song from 1162	Medium Foot	Protected	Superior	Drilled	Crossbow		9	4–6	0–6
Anti-cavalry squads		Heavy Foot	Protected	Average	Undrilled	–	Heavy Weapon	7	6–8	0–12
					Drilled			8		
Provincial or other poor quality infantry		Medium Foot	Protected	Poor	Undrilled	–	Heavy Weapon	5	8–10	0–32	0–64
		Medium Foot	Protected	Poor	Undrilled	Crossbow	–	4	8–10	0–32
			Unprotected					3		
		Medium Foot	Protected	Poor	Undrilled	Bow	–	4	8–10	0–16
			Unprotected					3		
Skirmishers		Light Foot	Unprotected	Average	Drilled	Bow	–	5	6–8	0–8
		Light Foot	Unprotected	Average	Drilled	Crossbow	–	5	6–8	
Southern auxiliaries		Medium Foot	Protected	Average	Undrilled	–	Light Spear	5	6–8	0–16
		Medium Foot	Protected	Average	Undrilled	–	Impact Foot, Swordsmen	7	6–8	
		Medium Foot	Protected	Average	Undrilled	–	Light Spear, Swordsmen	6	6–8	
		Light Foot	Unprotected	Average	Undrilled	Bow	–	5	6–8	0–8
		Light Foot	Unprotected	Average	Undrilled	Crossbow	–	5	6–8	
Huotong "fire tube" armed infantry	Only Southern Song from 1200	Light Foot	Unprotected	Average	Drilled	Firearm		4	4	0–4
Mongol mercenaries or deserters	Only Southern Song from 1250	Light Horse	Unprotected	Superior	Drilled	Bow	Swordsmen	12	4–6	0–8
				Average				10		
		Cavalry	Unprotected	Superior	Drilled	Bow	Swordsmen	13	4–6	
			Protected	Superior				15		
			Unprotected	Average	Drilled	Bow	Swordsmen	11		
			Protected	Average				12		

Light stone-throwers or heavy crossbow artillery	Only Northern Song	Light Artillery	–	Average	Drilled	Light Artillery	–	17	2	0–4
	Only Southern Song									0–6
Heavy stone-throwers	Only Northern Song	Heavy Artillery	–	Average	Drilled	Heavy Artillery	–	25	2	0–2
	Only Southern Song									0–4
Palisades or similar		Field Fortifications						3		0–24
Fortified Camp								24		0–1
Special Campaigns										
Northern Song conquest of Southern Tang 974 to 976										
Wuyue allies – Late Tang to Five Dynasties Chinese										
Yue Fei's Southern Song 1129 to 1141										
Replace all Heavy Weapon troops with retrained units		Heavy Foot	Protected	Average	Drilled	–	Heavy Weapon	8	6–8	All or none

XI XIA

This list covers the Tangut Xi Xia (Western Xia) state from 967 AD until their destruction by Genghis Khan in 1227.

The origin of the Xi Xia state lies in the last decades of the Tang dynasty when rulers of the descendants of the Qiang living on the western borders of China were appointed military governors (*jiedushi*) and in 883 were elevated to the position of Dukes of Xia – that is, controlling the Xia region. They maintained this position through the upheavals of the Five Dynasties period and were further raised to the position of King of Xiping in 954 by the Later Zhou ruler. The Song, needing a stable frontier, were happy to leave the situation as they found it, and in 967, when the then King of Xiping died, the Song posthumously recognised him as King of Xia – a tacit admission that the Xia were politically independent.

Nomad Auxiliary

Despite this independence, it was not until 1032 that the Xia ruler, Li Yuanhao, declared himself Emperor of the Xia dynasty. This is usually called the Xi Xia in Chinese records, although they called themselves the Da Xia (Great Xia). Li Yuanhao rapidly capitalised on the friction between the Song and Liao to try and extract from the Song a tributary arrangement such as the Liao benefited from. This involved intriguing with the Liao to give the Song the idea that they might be faced by a war on two fronts against two powerful enemies. The result of the war that followed from 1038 to 1045 was a military stalemate. Although the Song suffered badly at first as their army had not been at war for decades, they recovered, and the Xia were not able to make much progress. However, they did succeed in negotiating a valuable treaty, by which they were paid an annual indemnity. A short second war was fought in 1081–82, but this made little difference to the status quo.

Relations with the Jin following their defeat of the Northern Song were cordial, even though the Jin insisted on treating the Xia as an inferior – which in reality they were. By tacitly accepting this, the Xia did not bring down military retribution on themselves, and the Jin were satisfied to leave them be.

In 1205 the Mongols started to raid Xia territory, and in 1209 the Xia were forced to submit and contribute troops to the Mongol war against the Jin. In 1223 the Xia emperor Shenzong was forced to abdicate as a result of the alliance with the Mongols and his successor had little choice but to change sides and ally with the Jin. This brought down the wrath of Genghis Khan on the Xia and he personally led the army that was to destroy them. Although the campaign was successful and the Xi Xia state destroyed, Genghis himself died towards the end of the campaign in 1227.

TROOP NOTES

The Xi Xia cavalry are stated by one Chinese source as trying "... to break our formation or crush our infantry ..." and the crossbowmen alone would not be enough to stop them. Therefore, we classify them as Lancers, Swordsmen although bows may have been carried under steppe influence. The cavalry are recorded as dismounting to attack in difficult terrain.

Infantry are assumed to be based around Chinese types as the Xi Xia power was based in former Chinese western prefectures. They would probably be supplemented by irregular troops armed in traditional Qiang styles. Anti-cavalry squads represent Chinese infantry armed with a mixture of two-handed swords, axes, pole axes and shorter swords. One of the main roles of such troops in Song armies was to fight enemy cavalry. We assume they served the same function in Xi Xia armies, hence we have classified them as Heavy Foot.

XI XIA STARTER ARMY		
Commander-in-Chief	1	Field Commander
Sub-commanders	2	2 x Troop Commander
Cavalry	4 BGs	Each comprising 4 bases of cavalry: Superior, Armoured, Drilled Cavalry – Lancers, Swordsmen
Nomad auxiliaries	2 BGs	Each comprising 4 bases of nomad auxiliaries: Average, Unprotected, Undrilled Light Horse – Bow, Swordsmen
Regular infantry	2 BGs	Each comprising 6 bases of Chinese regular infantry: 3 Average, Protected, Drilled Medium Foot – Light Spear, Swordsmen, 3 Average, Protected, Drilled Medium Foot – Bow
Skirmishers	1 BG	8 bases of skirmishers: Average, Unprotected, Undrilled Light Foot – Bow
Camp	1	Unfortified camp
Total	9 BGs	Camp, 24 mounted bases, 20 foot bases, 3 commanders

BUILDING A CUSTOMISED LIST USING OUR ARMY POINTS

Choose an army based on the maxima and minima in the list below. The following special instructions apply to this army:

- Commanders should be depicted as Cavalry.
- Cavalry can always dismount as Medium Foot, Armoured, Superior, Drilled, Offensive Spearmen.

XI XIA								
Territory Types: Hilly, Agricultural, Developed								
C-in-C	Inspired Commander/Field Commander/Troop Commander					80/50/35	1	
Sub-commanders	Field Commander					50	0–2	
	Troop Commander					35	0–3	
Troop name	Troop Type				Capabilities		Points per base	Bases per BG	Total bases
	Type	Armour	Quality	Training	Shooting	Close Combat			
Core Troops									
Cavalry	Cavalry	Armoured	Superior	Drilled	–	Lancers, Swordsmen	17	4–6	8–24
Regular infantry	Medium Foot	Protected	Average	Drilled	–	Light Spear Swordsmen	7	1/2	8–36
	Medium Foot	Protected	Average	Drilled	Bow or Crossbow	–	7	1/2	6–8
Optional Troops									
Nomad auxiliaries	Light Horse	Unprotected	Average	Undrilled	Bow	Swordsmen	10	4–6	0–12
	Cavalry	Unprotected	Average	Undrilled	Bow	Swordsmen	10	4–6	
		Protected					11		
Anti-cavalry squads	Heavy Foot	Protected	Average	Undrilled	–	Heavy Weapon	7	4–8	0–8
				Drilled			8		
Irregular infantry	Medium Foot	Protected	Average	Undrilled	–	Light Spear, Swordsmen	6	6–8	0–48
			Poor				4		
Skirmishers	Light Foot	Unprotected	Average	Undrilled	Bow	–	5	6–8	0–8
"Fire tube" armed infantry	Only from 1200	Light Foot	Unprotected	Average	Drilled	Firearm	–	4	4	0–4
Light stone-throwers or heavy crossbow artillery	Light Artillery	–	Average	Drilled	Light Artillery	–	17	2	0–4
Heavy stone-throwers	Heavy Artillery	–	Average	Drilled	Heavy Artillery	–	25	2	0–2
Palisades or similar fortifications	Field Fortifications						3		0–24
Fortified camp							24		1
Allies									
Uighur allies – Later Horse Nomads									
Tibetan allies (Only before 1065)									

GHURID AFGHAN

The Ghurids were ethnic Afghans who were named from their region of origin – the Ghur mountains in Afghanistan between Herat and Ghazni, currently known as Hindustan.

The Ghurids ended Ghaznavid rule in India and captured their base in Lahore. The state they founded in India lasted from 1148 until 1206 AD. The sultans did not rule from an Indian capital but remained in Afghanistan while their

ghulam generals governed their Indian holdings. In 1206 Sultan Mu'izz ad-Din Muhammad was assassinated, following which the Ghurid Indian holdings broke away from Afghan rule to establish what became the Delhi Sultanate. The rump of the kingdom was conquered by the Khwarazmians in 1215.

This list covers Ghurid armies based in Ghur from 1100 to 1215, those based in Ghazni from

1148 to 1206 and those in India from 1148 to 1191, after which the Ghurid armies in India are covered by the Muslim Indian Sultanates list.

TROOP TYPES

The enigmatic *karwah* has been interpreted in the past as a bullock or buffalo hide stuffed with hay or straw and rolled along in front of troops to protect them from enemy arrows. G.H. Raverty's translation of the *Tabaqat-i-Nasiri* offers the perhaps more plausible interpretation that it was infantry body armour made of rawhide with cotton padding. "The troops of Ghur have a method, in the practise of fighting on foot, of making a certain article of one fold of raw bullock-hide, over both sides of which they lay cotton, and over all draw figured coarse cotton cloth, after the form of a screen [or breast work], and the name of that article of defence is karwah. When the foot soldiers of Ghur place this [screen] upon their shoulders, they are completely covered from head to foot by it; and when they close their ranks, they appear like unto a wall, and no missile or arms can take any effect on it, on account of the quantity of cotton with which it is stuffed." Either way, troops equipped with *karwah* seem best classified as normal Islamic infantry spearmen.

GHURID AFGHAN STARTER ARMY		
Commander-in-Chief	1	Field Commander
Sub-commanders	2	2 x Troop Commander
Ghilman	3 BGs	Each comprising 4 bases of ghilman: Superior, Armoured, Drilled Cavalry – Bow, Swordsmen
Turkish tribal cavalry	2 BGs	Each comprising 4 bases of Turkish tribal cavalry: Average, Unprotected, Undrilled Light Horse – Bow, Swordsmen
Afghan tribal cavalry	1 BG	4 bases of Afghan tribal cavalry: Average, Unprotected, Undrilled Light Horse – Javelins, Light Spear
Spearmen with karwah	3 BGs	Each comprising 8 bases of spearmen with karwah: Average, Protected, Undrilled Heavy Foot – Defensive Spearmen
Camp	1	Unfortified camp
Total	9 BGs	Camp, 24 mounted bases, 24 foot bases, 3 commanders

BUILDING A CUSTOMISED LIST USING OUR ARMY POINTS

Choose an army based on the maxima and minima in the list below. The following special instructions apply to this army:

- Commanders should be depicted as ghilman or Afghan tribal cavalry.
- The minimum marked * only applies if elephants, Indian allies or more than 8 bases of Turkish tribal cavalry are used.
- A Ghurid allied commander's contingent must conform to the Ghurid Afghan allies list below, but the troops in the contingent are deducted from the minima and maxima in the main list.
- Sistan and Indian allies cannot be used together.

GHURID AFGHAN

Territory Types: Mountains, Hilly, Agricultural

C-in-C	Inspired Commander/Field Commander/Troop Commander						80/50/35		1	
Sub-commanders	Field Commander						50		0–2	
	Troop Commander						35		0–3	
Ghurid allied commanders	Field Commander/Troop Commander						40/25		0–2	
Troop name	**Troop Type**				**Capabilities**		**Points per base**		**Bases per BG**	**Total bases**
	Type	Armour	Quality	Training	Shooting	Close Combat				
Core Troops										
Ghilman	Cavalry	Armoured	Superior	Drilled	Bow	Swordsmen	19		4–6	*4–12
Turkish tribal cavalry	Light Horse	Unprotected	Average	Undrilled	Bow	Swordsmen	10		4–6	4–36
	Cavalry	Unprotected	Average	Undrilled	Bow	Swordsmen	10		4–6	
		Protected					11			
Spearmen	Medium Foot	Protected	Average	Undrilled	–	Light Spear	5		6–8	24–84
		Unprotected					4			
Spearmen with *karwah*	Heavy Foot	Protected	Average	Undrilled	–	Defensive Spearmen	6			
Optional Troops										
Archers	Medium Foot	Unprotected	Average	Undrilled	Bow	–	5		6–8	0–8
	Light Foot	Unprotected	Average	Undrilled	Bow	–	5		6–8	
Afghan tribal cavalry	Light Horse	Unprotected	Average	Undrilled	Javelins	Light Spear	7		4–6	0–8
	Cavalry	Protected	Average	Undrilled	–	Light Spear, Swordsmen	9		4–6	
Khurasanian mercenaries	Cavalry	Armoured	Superior	Undrilled	Bow	Swordsmen	18		4	0–4
	Light Horse	Unprotected	Average	Undrilled	Bow	–	8		4	
Elephants	Elephants	–	Average	Undrilled	–	–	25		2	0–4
Slingers	Light Foot	Unprotected	Average	Undrilled	Sling	–	4		6–8	0–8
Allies										

Sistan allies – Khurasanian Dynasties – See Field of Glory Companion 7: *Decline and Fall: Byzantium at War*

Indian allies (from 1186 to 1191) – Later Hindu North Indian

GHURID ALLIES

Allied commander	Field Commander/Troop Commander						40/25		1	
Troop name	**Troop Type**				**Capabilities**		**Points per base**		**Bases per BG**	**Total bases**
	Type	Armour	Quality	Training	Shooting	Close Combat				
Ghilman	Cavalry	Armoured	Superior	Drilled	Bow	Swordsmen	19		4	0–4
Turkish tribal cavalry	Light Horse	Unprotected	Average	Undrilled	Bow	Swordsmen	10		4–6	4–12
	Cavalry	Unprotected	Average	Undrilled	Bow	Swordsmen	10		4–6	
		Protected					11			
Spearmen	Medium Foot	Protected	Average	Undrilled	–	Light Spear	5		6–8	8–24
		Unprotected					4			
Spearmen with *karwah*	Heavy Foot	Protected	Average	Undrilled	–	Defensive Spearmen	6			

JIN

The Jurchens were semi-sedentary tribes from the eastern part of Manchuria whom the Chinese traditionally divided into two – firstly the "tame" (literally "cooked") Jurchens and secondly the "wild" ("uncooked") Jurchens. It was from the second of these that the Imperial Jin dynasty was to dramatically arise in the later part of the 12th century, although their military impact was not felt until they rebelled against their Liao overlords in 1114. They were led by the ambitious and visionary Aguda, who had become leader of the recently united Jurchens on his brother's death in 1113.

Although they were not themselves nomads the Jurchens were heavily influenced by their neighbours and it was with an army of 10,000 cavalry that Aguda gained his first victory over a much larger Liao army led by the Liao emperor in 1114. The victory was so complete that Aguda was moved to declare his own Jin (Gold) dynasty in 1115.

Following this the Jin proceeded with a series of lightning campaigns to destroy the Liao, which was completed in 1125. The Jin were so successful so quickly not because of any inherent military superiority or dramatic decline in the quality of the Liao troops, but because Aguda allowed his generals great freedom of action, including the ability to make treaties. Also because of his extreme tenacity in seeking out and eliminating the leadership of the Liao and subsequently the Song, which saw both royal lines reduced to a single survivor. This combination presaged the methods of Genghis Khan.

Theoretically the Song had been allied to the Jin during the war with the Liao and the Chinese expected to be allowed to regain the Sixteen Prefectures. However, as they had not actually made any material contribution to the war the Jin refused. When the Song foolishly occupied the territory, the Jin retaliated by driving them out of north China, capturing all but one of the Imperial family and exiling them to the cold of Manchuria. War with the Song continued until 1142, with the Jin held at the line of the Yangtze, as many northern invaders had been, due to a lack of a suitable navy.

After the capture of the Northern Song capital Kaifeng in 1127, the Jin set up a puppet regime called the Chu to rule north China, but this proved ineffective and was soon dissolved. It was tried again in 1130, this time under the name of Qi, and lasted until 1187 when it was abolished. Neither puppet state was able to field armies on its own but did provide Chinese troops to Jin armies.

After peace had been established, with the Chinese forced to officially recognise a non-Chinese state as the senior partner for the first time, the two sides settled down to a mostly peaceful co-existence until the arrival of the Mongols once again changed the balance of power. During this mostly peaceful period, the majority of the Jurchen population was moved from Manchuria to north China, which had a negative effect on the military efficiency of many of them. It was also a time of tension within the Jin ruling class between those who wanted to adopt a more Chinese way of life and those who wished to retain the traditional values.

This was all made immaterial from 1208 when the Mongols started to raid and then invade the Jin realm. Despite the decline in efficiency of some Jurchen troops, they proved to be a tough and determined opponent for the Mongols, and it was not until 1234 that they finally fell. The last Jurchen emperor committed suicide in

Caizhou whilst besieged by both Mongol and Song armies.

This list covers the Jurchens from the start of Aguda's reign in 1113 until their final defeat by the Mongols in 1234.

TROOP NOTES

Whilst initially the Jurchen cavalry were not fully equipped, only 2 ranks of the 5 rank *guaizima* formation being armoured, they quickly adopted more complete armour from their defeated Liao and Song opponents. At the start of the Jin period the most heavily armoured cavalry were nicknamed "iron pagodas" and may have formed separate bodies on the battlefield. Tactics in the early period were a charge to close combat "shot in" by the rear 3 ranks who were archers. We classify this as Bow*, Lancers, Swordsmen.

As Liao and other troops were incorporated into the army, traditional steppe practice started to dominate, and so we allow greater numbers of Bow, Swordsmen cavalry.

Jurchen Cavalry

Eventually the *guaizima* formation probably disappeared. The formation of a formal bureau of military affairs in 1152 is taken as the start of this process.

By the last quarter of the 12th century, those Jurchens who had been settled in north China needed government assistance to avoid penury. One result of this was a decline in the quality of some Jin cavalry, although the wars against the Mongols show that many remained as effective as before.

Chinese infantry were rapidly included in the army following the defeat of the Liao and Northern Song. These are assumed to follow the existing Song patterns. Anti-cavalry squads represent Chinese infantry armed with a mixture of two-handed swords, axes, pole axes and shorter swords. One of the main roles of such troops in Song armies was to fight enemy cavalry. We assume they served the same function in Jin armies, hence we have classified them as Heavy Foot.

Later additional infantry, known as *Zhongxiao jun* ("loyal and filial troops"), were added, although these were noted as being less disciplined but still good fighters. Although there are no clear details we assume that they included missile-men and close combat infantry.

JIN STARTER ARMY (1170)		
Commander-in-Chief	1	Field Commander
Sub-commanders	2	2 x Troop Commander
Jurchen cavalry	3 BGs	Each comprising 4 bases of Jurchen cavalry: Superior, Armoured, Drilled Cavalry – Bow*, Lancers, Swordsmen
Tribal cavalry	2 BGs	Each comprising 4 bases of tribal cavalry: Average, Unprotected, Undrilled Light Horse – Bow, Swordsmen
Chinese infantry in mixed formations	1 BG	8 bases of Chinese infantry in mixed formations: 4 Average, Protected, Drilled Medium Foot – Crossbow, Light Spear, 4 Average, Protected, Drilled Medium Foot – Crossbow
Zhongxiao jun	2 BGs	Each comprising 8 bases of Zhongxiao jun: Average, Protected, Undrilled Medium Foot – Heavy Weapon
Camp	1	Unfortified camp
Total	8 BGs	Camp, 20 mounted bases, 24 foot bases, 3 commanders

BUILDING A CUSTOMISED LIST USING OUR ARMY POINTS

Choose an army based on the maxima and minima in the list below. The following special instructions apply to this army:

- Commanders should be depicted as Jurchen Cavalry.
- Only one set of troops marked * can be used.

JIN										
Territory Types: Before 1126 – Agricultural, Woodland. From 1126 – Agricultural, Developed, Hilly, Woodland										
C-in-C		Inspired Commander/Field Commander/Troop Commander					80/50/35		1	
Sub-commanders		Field Commander					50		0–2	
		Troop Commander					35		0–3	
Troop name		Troop Type				Capabilities		Points per base	Bases per BG	Total bases
		Type	Armour	Quality	Training	Shooting	Close Combat			
Core Troops										
Jurchen cavalry in "guaizima" formation	Only before 1180	Cavalry	Protected	Superior	Drilled	Bow*	Lancers, Swordsmen	15	4–6	0–48
			Armoured					19		
Jurchen, Khitan and similar cavalry	Any date	Cavalry	Armoured	Superior	Drilled	Bow	Swordsmen	19	4–6	0–6
	Only from 1152									0–36	8–54
Poor quality Jurchen cavalry	Only from 1180	Cavalry	Armoured	Average	Drilled	Bow	Swordsmen	15	4–6	6–36
			Protected					12		
Bohai and other tribal cavalry	Only before 1180	Light Horse	Unprotected	Average	Undrilled	Bow	Swordsmen	10	4–6	0–12
		Cavalry	Unprotected	Average	Undrilled	Bow	Swordsmen	10	4–6	
			Protected					11		
Optional Troops										
Anti-cavalry squads		Heavy Foot	Protected	Average	Undrilled	–	Heavy Weapon	7	4–8	0–8
					Drilled			8		
Chinese infantry in mixed formations		Medium Foot	Protected	Average	Drilled	Crossbow	Light Spear	7	1/2	6–8	*6–36
		Medium Foot	Protected	Average	Drilled	Crossbow	–	7	1/2	
		Medium Foot	Protected	Poor	Drilled	Crossbow	Light Spear	5	1/2	6–8
		Medium Foot	Protected	Poor	Drilled	Crossbow	–	5	1/2	
Chinese infantry in separate formations	Only from 1127	Medium Foot	Protected	Average	Drilled	–	Heavy Weapon	8	6	0–6
				Poor				6		
		Medium Foot	Protected	Average	Drilled	Crossbow	–	7	6–8	0–18	*6–36
				Poor				5		
		Medium Foot	Protected	Average	Drilled	Bow	–	7	6	0–6
				Poor				5		
Chinese artillery		Light Artillery	–	Average	Drilled	Light Artillery		17	2	0–2
Zhongxiao jun	Only from 1160	Medium Foot	Protected	Average	Undrilled	–	Heavy Weapon	7	6–8	6–18
		Medium Foot	Protected	Average	Undrilled	Crossbow		7	6–8	
Steppe mercenaries	Only from 1180	Cavalry	Armoured	Superior	Undrilled	Bow	Swordsmen	18	4	0–4
		Light Horse	Unprotected	Average	Undrilled	Bow	Swordsmen	10	4	
		Cavalry	Unprotected	Average	Undrilled	Bow	Swordsmen	10	4	
			Protected					11		
Huotong "fire tube" armed foot	Only from 1215	Light Foot	Unprotected	Average	Undrilled	Firearm	–	4	4	0–4
Fortified camp								24	1	
Allies										
Steppe allies (Only from 1126 to 1211) – Later Horse Nomad										

JIN ALLIES

Allied commander		Field Commander/Troop Commander					40/25		1	
Troop name		Troop Type				Capabilities		Points per base	Bases per BG	Total bases
		Type	Armour	Quality	Training	Shooting	Close Combat			
Jurchen cavalry in "guaizima" formation	Only before 1180	Cavalry	Protected	Superior	Drilled	Bow*	Lancers, Swordsmen	15	4–6	0–12	4–12
			Armoured					19		
Jurchen, Khitan and similar cavalry	Only from 1152	Cavalry	Armoured	Superior	Drilled	Bow	Swordsmen	19	4–6	0–12
Poor quality Jurchen cavalry	Only from 1180	Cavalry	Armoured	Average	Drilled	Bow	Swordsmen	15	4–6	4–12
			Protected					12		
Bohai and other tribal cavalry	Only before 1180	Light Horse	Unprotected	Average	Undrilled	Bow	Swordsmen	10	4	0–4
		Cavalry	Unprotected	Average	Undrilled	Bow	Swordsmen	10	4	
			Protected					11		
Chinese infantry in mixed formations	Only from 1127	Medium Foot	Protected	Average	Drilled	Crossbow	Light Spear	7	1/2	6–8	*0–12
		Medium Foot	Protected	Average	Drilled	Crossbow	–	7	1/2	
		Medium Foot	Protected	Poor	Drilled	Crossbow	Light Spear	5	1/2	6–8
		Medium Foot	Protected	Poor	Drilled	Crossbow	–	5	1/2	
Chinese infantry in separate formations		Medium Foot	Protected	Average	Drilled	–	Heavy Weapon	8	6	0–6	*0–12
				Poor				6		
		Medium Foot	Protected	Average	Drilled	Crossbow	–	7	6–8	0–18
				Poor				5		
		Medium Foot	Protected	Average	Drilled	Bow	–	7	6	0–6
				Poor				5		
Zhongxiao jun	Only from 1160	Medium Foot	Protected	Average	Undrilled	–	Heavy Weapon	7	4–6	0–6
		Medium Foot	Protected	Average	Undrilled	Crossbow	–	7	4–6	

LATE HEIAN TO MUROMACHI JAPANESE

This list covers Japanese armies in the late Heian period from 1040 to 1185 AD, through the Kamakura shogunate (1185–1333), the Nambokucho period (1336–1392) and the early Muromachi period (1392–1500). Armies were still small but increased in size dramatically towards the end of the period. Armies were led by powerful local warlords, daimyo, fighting either for the Imperial court, the Kamakura shogunate or on their own behalf, and based round relatives and retainers fighting as mounted archers.

Muromachi Commander

TROOP NOTES

During most of this period the bushi fought on horseback except when fighting in boats or behind fortifications. Towards the end of the period, especially during the Onin War of 1467–68, fought in the streets of Kyoto, which ushered in the Sengoku jidai, the Age of the Country at War, bushi increasingly fought on foot.

Infantry were the followers of the mounted warriors and were equipped to a lower standard, although the better armoured neared the level of the mounted troops. The naginata is first mentioned around the middle of the 12th century and replaced the earlier hoko spears. Numbers of foot followers were in the region of between 2 and 3 per mounted warrior. Throughout the period the bushi fought as horse archers and were closely supported by their followers on foot who carried

Samurai preparing for battle, by Richard Hook. Taken from Elite 125:
Samurai Commanders (1): 940–1576.

a mixture of bows, staff weapons – especially the *naginata* – and swords. There is no indication that the users of different weapons were separated out into units based on their weapon type.

From 1335 groups of followers led by samurai were armed with 4 metre long spears, *yari*, and at the same time a variety of long sword and similar weapons, including the *nagamaki* and *nodachi*, became popular for fighting on foot. The first use of the word *ashigaru*, referring to groups of follower-grade foot archers, appears about the same time.

We represent mixed battle groups of *bushi* and foot followers as Medium Foot, whether or not the *bushi* are themselves mounted. Prior to 1467, such battle groups should depict a mixture of mounted *bushi* and foot follower figures.

We recommend that they should be based on Mob depth bases each with 1 mounted *bushi* figure and 2 or 3 foot followers with mixed weaponry. From 1467 it is appropriate to depict the *bushi* in mixed battle groups as dismounted and use normal depth Medium Foot bases.

Bushi clash across the barricades

LATE HEIAN TO MUROMACHI JAPANESE STARTER ARMY (AFTER 1335 AD)		
Commander-in-Chief	1	Field Commander
Sub-commanders	2	2 x Troop Commander
Detached bushi	2 BGs	Each comprising 4 bases of detached bushi: Superior, Armoured, Undrilled Cavalry – Bow, Swordsmen
Bushi and followers	4 BGs	Each comprising 6 bases of bushi and followers: Average, Armoured, Undrilled Medium Foot – Bow*, Heavy Weapon
Detached yari–armed followers	2 BGs	Each comprising 6 bases of detached yari–armed followers: Average, Protected, Undrilled Medium Foot – Offensive Spearmen
Conscripts	1 BG	6 bases of conscripts: Poor, Unprotected, Undrilled Mob – No capabilities
Camp	1	Unfortified camp
Total	9 BGs	Camp, 8 mounted bases, 42 foot bases, 3 commanders

BUILDING A CUSTOMISED LIST USING OUR ARMY POINTS

Choose an army based on the maxima and minima in the list below. The following special instructions apply to this army:

- Commanders should be depicted as *bushi*.
- A Japanese allied commander's contingent

must conform to the Late Heian to Muromachi Japanese allies list below, but the troops in the contingent are deducted from the minima and maxima in the main list.

- From 1467 Cavalry detached *bushi* can always dismount as Superior, Armoured, Undrilled Medium Foot – Skilled Swordsmen.

Samurai fording a stream, by Richard Hook. Taken from Elite 125:
Samurai Commanders (1): 940–1576.

LATE HEIAN TO MUROMACHI JAPANESE

Territory Types: Agricultural, Developed, Hilly

C-in-C	Inspired Commander/Field Commander/Troop Commander				80/50/35		1
Sub-commanders	Field Commander				50		0–2
	Troop Commander				35		0–3
Japanese allied commanders	Field Commander/Troop Commander				40/25		0–2

Troop name	Troop Type				Capabilities		Points per base	Bases per BG	Total bases
	Type	Armour	Quality	Training	Shooting	Close Combat			
Core Troops									
Bushi and followers	Medium Foot	Armoured	Average	Undrilled	Bow*	Heavy Weapon	10	6–8	24–64
		Protected					8		
Optional Troops									
Conscripts, badly equipped followers or inji 'ruffians'	Mob	Unprotected	Poor	Undrilled	–	–	2	6–8	0–12
Armed ladies and boys to guard camp	Medium Foot	Unprotected	Poor	Undrilled	–	Heavy Weapon	4	4	0–4
Detached bushi	Any date	Cavalry	Armoured	Superior	Undrilled	Bow	Swordsmen	18	4–6	
	Only from 1467	Medium Foot	Armoured	Superior	Undrilled	–	Skilled Swordsmen	12	6–8	0–16
		Medium Foot	Armoured	Superior	Undrilled	–	Offensive Spearmen	12	6–8	
Detached followers		Medium Foot	Protected	Poor	Undrilled	Bow*	Heavy Weapon	6	6–8	1 BG per BG of detached bushi
Upgrade detached followers to yari-armed	Only from 1335	Medium foot	Protected	Average	Undrilled	–	Offensive Spearmen	7	6–8	Any BG of detached followers
				Poor				5		
Detached followers fighting behind standing shields	Only from 1335	Medium Foot	Armoured	Average	Undrilled	Bow	–	8	6–8	0–8
			Armoured	Poor				6		
			Protected	Average				6		
			Protected	Poor				4		
Palisade fieldworks	Field Fortifications						3		0–20
Allies									
Japanese Warrior Monk allies									

LATE HEIAN TO MUROMACHI JAPANESE ALLIES

Allied commander	Field Commander/Troop Commander				40/25		1

Troop name	Troop Type				Capabilities		Points per base	Bases per BG	Total bases
	Type	Armour	Quality	Training	Shooting	Close Combat			
Bushi and followers	Medium Foot	Armoured	Average	Undrilled	Bow*	Heavy Weapon	10	6–8	6–20
		Protected					8		
Detached bushi	Any date	Cavalry	Armoured	Superior	Undrilled	Bow	Swordsmen	18	4–6	
	Only from 1467	Medium Foot	Armoured	Superior	Undrilled	–	Skilled Swordsmen	12	6	0–6
		Medium Foot	Armoured	Superior	Undrilled	–	Offensive Spearmen	12	6	
Detached followers		Medium Foot	Protected	Poor	Undrilled	Bow*	Heavy Weapon	6	6–8	1 BG per BG of detached bushi
Upgrade detached followers to yari-armed	Only from 1335	Medium foot	Protected	Average	Undrilled	–	Offensive Spearmen	7	6–8	Any BG of detached followers
				Poor				5		

Scouting party, by Angus McBride. Taken from Elite 23: The Samurai.

Samurai and bushi resist the Mongol invasion, 1281, by Angus McBride. Taken from Elite 23: The Samurai.

JAPANESE WARRIOR MONK ALLIES

This list covers allied contingents supplied by the monks of the various Japanese Buddhist temple communities, including Nara and Mount Hiei. The term warrior monk comes from the translation of *Sohei, so* meaning a Buddhist priest or monk and *hei* meaning soldier or warrior. The monks tended to be belligerent to the point of foolhardiness and the Nara and Miidera monks were heavily suppressed after allying with the "wrong" side during the Gempei War (1180–85).

Warrior Monk

Monastic forces consisted of a hard core of trained warriors but the bulk of armies were made up of less well-trained and/or motivated members of the temple communities. Their overall effectiveness has probably been overrated under other rules systems. One well known tactic was to place their portable shrine, containing the *kami* (or spirit) of the temple, in front of the battle line and dare all comers to try and take it! One might simulate this on the wargames table by including a portable shrine on a commander's base and having him fight in the front rank of a battle group.

- The commander's base should be depicted as skilled fighting monks.

JAPANESE WARRIOR MONK ALLIES

Allied commander		Field Commander/Troop Commander						40/25		1	
Troop name		Troop Type				Capabilities		Points per base	Bases per BG	Total bases	
		Type	Armour	Quality	Training	Shooting	Close Combat				
Skilled fighting monks		Medium Foot	Unprotected	Average	Undrilled	–	Heavy Weapon	6	4–6	0–6	
			Protected					7			
Other Monks	Any	Medium Foot or Mob	Unprotected	Poor	Undrilled	–	Light Spear	2	6–8	8–24	
	Only from 1334	Medium Foot	Unprotected	Average	Undrilled	–	Heavy Weapon	6	6–8		
				Poor				4			
Mounted Monks		Cavalry	Protected	Average	Undrilled	Bow	–	9	2	0–2	

MONGOL CONQUEST

This list covers Mongol armies from 1206 AD until 1230 in Persia and 1260 in China. The armies that invaded Russia and Europe from 1223 are covered by the Mongol Invasion list in Field of Glory Companion 10: *Oath of Fealty*. Later Mongol armies in Russia are covered by the Tatar list in Field of Glory Companion 6: *Eternal Empire*, in Persia and the Near East by the Ilkhanid Mongol list in Field of Glory Companion 4: *Swords and Scimitars* and the Timurid list in Field of Glory Companion 6: *Eternal Empire*, in China by the Yuan Chinese list in this book, and in Central Asia and Mongolia by the Later Horse Nomad list in this book.

At the turn of the 13th century AD, the Mongolian plateau was home to a number of rival nomad *khanliks*, the most powerful being the Kereyds, Mongols, Naimans, Merkits and Tatars. The Jin rulers of northern China kept these in a state of turmoil by successively supporting different *khanliks* to prevent any one group from achieving dominance.

Born around 1162, Temujin was the son of the chieftain of a minor Mongol clan. After many vicissitudes in his youth, Temujin united the Mongol clans under his leadership by 1190. He then embarked on the conquest of the other nomad tribes, so that by 1206 he was absolute ruler of the Mongols, Kereyds, Naimans, Merkits, Tatars and Uighurs, and assumed the title of Khagan under the name Genghis Khan.

He then embarked on the conquest of the settled nations. By 1209 he had defeated and received the submission of the Xi Xia. Between 1211 and 1215 he conquered the northern part of the Jin Empire. By 1218, the Kara Khitai state (since 1211 under the rule of a section of the Naiman tribe which had fled west rather than submit to Genghis) was defeated and annexed.

Genghis Khan

In 1220 Genghis led a massive invasion of the Khwarazmian Empire in Persia and Central Asia, rapidly defeating its forces and storming its major cities, killing the Shah and forcing his son to flee into exile in India. The Mongol forces were then divided, part, under Genghis, sweeping through Afghanistan and northern India, while two tumens made a reconnaissance in force through the Caucasus into Russia. Georgia was devastated, the Genoese trading emporium of Kaffa in the Crimea was sacked, and a Russian army was defeated at the Kalka River in 1223.

The Xi Xia had repudiated their tributary status. On his return to Mongolia, Genghis led an invasion of their territory. The Western Xia state was destroyed, but Genghis died near the end of the campaign in 1227. His son Ögedei was elected as his successor in 1229. During his reign the Mongols completed the conquest of the Jin Empire by 1234 and in 1235 began the conquest of the Song, which was to take almost 45 years. Between 1236 and 1239 Mongol forces under Genghis' grandson Batu subjugated the Volga Bulgars, the Cumans and the Russian principalities. In 1241 they invaded central Europe, one division invading Hungary and the other Poland. The Hungarians were severely defeated at Mohi and the Poles at Liegnitz. Fortunately for Europe, Ögedei died the same year, and the Mongol leaders broke off the campaign to take part in the election of a new Great Khan.

The Mongol Empire was the largest contiguous empire in the history of the world, stretching from the borders of Poland and Hungary to the Sea of Japan.

On the death of the 4th Great Khan, Möngke, a grandson of Genghis, in 1259, the succession was disputed between his brothers. Khubilai was eventually victorious and accepted as Great Khan, but this succession war marked the end of the Mongol Empire as a single political unit. Thereafter, the Golden Horde in Russia, the Ilkhanate in Persia and the Chagatai Khanate in Central Asia were effectively independent. Khubilai proclaimed the Yuan dynasty in 1271 and crushed the last Song resistance in 1279.

TROOP NOTES

Mongol forces used normal nomad horse archer tactics. Their amazing military success can be attributed more to organisation and discipline than to tactical innovation. They also became expert at siege warfare, using engineers recruited from their settled subjects.

Breaking with Mongol tradition, Genghis appointed officers on the basis of merit rather than family connections. He retained the traditional decimal organisation of steppe armies, but formalised it into a permanent structure: The basic squad (*arbat*) consisted of ten men; ten *arbats* (100 men) made a *zuut*; ten *zuuts* (1,000 men) made a *myanghan* and ten *myanghans* (10,000 men) made a *tumen* – forming a strategic division of the army. He incorporated the forces of subjugated tribes into his army on the same basis. In conjunction with strictly imposed discipline and a new code of laws (the Yassa) regulating all aspects of life, this formal organisation made the Mongol army far more effective than its tribal predecessors.

Mongol Cavalry

MONGOL CONQUEST STARTER ARMY

Commander-in-Chief	1	Inspired Commander (Temüjin – Genghis Khan)
Sub-commanders	2	2 x Troop Commander
Best equipped Mongol cavalry	2 BGs	Each comprising 4 bases of best equipped Mongol cavalry: Superior, Armoured, Drilled Cavalry – Bow, Swordsmen
Other Mongol cavalry	2 BGs	Each comprising 4 bases of other Mongol cavalry: Superior, Protected, Drilled Cavalry – Bow, Swordsmen
Other Mongol cavalry	2 BGs	Each comprising 4 bases of other Mongol cavalry: Superior, Unprotected, Drilled Light Horse – Bow, Swordsmen
Other nomad cavalry	2 BGs	Each comprising 4 bases of other nomad cavalry: Average, Unprotected, Undrilled Light Horse – Bow, Swordsmen
Camp	1	Unfortified camp
Total	8 BGs	Camp, 32 mounted bases, 3 commanders

Mongol officer directing the siege of a Chinese city, by Angus McBride.
Taken from Men-at-Arms 105: The Mongols.

BUILDING A CUSTOMISED LIST USING OUR ARMY POINTS

Choose an army based on the maxima and minima in the list below. The following special instructions apply to this army:

- Commanders should be depicted as guard or best equipped Mongol cavalry.

- Guard and Mongol cavalry can always dismount. Light Horse dismount as Light Foot, Cavalry as Medium Foot. Armour, quality, training, and shooting and close combat capabilities are the same as when mounted.

- Jin or Korean allies cannot be used in Persia.

MONGOL CONQUEST

Territory Types: Steppes

C-in-C	Inspired Commander/Field Commander/Troop Commander						80/50/35	1	
Sub-commanders	Field Commander						50	0–2	
	Troop Commander						35	0–3	
Troop name	**Troop Type**				**Capabilities**		**Points per base**	**Bases per BG**	**Total bases**
	Type	Armour	Quality	Training	Shooting	Close Combat			
Core Troops									
Guard cavalry	Cavalry	Armoured	Elite	Drilled	Bow	Swordsmen	22	4	0–4
Best equipped Mongol cavalry	Cavalry	Armoured	Superior	Drilled	Bow	Swordsmen	19	4–6	4–18
Other Mongol cavalry	Light Horse	Unprotected	Superior	Drilled	Bow	Swordsmen	12	4–6	16–60
		Average					10		
	Cavalry	Unprotected	Superior	Drilled	Bow	Swordsmen	13	4–6	
		Unprotected	Average				11		
		Protected	Superior				15		
		Protected	Average				12		
Optional Troops									
Other nomad cavalry	Light Horse	Unprotected	Average	Undrilled	Bow	Swordsmen	10	4–6	0–12
	Cavalry	Unprotected	Average	Undrilled	Bow	Swordsmen	10	4–6	
		Protected					11		
Qidan or Jurchen cavalry	Only from 1212	Cavalry	Armoured	Superior	Drilled	Bow	Swordsmen	19	4–6	0–12
				Average				15		
Stone-throwers and bolt-shooters	Heavy Artillery	–	Average	Drilled	Heavy Artillery	–	20	2	0–4
Allies									
Jin allies (Only from 1214)									
Korean allies (Only from 1242) – Koryo Korean									
Uighur allies – Later Horse Nomad									

MONGOL CONQUEST ALLIES

Allied commander	Field Commander/Troop Commander						40/25	1	
Troop name	**Troop Type**				**Capabilities**		**Points per base**	**Bases per BG**	**Total bases**
	Type	Armour	Quality	Training	Shooting	Close Combat			
Best equipped Mongol cavalry	Cavalry	Armoured	Superior	Drilled	Bow	Swordsmen	19	4–6	0–6
Other Mongol cavalry	Light Horse	Unprotected	Superior	Drilled	Bow	Swordsmen	12	4–6	6–16
			Average				10		
	Cavalry	Unprotected	Superior	Drilled	Bow	Swordsmen	13	4–6	
		Unprotected	Average				11		
		Protected	Superior				15		
		Protected	Average				12		

Wounded Mongols at the siege of Kaifeng, 1232, by Wayne Reynolds. Taken from
Warrior 84: Mongol Warrior 1200–1350.

MUSLIM INDIAN SULTANATES

This list covers Muslim Indian armies from 1192 to 1500 AD.

After the conquest of the rump Ghaznavid territories in India by the Ghurids, the next major involvement of Muslim armies was under the Ghurid Sultan Mu'izz ad-Din Muhammad who attempted to conquer the whole of northern India. Following a series of set backs, during which he was nearly killed at the first battle of Tarain, he recruited a large cavalry army, reputedly 120,000 strong, and at the second battle of Tarain in 1192 he destroyed the opposing Hindu army and went on to conquer Delhi. This use of large numbers of mainly Turkish cavalry set the basis for all following Muslim armies in India and is thus taken as the start date for this list.

Following the assassination of Sultan Mu'izz ad-Din Muhammed in 1206, rule of the Ghurid north Indian territories fell to his senior Ghilman (the *bandagan i-khass*) who, whilst continuing in theory to recognise the overlordship of Ghur, were in fact independent rulers. These rulers quickly adopted the title Sultan and a series of fledgling states was formed. Early armies especially were often made up of uneasy alliances between these rulers.

Hindu Archers

The best known of the Muslim Indian Sultanates was that based in Delhi. On the death of Mu'izz ad-Din, one of his generals, Qutb-ud-din Aybak, proclaimed himself Sultan of Delhi. In a series of wars the Delhi Sultanate extended its way east to Bengal and south to the Deccan, however, whilst this was being undertaken, the Sultanate itself experienced repeated threats from the north-west and internal revolts from independent-minded nobles. The Delhi Sultanate consisted of six distinct dynasties: the Shamsid dynasty (1210–1266), the Ghiyathid dynasty (1266–1290), the Khilji dynasty (1290–1320), the Tughlaq dynasty (1320–1413), the Sayyid dynasty (1414–1451), and the Lodhi dynasty (1451–1526).

The Bahmani Sultanate was created in 1347. In the second half of the 15th century, its Sultan Mohammed Shah III Lashkari fielded a personal force of 300 elephants, 10,000 cavalry and 20,000 infantry. In addition, a number of nobles, both Muslim and Hindu, could contribute troops to the army. The Bahmani Sultanate had decentralized power with several khans having private armies of over 10,000 men. As a result, when the Bahmani Sultanate fell in about 1490, it was divided into five Deccan successor states.

Other Muslim Dynasties in India included Nair or Kozhikode and the Muzaffarid dynasty of Gujarat which was established in 1391.

In the early 16th century, the Timurid ruler of Fergana, Bābur, a direct descendant of Timur, invaded India and founded the Mughal Empire, which lasted until 1857

TROOP NOTES

Gunpowder skirmishers include "grenade" throwers (*ra'd-andaz*), firework throwers (*atash-baz*) and those using hand held rockets (*taksh-andaz*).

MUSLIM INDIAN SULTANATES STARTER ARMY (AFTER 1340 AD)

Commander-in-Chief	1	Troop Commander
Sub-commanders	2	2 x Troop Commander
Mamluk, *murattab* or similar cavalry	3 BGs	Each comprising 4 bases of Mamluk, murattab or similar cavalry: Superior, Armoured, Drilled Cavalry – Bow, Swordsmen
Horse archers	1 BG	4 bases of horse archers: Average, Unprotected, Undrilled Light Horse – Bow
Elephants	2 BGs	Each comprising 2 bases of elephants: Average, Undrilled Elephants
Hindu javelinmen	1 BG	6 bases of Hindu javelinmen: Average, Unprotected, Undrilled Light Foot – Javelins, Light Spear
Gunpowder skirmishers	1 BG	4 bases of gunpowder skirmishers: Average, Unprotected, Undrilled Light Foot – Firearm
Hindu swordsmen	1 BG	6 bases of Hindu swordsmen: Average, Unprotected, Undrilled Medium Foot – Swordsmen
Hindu archers	2 BGs	Each comprising 6 bases of Hindu archers: Average, Unprotected, Undrilled Medium Foot – Bow
Camp	1	Unfortified camp
Total	11 BGs	Camp, 20 mounted bases, 28 foot bases, 3 commanders

BUILDING A CUSTOMISED LIST USING OUR ARMY POINTS

Choose an army based on the maxima and minima in the list below. The following special instructions apply to this army:

- Commanders should be depicted as mamluks.

- A Muslim Indian allied commander's contingent must conform to the Muslim Indian Sultanates allies list below, but the troops in the contingent are deducted from the minima and maxima in the main list.

- Minima marked * only apply if any infantry are used or after 1266.

MUSLIM INDIAN SULTANATES

Territory Types: Agricultural, Developed, Hilly

C-in-C		Inspired Commander/Field Commander/Troop Commander				80/50/35		1	
Sub-commanders		Field Commander				50		0–2	
		Troop Commander				35		0–3	
Muslim Indian allied commander		Field Commander/Troop Commander				40/25		0–2	

Troop name		Troop Type				Capabilities		Points per base	Bases per BG	Total bases
		Type	Armour	Quality	Training	Shooting	Close Combat			
Core Troops										
Elephants		Elephants	–	Average	Undrilled	–	–	25	2	2–8
Mamluk, murattab, and similar cavalry	Before 1220	Cavalry	Armoured	Superior	Drilled	Bow	Swordsmen	19	4–6	4–16
	From 1220	Cavalry	Armoured	Superior	Drilled	Bow	Swordsmen	19	4–6	8–36
Lesser cavalry, Indians and *duaspa*	Only from 1296	Cavalry	Armoured	Average	Undrilled	Bow	Swordsmen	14	4–6	
			Protected					11		
Turkish tribal cavalry, ghazis, etc.	Only before 1220	Cavalry	Protected	Average	Undrilled	Bow	Swordsmen	11	4–6	6–40
			Unprotected					10		
		Light Horse	Unprotected	Average	Undrilled	Bow	Swordsmen	10	4–6	
Hindu swordsmen, *paik*		Medium Foot	Unprotected	Average	Undrilled	–	Swordsmen	5	6–8	*6–24
Hindu archers, *dhanuk*		Medium Foot	Unprotected	Average	Undrilled	Bow	–	5	6–8	*12–36
Camp followers		Mob	Unprotected	Poor	Undrilled	–	–	2	8–12	0–12
Optional Troops										
Afghan horse		Light Horse	Unprotected	Average	Undrilled	Javelins	Light Spear	7	4	0–4
Horse archers or mercenary nomads		Light Horse	Unprotected	Average	Undrilled	Bow	–	8	4	0–4
		Light Horse	Unprotected	Average	Undrilled	Bow	Swordsmen	10	4	
Hindu javelinmen		Light Foot	Unprotected	Average	Undrilled	Javelins	Light Spear	4	4–6	0–6
Afghan spearmen		Medium Foot	Protected	Average	Undrilled	–	Light Spear	5	6–8	0–8
Afghan archers		Medium Foot	Unprotected	Average	Undrilled	Bow	–	5	6–8	0–8
		Light Foot	Unprotected	Average	Undrilled	Bow	–	5	6–8	
Abyssinian bodyguard	Only from 1340	Medium Foot	Protected	Average	Drilled	–	Impact Foot, Swordsmen	8	4	0–4
Gunpowder skirmishers	Only from 1340	Light Foot	Unprotected	Average	Undrilled	Firearm	–	4	4	0–4
Handgunners	Only from 1470	Light foot	Unprotected	Average	Undrilled	Firearm	–	4	4	
Bolt-shooters		Light Artillery	–	Average	Undrilled	Light Artillery	–	15	2	0–2
Stone-throwers		Heavy Artillery	–	Average	Undrilled	Heavy Artillery	–	20	2	
Bombards	Only from 1365	Heavy Artillery	–	Average	Undrilled	Heavy Artillery	–	20	2	
Rocket troops	Only from 1340	Light Artillery	–	Average	Undrilled	Light Artillery	–	15	2	0–6
Allies										
Hindu Indian allies (Only from 1296) – Later Hindu South Indian										

MUSLIM INDIAN SULTANATE ALLIES

Allied commander		Field Commander/Troop Commander						40/25		1
Troop name		**Troop Type**				**Capabilities**		**Points per base**	**Bases per BG**	**Total bases**
		Type	Armour	Quality	Training	Shooting	Close Combat			
Elephants		Elephants	–	Average	Undrilled	–	–	25	2	2
Mamluk, *murattab*, and similar cavalry	Before 1220	Cavalry	Armoured	Superior	Drilled	Bow	Swordsmen	19	4–6	4–6
	From 1220	Cavalry	Armoured	Superior	Drilled	Bow	Swordsmen	19	4–6	4–16
Lesser cavalry, Indians and *duaspa*	Only from 1296	Cavalry	Armoured	Average	Undrilled	Bow	Swordsmen	14	4–6	
			Protected					11		
Turkish tribal cavalry, ghazis, etc.	Only before 1220	Cavalry	Protected	Average	Undrilled	Bow	Swordsmen	11	4–6	4–16
			Unprotected					10		
		Light Horse	Unprotected	Average	Undrilled	Bow	Swordsmen	10	4–6	
Hindu swordsmen, *paik*		Medium Foot	Unprotected	Average	Undrilled	–	Swordsmen	5	6–8	*6–8
Hindu archers, *dhanuk*		Medium Foot	Unprotected	Average	Undrilled	Bow	–	5	6–8	*6–12

MEDIEVAL INDONESIAN OR MALAY

This list covers Indonesian and Malay armies from 1222 to 1500 AD.

The Indonesians consider ten main ethnic groups to occupy the islands. These are geographically based around Central Java, Bali, West Sumatra, South Sulawesi, East Nusa-Tenggara, Central Sulawesi, West Kalimantan, Maluku, East Java and Papua.

Throughout much of this era Indonesia was consumed by both civil wars and an Islamic Jihad aimed at converting the islands. Balinese Hinduism was distinctly anti-Muslim.

SINGOSARI-MAJAPAHIT KINGDOM

A Javanese/Indonesian state located in eastern Java which was founded c.1222, when the town of Singosari destroyed its rival Kediri/Mataram after years of civil war. It lasted until 1518. At the height of its power it controlled all of Indonesia and Malaysia, although historians from rival cities maintain that it actually only controlled parts of several key islands.

Following the foundation of the kingdom, it quickly expanded control over the islands of

Madura, Bali, numerous smaller islands and even conquered part of southern Sumatra.

A brief civil war between 1289 and 1300 saw Mongol (Yuan Chinese) intervention to aid one of the factions. The Mongol-supported faction won, but soon turned on their allies and drove the Mongols out of the country. The capital of the kingdom shifted at about this time to Majapahit. The kingdom then expanded into an empire. In 1377 even several of the Srivijayan cities were vassals of Majapahit. The Paregreg civil war of Majapahit ended in 1406. Prince Paramisora of Blambangan in East Java, the loser in this war, fled for Tumasik and then to the Malacca Peninsula. There he established the kingdom of Malacca in 1406.

The Empire won the war and was able to hold onto the core of its power but lost control over most of the rival towns. Now only a local power, the Majapahit city-state was crushed in 1518 by Malacca.

TROOP NOTES

Indonesia and Malay troops were known for their fierce attack and disregard for their own safety.

The use of the spear and blades dominated Indonesian warfare. A statue in Alor, Indonesia, shows a warrior with a light spear and long wooden shield. From the start of the 13th century many of the troops armed with bows, spears and blowguns also carried a *kerambit*. The *kerambit* had a unique curved blade shape that symbolised a "tiger claw".

The Buginese and Makasar people from South Sulawesi region were known as tough sailors, mercenaries and fearless warriors. Artwork shows them armed with swords and javelins. A drawing of a Papuan warrior shows him with a light spear and shield that reaches from the feet to the neck. A drawing of a West Kalimantan warrior has him with a *kris* and smaller shield.

Indonesia has never known a standardized appearance of its warriors. Malukunese, as did most Indonesians, wore little to the battlefield and only carried long or small round shields for protection. Malukunese warriors favored a *parang sawalaku*. Its blade is as heavy and as wide as an English broad sword, with a long wooden end. The length of the entire thing is similar to a falchion's.

Kris blades date back to the 600s in Malaysia, Indonesia and the southern Philippines. The blade of a *kris* is of asymmetric form, with the blade wider on one side than the other. The blade can be either straight or with an uneven number of waves. The most remarkable feature is the pattern on the surface of the blade.

Skirmishers are assumed to be armed with a mixture of blow-pipes and other missile weapons, and assorted bladed hand-to-hand weapons. We treat the mixture as Javelins, Light Spear.

Cavalry and elephants were unavailable in some areas.

MEDIEVAL INDONESIAN OR MALAY STARTER ARMY		
Commander-in-Chief	1	Field Commander
Sub-commanders	2	2 x Troop Commander
Noble cavalry	1 BG	4 bases of noble cavalry: Average, Protected, Undrilled Light Horse – Javelins, Light Spear
Elephants	3 BGs	Each comprising 2 bases of elephants: Average, Undrilled Elephants
Warriors	4 BGs	Each comprising 8 bases of warriors: Average, Protected, Undrilled Medium Foot – Impact Foot, Swordsmen
Skirmishers	1 BG	8 bases of skirmishers: Average, Unprotected, Undrilled Light Foot – Javelins, Light Spear
Archers	1 BG	8 bases of archers: Average, Unprotected, Undrilled Light Foot – Bow
Camp	1	Unfortified camp
Total	10 BGs	Camp, 10 mounted bases, 48 foot bases, 3 commanders

BUILDING A CUSTOMISED LIST USING OUR ARMY POINTS

Choose an army based on the maxima and minima in the list below. The following special instructions apply to this army:

- Commanders should be depicted on elephants, as noble cavalry or warriors, or, if Javanese, in a chariot.
- Javanese allied contingents cannot include elephants.

MEDIEVAL INDONESIAN OR MALAY

Territory Types: Agricultural, Tropical, Hilly, Mountains

C-in-C	Inspired Commander/Field Commander/Troop Commander					80/50/35		1	
Sub-commanders	Field Commander					50		0–2	
	Troop Commander					35		0–3	

Troop name		Troop Type				Capabilities		Points per base	Bases per BG	Total bases
		Type	Armour	Quality	Training	Shooting	Close Combat			
Core Troops										
Archers		Medium Foot	Unprotected	Average	Undrilled	Bow	–	5	6–8	8–36
		Light Foot	Unprotected	Average	Undrilled	Bow	–	5	6–8	
Warriors		Medium Foot	Protected	Average	Undrilled	–	Impact Foot, Swordsmen	7	8–12	24–120
			Unprotected					6		
Skirmishers		Light Foot	Unprotected	Average	Undrilled	Javelins	Light Spear	4	6–8	0–24
Elephants	Only Singosari-Majapahit before 1406, Malay or Sumatran	Elephants	–	Average	Undrilled	–	–	25	2	0–8
Optional Troops										
Noble horse		Light Horse	Protected	Average	Undrilled	Javelins	Light Spear	8	4–6	0–6
Uniformed light cavalry	Only Singosari-Majapahit	Light Horse	Unprotected	Average	Drilled	Javelins	Light Spear	7	4	0–4
Levy Foot		Medium Foot	Unprotected	Poor	Undrilled	–	Light Spear	2	8–10	0–20
Peasants		Mob	Unprotected	Poor	Undrilled	–	–	2	10–12	
Handgunners	Only from 1435	Light Foot	Unprotected	Average	Undrilled	Firearm	–	4	4–6	0–6
Cannon	Only from 1400	Light Artillery	–	Average	Undrilled	Light Artillery	–	15	2	0–2
Turkish mercenary cannon	Only Malacca Malay from 1435	Heavy Artillery	–	Average	Undrilled	Heavy Artillery	–	20	2	
Allies										
Only Malay										
Javanese allies (Only Malacca Malay from 1435) – Medieval Indonesian or Malay										
Sinhalese allies (Only from 1240 to 1270) – Later Hindu South Indian										
Ming Chinese allies (Only from 1409 to 1435) – Ming Chinese										
Only Singosari-Majapahit										
Javanese allies (Only from 1270 to 1390) – Medieval Indonesian or Malay										
Yuan Chinese allies (Only from 1289 to 1300) – Yuan Chinese										

MEDIEVAL INDONESIAN OR MALAY ALLIES

Allied commander	Field Commander/Troop Commander					40/25		1	
Troop name	Troop Type				Capabilities		Points per base	Bases per BG	Total bases
	Type	Armour	Quality	Training	Shooting	Close Combat			
Archers	Medium Foot	Unprotected	Average	Undrilled	Bow	–	5	6–8	6–12
	Light Foot	Unprotected	Average	Undrilled	Bow	–	5	6–8	
Warriors	Medium Foot	Protected	Average	Undrilled	–	Impact Foot, Swordsmen	7	8–12	8–32
		Unprotected					6		
Skirmishers	Light Foot	Unprotected	Average	Undrilled	Javelins		4	6–8	0–8
Elephants	Elephants	–	Average	Undrilled	–		25	2	0–2

YUAN CHINESE

In 1259 AD the Mongol Great Khan Möngke died and was succeeded, although this was disputed, by his brother Khubilai, who was at the time in command of the Mongol armies in China attempting to complete the conquest of the Southern Song. During his time in China, Khubilai had come to recognise the benefits that could be gained from incorporating Chinese practices into the Mongol system. When he became Great Khan he was in a position to implement this, at least in the part of the Mongol realm where his writ was obeyed.

His first, and most important, military act was to finish the conquest of Song which was undertaken by the end of 1279. This was achieved by realising that, due to the nature of the terrain in the south, an effective river navy was required. Even with this it took many years of often brutal fighting and sieges to finally eliminate the Song and once again unify China under the rule of a single "Son of Heaven", even if he was a Mongol.

At the same time Khubilai was forced to defend his position as Mongol Great Khan against his brother Arigh Böke, whom he finally defeated

Khubilai Khan

in 1264. Despite his victory, this civil war effectively marked the end of the unified Mongol realm as the other Khans recognised Khubilai's supremacy only nominally at best, and wars had to be conducted against some.

Following the success in southern China, additional expeditions were undertaken, but these were much less successful – probably because they took place in countries where the terrain was even less suitable for the Mongol way of war than south China. Even the additional Chinese manpower was not able to offset these disadvantages. The most famous of these failed expeditions were the two attempted invasions of Japan in 1274 and 1281, the second of which was wrecked by storms, the *kamikaze* ('divine wind') of Japanese legend.

Following Khubilai's death, the Yuan Empire rapidly declined under a series of short lived emperors who were often murdered as a result of political machinations within the Mongol hierarchy. As with the Jurchens before them, those Mongols who moved to north China soon found themselves in dire straits, often being exploited by their subject Chinese and reduced to penury. This obviously had an impact on the efficiency of the army, which relied on the Mongol cavalry to provide its strike troops, even though the majority of soldiers would now be Chinese or other subjects. There were also conflicts within the elite over the degree of sinicisation that was acceptable or desirable.

From the 1330s the state started to rapidly disintegrate and the political instability of the Empire was compounded by the appearance of a large scale messianic religious movement, known as the Red Turbans, amongst the Chinese population. Armed rebellions started in the

1340s as the government tried to suppress the movement, and this further weakened the Yuan. Over the next 20 years the whole of the Yangtze region fell away from Yuan control, and came under the control of the emerging Ming dynasty. In 1368, in the face of overwhelming odds, the last Yuan emperor fled to the Mongolian steppes.

This list covers the armies of Yuan dynasty China from 1260 to 1368.

TROOP NOTES

The Chinese term *dao* includes any single edged bladed weapon including polearms as well as swords. As well as polearms, many of the swords used, such as the *zhanmadao* and *mazhadao*, were large enough to qualify as Heavy Weapon.

Mixed infantry battle groups represent troops depicted with a front rank of men carrying shields and spears, and rear ranks of crossbowmen or

Yuan troops, by David Sque. Taken from Men-at-Arms 251: Medieval Chinese Armies 1260–1520.

archers. This appears to have been a continuation of Song practice and we classify them similarly.

It is during the Yuan period that gunpowder artillery starts to become a common feature of Chinese armies. Both small cannon and rockets were used in substantial numbers by the end of the dynasty, although man-carried firearms remained relatively rare.

YUAN CHINESE STARTER ARMY (BEFORE 1300 AD)		
Commander-in-Chief	1	Field Commander
Sub-commanders	2	2 x Troop Commander
Guard cavalry	2 BGs	Each comprising 4 bases of Guard cavalry: Superior, Armoured, Drilled Cavalry – Bow, Swordsmen
Mongol cavalry	2 BGs	Each comprising 4 bases of Mongol cavalry: Average, Unprotected, Undrilled Light Horse – Bow, Swordsmen
Chinese guard halberdiers	1 BG	6 bases of Chinese guard halberdiers: Superior, Armoured, Drilled Heavy Foot – Heavy Weapon
Anti-cavalry squads	1 BG	6 bases of anti-cavalry squads: Average, Protected, Undrilled Heavy Foot – Heavy Weapon
Chinese crossbowmen in mixed formation	1 BG	8 bases of Chinese crossbowmen in mixed formation: 4 Average, Protected, Drilled Medium Foot – Crossbow, Light Spear, 4 Average, Protected, Drilled Medium Foot – Crossbow
Chinese archers in mixed formation	1 BG	8 bases of Chinese archers in mixed formation: 4 Average, Protected, Drilled Medium Foot – Bow, Light Spear, 4 Average, Protected, Drilled Medium Foot – Bow
Handgunners	1 BG	4 bases of handgunners: Average, Unprotected, Drilled Light Foot – Firearm
Camp	1	Unfortified camp
Total	9 BGs	Camp, 16 mounted bases, 34 foot bases, 3 commanders

BUILDING A CUSTOMISED LIST USING OUR ARMY POINTS

Choose an army based on the maxima and minima in the list below. The following special instructions apply to this army:

- Commanders should be depicted as guard cavalry. Before 1300, the C-in-C could be depicted on an elephant.
- Guard and Mongol cavalry can always dismount. Light Horse dismount as Light Foot, Cavalry as Medium Foot. Armour, quality, training, and shooting and close combat capabilities are the same as when mounted.
- The minimum marked * only applies if mixed formations are not used.
- Javanese cannot be used with other allies nor with Southern tribal troops.
- Uighur or Mongol allies cannot be used with Southern tribal troops

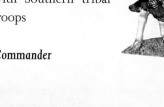

Field Commander

YUAN CHINESE

Territory Types: Agricultural, Developed, Hilly, Steppes

C-in-C		Inspired Commander/Field Commander/Troop Commander				80/50/35	1	
Sub-commanders		Field Commander				50	0–2	
		Troop Commander				35	0–3	

Troop name		Troop Type				Capabilities		Points per base	Bases per BG	Total bases
		Type	Armour	Quality	Training	Shooting	Close Combat			
Core Troops										
Guard cavalry		Cavalry	Armoured	Superior	Drilled	Bow	Swordsmen	19	4–6	4–12
Mongol cavalry	Before 1300	Light Horse	Unprotected	Superior	Drilled	Bow	Swordsmen	12	4–6	6–24
				Average				10		
		Cavalry	Unprotected	Superior	Drilled	Bow	Swordsmen	13	4–6	
			Unprotected	Average				11		
			Protected	Superior				15		
			Protected	Average				12		
	From 1300	Light Horse	Unprotected	Average	Drilled	Bow	Swordsmen	10	4–6	0–12
		Cavalry	Unprotected	Average	Drilled	Bow	Swordsmen	11	4–6	6–12
			Unprotected	Poor				9		
			Protected	Average				12		
			Protected	Poor				10		
Separately deployed Chinese spear- and dao-men		Medium Foot	Protected	Average	Drilled	–	Heavy Weapon	8	6–8	*6–24
				Poor	Undrilled			5		
Chinese crossbowmen in mixed formations		Medium Foot	Protected	Average	Drilled	Crossbow	Light Spear	7	1/2	6–8	6–12
		Medium Foot	Protected	Average	Drilled	Crossbow	–	7	1/2	
		Medium Foot	Protected	Poor	Undrilled	Crossbow	Light Spear	4	1/2	6–8	
		Medium Foot	Protected	Poor	Undrilled	Crossbow	–	4	1/2	
Separately deployed Chinese crossbowmen		Medium Foot	Protected	Average	Drilled	Crossbow	–	7	6–8	
			Protected	Poor	Undrilled			4		
			Unprotected	Poor	Undrilled			3		
Chinese archers in mixed formations		Medium Foot	Protected	Average	Drilled	Bow	Light Spear	7	1/2	6–8	6–18
		Medium Foot	Protected	Average	Drilled	Bow	–	7	1/2	
		Medium Foot	Protected	Poor	Undrilled	Bow	Light Spear	4	1/2	6–8	
		Medium Foot	Protected	Poor	Undrilled	Bow	–	4	1/2	
Separately deployed Chinese archers		Medium Foot	Protected	Average	Drilled	Bow	–	7	6–8	
			Protected	Poor	Undrilled			4		
			Unprotected	Poor	Undrilled			3		
Optional Troops										
Chinese cavalry	Only before 1300	Cavalry	Armoured	Average	Drilled	Bow	Swordsmen	15	4–6	0–6
			Armoured	Poor				12		
			Protected	Average				12		
			Protected	Poor				10		
Southern tribal cavalry		Cavalry	Protected	Average	Undrilled	–	Light Spear, Swordsmen	9	4–6	0–8
		Cavalry	Protected	Average	Undrilled	Crossbow	–	8	4–6	
Chinese guard halberdiers		Heavy Foot	Armoured	Superior	Drilled	–	Heavy Weapon	13	4–6	0–6
				Average				10		0–12
Anti-cavalry squads		Heavy Foot	Protected	Average	Undrilled	–	Heavy Weapon	7	4–8	0–8
					Drilled			8		
Southern tribal foot		Medium Foot	Protected	Average	Undrilled	–	Light Spear	5	6–8	0–8
		Medium Foot	Protected	Average	Undrilled	–	Impact Foot, Swordsmen	7	6–8	
		Medium Foot	Protected	Average	Undrilled	–	Light Spear, Swordsmen	6	6–8	

Troop name		Type	Armour	Quality	Training	Shooting	Close Combat	Points per base	Bases per BG	Total bases	
Chinese or southern tribal skirmishers		Light Foot	Unprotected	Average	Drilled or Undrilled	Bow	—	5	6–8	0–8	
		Light Foot	Unprotected	Average	Drilled or Undrilled	Crossbow	—	5	6–8		
Handgunners	Only from 1288	Light Foot	Unprotected	Average	Drilled or Undrilled	Firearm	—	4	4	0–4	
Stone-throwers		Heavy Artillery	—	Average	Drilled or Undrilled	Heavy Artillery	—	20	2	0–2	
Light guns	Only from 1300	Light Artillery	—	Average	Drilled	Light Artillery	—	17	2	0–2	0–6
					Undrilled			15			
Portable rocket launchers	Only from 1340	Light Artillery	—	Average	Drilled	Light Artillery	—	17	2	0–4	
					Undrilled			15			
Allies											
Chinese allies (Only before 1262) – Jin											
Javanese allies (Only in 1293) – Medieval Indonesian or Malay											
Koryo Korean allies											
Mongol allies – Mongol Conquest before 1266, Later Horse Nomad from 1266											
Uighur allies (Only before 1330) – Later Horse Nomad											

YUAN CHINESE ALLIES

Allied commander			Field Commander/Troop Commander					40/25		1	
Troop name		**Troop Type**				**Capabilities**		**Points per base**	**Bases per BG**	**Total bases**	
		Type	Armour	Quality	Training	Shooting	Close Combat				
Guard cavalry		Cavalry	Armoured	Superior	Drilled	Bow	Swordsmen	19	4	0–4	
Mongol cavalry	Before 1300	Light Horse	Unprotected	Superior	Drilled	Bow	Swordsmen	12	4–6	4–8	
				Average				10			
		Cavalry	Unprotected	Superior	Drilled	Bow	Swordsmen	13	4–6		
			Unprotected	Average				11			
			Protected	Superior				15			
			Protected	Average				12			
	From 1300	Light Horse	Unprotected	Average	Drilled	Bow	Swordsmen	10	4	0–4	
		Cavalry	Unprotected	Average	Drilled	Bow	Swordsmen	11	4	4	
			Unprotected	Poor				9			
			Protected	Average				12			
			Protected	Poor				10			
Separately deployed Chinese spear- and dao-men		Medium Foot	Protected	Average	Drilled	—	Heavy Weapon	8	6–8	*6–8	
				Poor	Undrilled			5			
Chinese crossbowmen in mixed formations		Medium Foot	Protected	Average	Drilled	Crossbow	Light Spear	7	1/2	4–6	
		Medium Foot	Protected	Average	Drilled	Crossbow	—	7	1/2		
		Medium Foot	Protected	Poor	Undrilled	Crossbow	Light Spear	4	1/2	4–6	0–6
		Medium Foot	Protected	Poor	Undrilled	Crossbow	—	4	1/2		
Separately deployed Chinese crossbowmen		Medium Foot	Protected	Average	Drilled	Crossbow	—	7	4–6		
			Protected	Poor	Undrilled			4			
			Unprotected	Poor	Undrilled			3			6–12
Chinese archers in mixed formations		Medium Foot	Protected	Average	Drilled	Bow	Light Spear	7	1/2	6–8	
		Medium Foot	Protected	Average	Drilled	Bow	—	7	1/2		
		Medium Foot	Protected	Poor	Undrilled	Bow	Light Spear	4	1/2	6–8	0–8
		Medium Foot	Protected	Poor	Undrilled	Bow	—	4	1/2		
Separately deployed Chinese archers		Medium Foot	Protected	Average	Drilled	Bow	—	7	6–8		
			Protected	Poor	Undrilled			4			
			Unprotected	Poor	Undrilled			3			

MEDIEVAL BURMESE

This lists covers the years when control of Burma shifted between the three main ethnic groups in the region and includes the long era of war with Siam. The Empire would shift between being dominated by the ethnic Burman, Shan and Mon. Throughout the period, small city-states continued to dot Burma and often provided vital manpower resources to the dynastic power or a new rival rising to challenge them.

The dynasties covered include Shan-Pinya (1312–1364), Shan-Sagaing (1312–1364), the Ava Dynasty (1364–1555), the southern Mon-Honswadi (Hanthawaddy) Dynasty (1287–1539) and the Burman-Toungoo Dynasty (1486–1750). The Honswadi Dynasty was a Mon dynasty based at Martaban and then shifted to Pegu. The Ava Dynasty was a coalition between the Shan and Burmans from 1364 until 1426. From 1426 until 1527, it was considered a Burman dynasty.

The Shan Nam-Mao-Long Dynasty reached its peak during the reign of Hso Hkan Hpa, from 1220 to 1230, when he conquered or made vassals all of the ethnic Shan towns in his region. One of the capitals of this Empire was Se-Lan. The Shan defeated the Chinese and Assam in 1229 plus they established an Indian vassal kingdom of Tai-Ahom. In Upper Burma after 1300, three Shan princes, called the Shan brothers, supported by the Yuan, held power.

The Toungoo Dynasty arose after many Burmans fled from Shan domination and established a population center around Toungoo located on the Sittang River. The Burman and the Shan kingdoms continued to remain in a permanent state of warfare. The Toungoo kingdom survived, despite being located between the Mon and Shan hostile regions.

This list covers Burmese armies from 1287 to 1500 AD.

TROOP NOTES

Mong troops represent troops contributed by towns dominated by an ethnic group other than the Dynastic central power. A Mong was the common term for the many small walled towns in Burma. Ethnic troops are those men provided by other towns with the same ethnic background as the rulers. Ethnic and Mong cavalry were not in high demand for campaigns, so are considered optional. Dynastic troops are essentially guard troops from the current capital and very loyal to the king. Unshielded troops classified as Protected wear quilted cotton armour.

Levy craftsmen represent the large numbers of peasants who responded to the muster call with only hammers and other tools. Their primary task was to build a palisade for the army each night.

Most Shan dynastic armies contained a core of full time guards often containing mercenaries. The bulk of the troops would be poorly armed tribal levies. Shan tribesmen were exceptional spearmen.

Fewer elephants were located in the Lower Burmese Mon region. Drawings indicate that warriors carried a sword and occasionally a spear. Their shield was round and could cover the entire torso. It was mainly used for protection from arrows while advancing into contact. It was often slung to the back when charging into contact.

The Burman were considered to be the best archers and drilled infantry. The Burman dynasties were known for hiring Shan spearmen as their bodyguards. The distinctive Burman cone

shaped headdress was a mark of its 'regular' soldiers during the Pagan Empire but may not have been used in the Burman-Toungoo Empire. The upper class would wear breast-plate and sometimes mail armour into battle.

Generally mercenaries came from groups of exiles from other Mongs or ethnic groups. For example the Talaings of Pegu employed 300 exiled Shan in 1330. Non-ethnic mercenaries were generally reliable when not fighting their own ethnic people. When fighting a similar ethnic group, they tended to be unreliable, even if the enemy was responsible for their exile status.

MEDIEVAL BURMESE STARTER ARMY (SHAN)		
Commander-in-Chief	1	Troop Commander
Sub-commanders	2	2 x Troop Commander
Elephants	4 BGs	Each comprising 2 bases of elephants: Average, Undrilled Elephants
Ethnic cavalry	2 BGs	Each comprising 4 bases of ethnic cavalry: Average, Unprotected, Undrilled Cavalry – Light Spear
Shan spearmen	2 BGs	Each comprising 10 bases of Shan spearmen: Average, Unprotected, Undrilled Medium Foot – Defensive Spearmen
Dynastic archers	4 BGs	Each comprising 6 bases of dynastic archers: Average, Unprotected, Drilled Light Foot – Bow
Levy craftsmen	1 BG	10 bases of levy craftsmen: Poor, Unprotected, Undrilled Mob – no capabilities
Camp	1	Unfortified camp
Total	13 BGs	Camp, 16 mounted bases, 54 foot bases, 3 commanders

BUILDING A CUSTOMISED LIST USING OUR ARMY POINTS

Choose an army based on the maxima and minima in the list below. The following special instructions apply to this army:

- Commanders should be depicted as guards.
- Minima marked * apply only to armies of dynasties of that nationality. If used in the armies of dynasties of other nationalities, the maxima of such troops are halved. Burman in a non-Burman dynasty army must all be Undrilled. (Mon dynasties = Mon-Honswadi. Burman dynasties = Ava and Toungoo. Shan dynasties = Ava before 1426, Pinya, Saigang and Nam-Mao-Long. Ava before 1426 counts as both Burman and Shan, but asterisked minima are halved.)
- Shan spearmen must all be graded the same.
- Minima marked ** apply only if any troops so marked are used.
- Minima marked *** apply only to allied contingents of that nationality. Burman in a non-Burman contingent must all be Undrilled.

MEDIEVAL BURMESE

Territory Types: Agricultural, Hilly, Tropical, Woodlands

Troop name		Troop Type				Capabilities		Points per base	Bases per BG	Total bases
		Type	Armour	Quality	Training	Shooting	Close Combat			
Core Troops										
Elephants	Burman or Shan dynasties	Elephants	–	Average	Undrilled	–	–	25	2	4–12
	Mon dynasties									2–8
Dynastic archers		Medium Foot	Protected	Average	Drilled	Bow	–	7	6–8	12–48
			Unprotected					6		
		Medium Foot	Protected	Average	Drilled	Crossbow	–	7	6–8	
			Unprotected					6		
		Light Foot	Unprotected	Average	Drilled	Bow	–	5	6–8	
		Light Foot	Unprotected	Average	Drilled	Crossbow	–	5	6–8	
Mon warriors		Medium Foot	Protected	Average	Undrilled	–	Swordsmen	6	6–10	*12–32
Burman spearmen		Medium Foot	Protected	Average	Undrilled	–	Light Spear	5	6–8	*12–36
					Drilled			6		
Shan spearmen		Medium Foot	Unprotected	Average	Undrilled	–	Light Spear	4	6–10	*12–24
		Medium Foot	Unprotected	Average	Undrilled	–	Defensive Spearmen	5	6–10	
Optional Troops										
Guard horse		Cavalry	Protected	Average	Drilled	–	Light Spear	8	4	0–4
Mong cavalry		Cavalry	Unprotected	Poor	Undrilled	–	Light Spear	4	4–6	0–8
Ethnic cavalry		Cavalry	Unprotected	Average	Undrilled	–	Light Spear	6	4–6	
Guard archers		Medium Foot	Protected	Average	Drilled	Bow	–	7	6–8	0–8
		Medium Foot	Protected	Average	Drilled	Crossbow	–	7	6–8	
Ethnic archers		Medium Foot	Unprotected	Average	Undrilled	Bow	–	5	6–8	0–16 / 0–16
		Medium Foot	Unprotected	Average	Undrilled	Crossbow	–	5	6–8	
		Light Foot	Unprotected	Average	Undrilled	Bow	–	5	6–8	0–12
Mong spearmen		Medium Foot	Unprotected	Poor	Undrilled	–	Light Spear	2	6–8	**6–24
Mong archers		Medium Foot	Unprotected	Poor	Undrilled	Bow	–	3	6–8	**8–24 / 0–24
Levy craftsmen or other peasants		Mob	Unprotected	Poor	Undrilled	–	–	2	10–12	0–24
Handgunners	Only from 1400	Light Foot	Unprotected	Average	Undrilled	Handgun	–	4	4	0–4
Stone-throwers		Light Artillery	–	Average	Undrilled	Light Artillery		15	2	0–2
Bolt-shooters		Light Artillery	–	Average	Undrilled	Light Artillery		15	2	
Cannon	Only from 1400	Heavy Artillery	–	Average	Undrilled	Heavy Artillery		20	2	0–2
Fortified camp								24		0–1
Allies										
Thai Allies										

MEDIEVAL BURMESE ALLIES

Allied commander		Field Commander/Troop Commander						40/25		1	
Troop name		**Troop Type**				**Capabilities**		**Points per base**	**Bases per BG**	**Total bases**	
		Type	Armour	Quality	Training	Shooting	Close Combat				
Elephants	Burman or Shan dynasties	Elephants	–	Average	Undrilled	–	–	25	2	2–4	
	Mon dynasties									0–2	
Dynastic archers		Medium Foot	Protected	Average	Drilled	Bow	–	7	6–8	6–16	
		Medium Foot	Protected	Average	Drilled	Crossbow	–	7	6–8		
		Light Foot	Unprotected	Average	Drilled	Bow	–	5	6–8		
		Light Foot	Unprotected	Average	Drilled	Crossbow	–	5	6–8		
Mon warriors		Medium Foot	Protected	Average	Undrilled	–	Swordsmen	6	6–8	***6–8	
Burman spearmen		Medium Foot	Protected	Average	Undrilled	–	Light Spear	5	6–8	***6–12	
					Drilled			6			
Shan spearmen		Medium Foot	Unprotected	Average	Undrilled	–	Light Spear	4	6–8	***6–8	
		Medium Foot	Unprotected	Average	Undrilled	–	Defensive Spearmen	5	6–8		
Ethnic archers		Medium Foot	Unprotected	Average	Undrilled	Bow	–	5	4–6	0–6	0–6
		Medium Foot	Unprotected	Average	Undrilled	Crossbow	–	5	4–6		
		Light Foot	Unprotected	Average	Undrilled	Bow	–	5	4	0–4	
Mong spearmen		Medium Foot	Unprotected	Poor	Undrilled	–	Light Spear	2	6–8	0–8	0–8
Mong archers		Medium Foot	Unprotected	Poor	Undrilled	Bow	–	3	6–8	0–8	
Levy craftsmen or other peasants		Mob	Unprotected	Poor	Undrilled	–	–	2	10–12	0–8	

MING CHINESE

The Ming dynasty is unique amongst the major Chinese dynasties that unified China in that it originated in the south rather than in the north. This was a reflection of the growing prosperity and increasing population of the region following centuries of warfare raging across the north China plains. The Ming founder, Zhu Yuanzhang, was by birth a peasant from a very poor family. Most of his immediate family starved to death and he survived by joining a Buddhist monastery.

Zhu Yuanzhang rose to power in the messianic Buddhist Red Turbans movement in the 1330s and by 1356 AD he had gained control of a significant army based on Red Turban members and other southern rebels. To this was added 36,000 Yuan troops who abandoned the city of Nanjing as Zhu was about to attack it. As was normal in the south of China, most of the

Ming Commander

most important engagements were naval. Zhu gained control of the vital Yangtze valley in a series of massive naval engagements in the huge lakes of the region, culminating in the Lake Poyang campaign in 1363, after which Zhu was the dominant power in south China.

Zhu Yuanzhang proclaimed the start of his Ming dynasty in 1368 in his then capital of Nanjing, taking the reign title Hongwu, "Overflowing Martiality". From this he is known as the Hongwu Emperor. Following this proclamation he sent his armies to conquer the north, especially the Yuan capital Dadu which was quickly captured and renamed Beiping, "The North is Conquered". The name was later changed in the reign of the third Ming emperor to its modern name of Beijing, "Northern Capital".

The Mongols, although driven from the Chinese throne, remained persistent enemies of the Ming and early in the dynasty a number of

Ming infantry, by David Sque. Taken from Men-at-Arms 251: Medieval Chinese Armies 1260–1520.

campaigns were sent into the steppe to try and impose Chinese authority. The most successful of these were those undertaken by the martial Yongle Emperor (1402–1424), who had actually usurped the throne himself, and whilst he reigned the Ming were in a position of dominance. After his death the situation deteriorated and reached its lowest ebb when an ill-advised expedition in 1449, including the Zhengtong Emperor, was defeated and the Emperor himself captured by the Oyirod Mongols. The Emperor was released the following year, partly as the Mongols did not know what to do with him. However, the whole affair was a severe blow to the Ming military, which subsequently went into decline and adopted a defensive posture in relation to the steppe which resulted in the creation of the Great Wall of China.

This list covers the armies of Ming dynasty China from 1356 to 1500.

TROOP NOTES

Mixed infantry battle groups represent troops depicted with a front rank of men carrying shields and spears, and rear ranks of crossbowmen or archers. This appears to have been a continuation of Song practice and we classify them similarly.

Ming armies continued to expand the number and range of gunpowder weapons in use and formed bodies of infantry using handguns started to appear, although in limited numbers. It is probable that the widespread adoption of handguns by the infantry was held back by their relative lack of effect against Mongol cavalry, which remained the most dangerous enemy of the Ming throughout this period. The Great Wall may be one way that the Chinese attempted to maximise the effect of their technology and at the same time limit the Mongols' own advantages.

Ming rocket launchers, by David Sque. Taken from Men-at-Arms 251: Medieval Chinese Armies 1260–1520.

MING CHINESE STARTER ARMY (BEFORE 1450 AD)

Commander-in-Chief	1	Field Commander
Sub-commanders	2	2 x Troop Commander
Guard cavalry	1 BG	4 bases of Guard cavalry: Superior, Armoured, Drilled Cavalry – Bow, Swordsmen
Chinese cavalry	2 BGs	Each comprising 4 bases of Chinese cavalry: Average, Protected, Drilled Cavalry – Bow, Swordsmen
Mongol cavalry	1 BG	4 bases of Mongol cavalry: Average, Unprotected, Drilled Light Horse – Bow, Swordsmen
Anti-cavalry squads	1 BG	4 bases of anti-cavalry squads: Average, Protected, Drilled Heavy Foot – Heavy Weapon
Separately deployed Chinese spear- and dao-men	2 BGs	Each comprising 6 bases of separately deployed Chinese spear- and dao-men: Average, Protected, Drilled Medium Foot – Heavy Weapon
Chinese crossbowmen in mixed formations	1 BG	6 bases of Chinese crossbowmen in mixed formations: 3 Average, Protected, Drilled Medium Foot – Crossbow , Light Spear, 3 Average, Protected, Drilled Medium Foot – Crossbow
Chinese archers in mixed formations	1 BG	6 bases of Chinese archers in mixed formations: 3 Average, Protected, Drilled Medium Foot – Bow, Light Spear, 3 Average, Protected, Drilled Medium Foot – Bow
Handgunners	1 BG	4 bases of handgunners: Average, Unprotected, Drilled Light Foot – Firearm
Portable rocket launchers	1 BG	2 bases of portable rocket launchers: Average, Drilled Light Artillery – Light Artillery
Palisades	2	2 sections of Field Fortifications
Camp	1	Unfortified camp
Total	11 BGs	Camp, 16 mounted bases, 34 foot bases, 3 commanders

BUILDING A CUSTOMISED LIST USING OUR ARMY POINTS

Choose an army based on the maxima and minima in the list below. The following special instructions apply to this army:

- Commanders should be depicted as guard cavalry.

- The minima marked * apply if any foot are used but mixed formations are not used.
- The minima marked ** apply if any foot are used.
- Mongol allies cannot be used with Burman or Shan allies or Southern tribesmen.

MING CHINESE

Territory Types: Agricultural, Developed, Hilly, Tropical

C-in-C	Inspired Commander/Field Commander/Troop Commander	80/50/35	1
Sub-commanders	Field Commander	50	0–2
	Troop Commander	35	0–3

Troop name		Troop Type				Capabilities		Points per base	Bases per BG	Total bases
		Type	Armour	Quality	Training	Shooting	Close Combat			
Core Troops										
Guard cavalry	Before 1450	Cavalry	Armoured	Superior	Drilled	Bow	Swordsmen	19	4–6	0–12
	From 1450									0–6
Chinese cavalry	Before 1450	Cavalry	Armoured	Average	Drilled	Bow	Swordsmen	15	4–6	6–20
			Protected					12		
	From 1450	Cavalry	Armoured	Average	Drilled	Bow	Swordsmen	15	4–6	0–8
			Protected					12		
		Cavalry	Armoured	Average	Undrilled	Bow	Swordsmen	14	4–6	4–12
			Armoured	Poor				11		(4–12)
			Protected	Average				11		
			Protected	Poor						
Mongol or Jurchen cavalry		Light Horse	Unprotected	Average	Drilled or Undrilled	Bow	Swordsmen	10	4–6	Before 1450 4–12, From 1450 0–8
		Cavalry	Unprotected	Average	Drilled	Bow	Swordsmen	11	4–6	
			Unprotected		Undrilled			10		
			Protected		Drilled			12		
			Protected		Undrilled			11		
Separately deployed Chinese spear- and dao-men	Only before 1450	Medium Foot	Protected	Average	Drilled	–	Heavy Weapon	8	6–8	*6–24 (*6–32)
	Any date	Medium Foot	Protected	Average	Undrilled	–	Heavy Weapon	7	6–8	0–32
				Poor				5	6–8	
Chinese crossbowmen in mixed formations	Only before 1450	Medium Foot	Protected	Average	Drilled	Crossbow	Light Spear	7	1/2 (6–8)	**6–12
		Medium Foot	Protected	Average	Drilled	Crossbow	–	7	1/2	
Separately deployed Chinese crossbowmen		Medium Foot	Protected	Average	Drilled	Crossbow	–	7	6–8	
Chinese crossbowmen in mixed formations	Any date	Medium Foot	Protected	Average	Undrilled	Crossbow	Light Spear	6	1/2 (6–8)	**6–16
		Medium Foot	Protected	Average	Undrilled	Crossbow	–	6	1/2	
		Medium Foot	Protected	Poor	Undrilled	Crossbow	Light Spear	4	1/2 (6–8)	0–16
		Medium Foot	Protected	Poor	Undrilled	Crossbow	–	4	1/2	
Separately deployed Chinese crossbowmen		Medium Foot	Protected	Average	Undrilled	Crossbow	–	6	6–8	
			Protected	Poor				4		
			Unprotected	Poor				3		
Chinese archers in mixed formations	Only before 1450	Medium Foot	Protected	Average	Drilled	Bow	Light Spear	7	1/2 (6–8)	**6–18
		Medium Foot	Protected	Average	Drilled	Bow	–	7	1/2	
Separately deployed Chinese archers		Medium Foot	Protected	Average	Drilled	Bow	–	7	6–8	
Chinese archers in mixed formations	Any date	Medium Foot	Protected	Average	Undrilled	Bow	Light Spear	6	1/2 (6–8)	**6–24
		Medium Foot	Protected	Average	Undrilled	Bow	–	6	1/2	
		Medium Foot	Protected	Poor	Undrilled	Bow	Light Spear	4	1/2 (6–8)	0–24
		Medium Foot	Protected	Poor	Undrilled	Bow	–	4	1/2	
Separately deployed Chinese archers		Medium Foot	Protected	Average	Undrilled	Bow	–	6	6–8	
			Protected	Poor				4		
			Unprotected	Poor				3		

Optional Troops									
Chinese anti-cavalry squads	Heavy Foot	Protected	Average	Undrilled	—	Heavy Weapon	7	4–8	0–8
				Drilled			8		
Chinese handgunners	Medium Foot	Protected	Average	Drilled	Firearm	—	6	4–8	0–8
	Medium Foot	Protected	Average	Undrilled	Firearm	—	5	4–8	
	Light Foot	Unprotected	Average	Drilled or Undrilled	Firearm	—	4	4–8	
Southern tribal foot	Medium Foot	Protected	Average	Undrilled	—	Light Spear	5	6–8	0–12
	Medium Foot	Protected	Average	Undrilled	—	Impact Foot, Swordsmen	7	6–8	
	Medium Foot	Protected	Average	Undrilled	—	Light Spear, Swordsmen	6	6–8	
Chinese or southern tribal skirmishers	Light Foot	Unprotected	Average	Drilled or Undrilled	Bow	—	5	6–8	0–8
	Light Foot	Unprotected	Average	Drilled or Undrilled	Crossbow	—	5	6–8	
Chinese militia	Only from 1450	Mob	Unprotected	Poor	Undrilled	—	2	10–12	0–24
Portable rocket launchers	Light Artillery	—	Average	Drilled	Light Artillery	—	17	2	0–8
				Undrilled			15		
Light guns	Light Artillery	—	Average	Drilled	Light Artillery	—	17	2	0–2
				Undrilled			15		0–10
Heavy rocket launchers	Heavy Artillery	—	Average	Drilled or Undrilled	Heavy Artillery	—	20	2	0–4
Stone-throwers	Heavy Artillery	—	Average	Drilled or Undrilled	Heavy Artillery	—	20	2	0–2
Palisades	Field Fortifications						3		0–24
Allies									
Burman or Shan allies (Only from 1440–1454) – Medieval Burmese									
Mongol allies – Later Horse Nomad									

MING CHINESE ALLIES

Allied commander		Field Commander/Troop Commander						40/25	1	
Troop name		**Troop Type**				**Capabilities**		**Points per base**	**Bases per BG**	**Total bases**
		Type	Armour	Quality	Training	Shooting	Close Combat			
Guard cavalry	Only before 1450	Cavalry	Armoured	Superior	Drilled	Bow	Swordsmen	19	4	0–4
Chinese cavalry	Before 1450	Cavalry	Armoured	Average	Drilled	Bow	Swordsmen	15	4–6	4–6
			Protected					12		
	From 1450	Cavalry	Armoured	Average	Drilled	Bow	Swordsmen	15	4	0–4
			Protected					12		4–6
	From 1450	Cavalry	Armoured	Average	Undrilled	Bow	Swordsmen	14	4–6	0–6
			Armoured	Poor				11		
			Protected	Average				11		
			Protected	Poor				9		
Mongol or Jurchen cavalry		Light Horse	Unprotected	Average	Drilled or Undrilled	Bow	Swordsmen	10	4	
		Cavalry	Unprotected	Average	Drilled	Bow	Swordsmen	11	4	0–4
			Unprotected		Undrilled			10		
			Protected		Drilled			12	4	
			Protected		Undrilled			11		
Separately deployed Chinese spear- and dao-men	Only before 1450	Medium Foot	Protected	Average	Drilled	—	Heavy Weapon	8	6–8	*6–8
	Any date	Medium Foot	Protected	Average	Undrilled	—	Heavy Weapon	7	6–8	
				Poor				5		
Chinese crossbowmen in mixed formations	Only before 1450	Medium Foot	Protected	Average	Drilled	Crossbow	Light Spear	7	1/2	6
		Medium Foot	Protected	Average	Drilled	Crossbow	—	7	1/2	0–6
Separately deployed Chinese crossbowmen	Only before 1450	Medium Foot	Protected	Average	Drilled	Crossbow	—	7	4–6	
Chinese crossbowmen in mixed formations	Any date	Medium Foot	Protected	Average	Undrilled	Crossbow	Light Spear	6	1/2	4–6
		Medium Foot	Protected	Average	Undrilled	Crossbow	—	6	1/2	0–6
		Medium Foot	Protected	Poor	Undrilled	Crossbow	Light Spear	4	1/2	4–6
		Medium Foot	Protected	Poor	Undrilled	Crossbow	—	4	1/2	
Separately deployed Chinese crossbowmen		Medium Foot	Protected	Average				6		**6–12
			Protected	Poor	Undrilled	Crossbow	—	4	4–6	
			Unprotected	Poor				3		
Chinese archers in mixed formations	Only before 1450	Medium Foot	Protected	Average	Drilled	Bow	Light Spear	7	1/2	6–8
		Medium Foot	Protected	Average	Drilled	Bow	—	7	1/2	0–8
Separately deployed Chinese archers	Only before 1450	Medium Foot	Protected	Average	Drilled	Bow	—	7	6–8	
Chinese archers in mixed formations	Any date	Medium Foot	Protected	Average	Undrilled	Bow	Light Spear	6	1/2	6–8
		Medium Foot	Protected	Average	Undrilled	Bow	—	6	1/2	
		Medium Foot	Protected	Poor	Undrilled	Bow	Light Spear	4	1/2	6–8
		Medium Foot	Protected	Poor	Undrilled	Bow	—	4	1/2	0–8
Separately deployed Chinese archers		Medium Foot	Protected	Average				6		
			Protected	Poor	Undrilled	Bow	—	4	6–8	
			Unprotected	Poor				3		

YI KOREAN

During the Yi Dynasty era, the Koreans had military conflicts with various neighbours including Japan, nomadic tribes from Manchuria, Ming dynasty China and various warlords fleeing from China. Political instability in those countries had a ripple effect on Korea. As long as conditions were quiet in China, the border with Korea remained calm. However when rebellions occurred, various refugees and rebel remnants crossed the border. These crossings were followed by Ming threats and demands for the refugees' return. As a result, sometimes the Koreans would have to conduct campaigns against these bands and/or defend against Ming retaliatory raids.

Stability in Japan meant that Japanese *shoguns* would consider campaigns against China or Korea. As long as the Japanese were involved with factional fighting, only Japanese pirate raids would threaten Korea. Likewise in Manchuria, as long as the nomadic tribes were divided, only light raiding activities affected the Korean border areas. Once the tribes were united, as under the Manchus, then serious invasions of Korea could be expected.

In regards to the strict Korean social caste system, one advantage of having the *Yang-ban*, a military professional class, was that military

Korean Commanders

training and attendance at military schools was provided to all designated youth. This resulted in a high level of military training for Korean soldiers. One disadvantage of the caste system is that it was almost impossible for a soldier to be promoted above his station based on merit or valour.

This list covers Yi Korean armies from 1388 to 1500 AD.

TROOP NOTES

Until the reforms of 1400, the Yi Dynasty used Koryo military formations. The Yi military underwent further reforms between 1457 and 1464. At this time the special *To-bang*, *Tae-gak* and private armies were outlawed and replaced with a new smaller "soldier" class. This was supported by more extensive conscription laws.

The highest troop classification were bodyguards who acted as government policemen rather than soldiers and were regarded as highly loyal but poor combat troops. The *Yang-ban* provided the next level of troops who were regarded as the best warriors. These troops, often referred to as "armoured soldiers", were brigaded in elite units and assigned either to the capital or to the frontier. They would often fight mounted (depicted charging in a wedge in many paintings) and would have the best armour and equipment. The third level was the common soldiers. By 1469, these were full-time volunteers from the lower social classes. They were often deployed as garrison troops in the less threatened regions or to supplement the garrison of a vital region. The fourth level was the conscripts who were often impressed into service only under emergency conditions. They were trained mainly as "spearmen" though some operated as archers.

"Spearmen" used a mixture of conventional spears, halberds and tridents. We classify the mixture as Heavy Weapon. Classification of "soldiers" is based on several drawings of troops from the Yi era who are armed with a trident and bow, and shown in battle scenes using a long sword. Protected troops wear armour under their outer garments.

Kwang-Gun Spearmen

YI KOREAN STARTER ARMY		
Commander-in-Chief	1	Field Commander
Sub-commanders	2	2 x Troop Commander
Guards	2 BGs	Each comprising 4 bases of guards: Superior, Armoured, Drilled Cavalry – Lancers, Swordsmen
Kwang-gun cavalry	1 BG	4 bases of regular cavalry: Average, Armoured, Drilled Cavalry – Lancers, Swordsmen
Light cavalry	1 BG	4 bases of light cavalry: Average, Unprotected, Drilled Light Horse – Bow
"Soldiers"	1 BG	8 bases of "soldiers": Superior, Protected, Drilled Medium Foot – Bow*, Light Spear, Swordsmen
Kwang-gun "spearmen" and archers in mixed battle groups	2 BGs	Each comprising 8 bases of Kwang-gun "spearmen" and archers in mixed battle groups: 3 Average, Protected, Drilled Medium Foot – Heavy Weapon, 3 Average, Protected, Drilled Medium Foot – Bow
Conscript "spearmen" and archers	1 BG	10 bases of conscript "spearmen" and archers: 5 Poor, Unprotected, Undrilled Medium Foot – Heavy Weapon, 5 Poor, Unprotected, Undrilled Medium Foot – Bow
Conscript skirmishing archers	1 BG	8 bases of conscript skirmishing archers: Poor, Unprotected, Drilled Light Foot – Bow
Camp	1	Unfortified camp
Total	9 BGs	Camp, 16 mounted bases, 42 foot bases, 3 commanders

BUILDING A CUSTOMISED LIST USING OUR ARMY POINTS

Choose an army based on the maxima and minima in the list below. The following special instructions apply to this army:

- Commanders should be depicted as guards.
- The total number of bases of *Kwang-gun* foot in the army cannot exceed the total number of bases of conscript foot by more than 50%.
- *Kwang-gun* mixed battle groups can be half "spearmen", half archers or half "spearmen", half crossbowmen.
- The total number of bases of *Kwang-gun* "spearmen" in the army cannot exceed the total number of *Kwang-gun* archers and crossbowmen.
- The total number of bases of *Kwang-gun* Medium Foot crossbowmen in the army cannot exceed the number of bases of *Kwang-gun* Medium Foot archers.
- "Soldiers" cannot be used with *To-bang* or *Tae-gak* guards.

YI KOREAN									
Territory Types: Developed, Mountains, Hilly, Woodlands									
C-in-C	Inspired Commander/Field Commander/Troop Commander						80/50/35	1	
Sub-commanders	Field Commander						50	0–2	
	Troop Commander						35	0–3	
Troop name	Troop Type				Capabilities		Points per base	Bases per BG	Total bases
	Type	Armour	Quality	Training	Shooting	Close Combat			
Core Troops									
Guards	Cavalry	Armoured	Superior	Drilled	–	Lance, Swordsmen	17	4–6	4–12
			Average				13		
Light cavalry	Light Horse	Unprotected	Average	Drilled	Bow	–	8	4–6	0–12
Kwang-gun cavalry	Cavalry	Armoured	Average	Drilled	–	Lancers, Swordsmen	13	4–8	4–18
Nomad nobles	Cavalry	Armoured	Average	Undrilled	Bow	Swordsmen	18	4–6	0–8
Other nomad mercenaries	Light Horse	Unprotected	Average	Undrilled	Bow	Swordsmen	10	4–6	0–12
	Cavalry	Unprotected	Average	Undrilled	Bow	Swordsmen	10	4–6	
		Protected					11		
Irregular cavalry	Cavalry	Unprotected	Poor	Undrilled	–	Light Spear	4	4–6	0–6
Separately deployed Kwang-gun "spearmen"	Medium Foot	Protected	Average	Drilled	–	Heavy Weapon	8	6–8	6–24
Kwang-gun "spearmen" in mixed battle groups	Medium Foot	Protected	Average	Drilled	–	Heavy Weapon	8	1/2	
Kwang-gun archers in mixed battle groups	Medium Foot	Protected	Average	Drilled	Bow	–	7	1/2	6–8
Kwang-gun crossbowmen in mixed battle groups	Medium Foot	Protected	Average	Drilled	Crossbow	–	7		6–24
Separately deployed Kwang-gun archers	Medium Foot	Protected	Average	Drilled	Bow	–	7	6–8	
Separately deployed Kwang-gun crossbowmen	Medium Foot	Protected	Average	Drilled	Crossbow	–	7	6–8	
Conscript "spearmen"	Medium Foot	Unprotected	Poor	Undrilled	–	Heavy Weapon	4	1/2	8–10
Conscript archers	Medium Foot	Unprotected	Poor	Undrilled	Bow	–	3	1/2	10–50

Optional Troops									
Skirmishers	Light Foot	Unprotected	Average	Undrilled	Javelins	Light Spear, Swordsmen	5	1/2	0–16
	Light Foot	Unprotected	Average	Undrilled	Bow	–	5	1/2	
Foot Nomads	Light Foot	Unprotected	Average	Undrilled	Bow	–	5	6–8	0–8
Conscript skirmishing archers	Light Foot	Unprotected	Poor	Undrilled	Bow	–	3	6–8	0–8
To-bang Guard	Medium Foot	Protected	Superior	Drilled	–	Heavy Weapon	10	6–8	0–8
Tae-gak Guard	Medium Foot	Protected	Superior	Drilled	Crossbow	–	9	6–8	0–8
"Soldiers"	Medium Foot	Protected	Superior	Drilled	Bow*	Light Spear, Swordsmen	10	6–8	0–16
Peasants	Mob	Unprotected	Poor	Undrilled	–	–	2	10–12	0–24
Handgunners	Light Foot	Unprotected	Average	Drilled	Firearms	–	4	4	0–4
Stone-throwers	Heavy Artillery	–	Average	Undrilled	Heavy Artillery	–	20	2	0–2
Bolt-shooters	Heavy Artillery	–	Average	Undrilled	Heavy Artillery	–	20	2	0–4
Field fortifications	Field Fortifications						3		0–24
Allies									
Nomad allies – Later Horse Nomad									
Chinese allies – Ming Chinese									

APPENDIX 1 – USING THE LISTS

To give balanced games, armies can be selected using the points system. The more effective the troops, the more each base costs in points. The maximum points for an army will usually be set at between 600 and 800 points for a singles game for 2 to 4 hours play. We recommend 800 points for 15mm singles tournament games (650 points for 25mm) and 1000 points for 15mm doubles games.

The army lists specify which troops can be used in a particular army. No other troops can be used. The number of bases of each type in the army must conform to the specified minima and maxima. Troops that have restrictions on when they can be used cannot be used with troops with a conflicting restriction. For example, troops that can only be used "before 209 BC" cannot be used with troops that can only be used "from 209 BC". All special instructions applying to an army list must be adhered to. They also apply to allied contingents supplied by the army.

All armies must have a C-in-C and at least one other commander. No army can have more than 4 commanders in total, including C-in-C, sub-commanders and allied commanders.

All armies must have a supply camp. This is free unless fortified. A fortified camp can only be used if specified in the army list. Field fortifications and portable defences can only be used if specified in the army list.

Allied contingents can only be used if specified in the army list. Most allied contingents have their own allied contingent list, to which they must conform unless the main army's list specifies otherwise.

BATTLE GROUPS

All troops are organized into battle groups. Commanders, supply camps and field fortifications are not troops and are not assigned to battle groups. Portable defences are not troops, but are assigned to specific battle groups.

Battle groups must obey the following restrictions:

- The number of bases in a battle group must correspond to the range specified in the army list.
- Each battle group must initially comprise an even number of bases. The only exception to this rule is that battle groups whose army list specifies them as 2/3 of one type and 1/3 of another, can comprise 9 bases if this is within the battle group size range specified by the list.
- A battle group can only include troops from one line in a list, unless the list specifies a mixed formation by specifying fractions of the battle group to be of types from two lines. e.g. 2/3 spearmen, 1/3 archers.

Warring States Infantry Battlegroup

- All troops in a battle group must be of the same quality and training. When a choice of quality or training is given in a list, this allows battle groups to differ from each other. It does not permit variety within a battle group.
- Unless specifically stated otherwise in an army list, all troops in a battle group must be of the same armour class. Excluding Light Foot, all of the bases in a mixed battle group must be of the same armour class. When a choice of armour class is given in a list, this allows battle groups to differ from each other. It does not permit variety within a battle group.

EXAMPLE LISTS

Here is a section of the Warring States to Western Han Chinese list, which will help us to explain the basics and some special features. The lists specify the following items for each historical type included in the army:

- Troop Type - comprising Type, Armour, Quality and Training.
- Capabilities – comprising Shooting and Close Combat capabilities.
- Points cost per base.
- Minimum and maximum number of bases in each battle group.
- Minimum and maximum number of bases in the army.

Troop name		Troop Type				Capabilities		Points per base	Bases per BG	Total bases
		Type	Armour	Quality	Training	Shooting	Close Combat			
Chariots, *che*	Only before 209 BC	Heavy Chariots	–	Superior	Drilled	Crossbow	–	21	4–6	4–8
				Average				17		
	Only from 209 to 100 BC	Heavy Chariots	–	Average	Drilled	Crossbow	–	17	4–6	0–8
Cavalry	Only before 209 BC	Cavalry	Armoured	Average	Drilled	Crossbow	Swordsmen	14	4–6	0–6
			Protected					11		
			Unprotected					10		
		Cavalry	Armoured	Average	Drilled	–	Light Spear, Swordsmen	13	4–6	
			Protected					10		
			Unprotected					9		
	Only from 209 BC	Cavalry	Armoured	Average	Drilled	Crossbow	Swordsmen	14	4–6	4–12
			Protected					11		
			Unprotected					10		
		Cavalry	Armoured	Average	Drilled	–	Light Spear, Swordsmen	13	4–6	
			Protected					10		
			Unprotected					9		
Horse archers	Only Zhao or (from 200 BC) Han	Light Horse	Unprotected	Average	Drilled	Bow	–	8	4–6	0–12
	Others									0–6
Separately deployed close combat foot, *duanbing*		Medium Foot	Armoured	Average	Drilled	–	Heavy Weapon	10	6–8	*6–32
			Protected					8		
Mixed BGs of close combat foot and crossbowmen		Medium Foot	Armoured	Average	Drilled	–	Heavy Weapon	10	1/2	6–8
			Protected					8		
		Medium Foot	Armoured	Average	Drilled	Crossbow	–	9	1/2	*6–32
			Protected					7		
Separately deployed crossbowmen, *nu*		Medium Foot	Protected	Average	Drilled	Crossbow	–	7	6–8	

SPECIAL FEATURES:

- Before 209 BC, chariots can be of Superior or Average Quality. They must be organized in battle groups of 4 or 6 bases. All the bases in a battle group must be of the same Quality but different battle groups can be of different Quality. The army must include a minimum of 4 bases of chariots and cannot include more than 8.

- Between 209 BC and 100 BC, chariots can only be of Average Quality. They must be organized in battle groups of 4 or 6 bases. The army need not include any chariots but can include up to 8 bases of them.

- After 100 BC, the army cannot include any chariots.

- Cavalry can be Armoured, Protected or Unprotected. They must be organized in battle groups of 4 or 6 bases. All the bases in a battle group must have the same armour level, but different battle groups can have different armour levels. The list gives the different points costs. Cavalry can have Crossbow and Swordsmen capabilities or Light Spear and Swordsmen capabilties. All the bases in a battle group must have the same capabilities, but different battle groups can have different capabilities. Before 209 BC the army can include up to 6 bases of cavalry. From 209 BC the army must include at least 4 bases of cavalry and can include up to 12.

- Horse archers must be organized in battle groups of 4 or 6 bases. A Zhao army, or a Han

156

army from 200 BC, can have up to 12 bases of horse archers in the army. Other states, or Han armies before 200 BC, can only have 6.

- Close combat troops and crossbowmen can either be deployed in mixed battle groups or separately. The special instructions for the Warring States to Western Han Chinese list specify that 'Medium Foot "close combat foot" and crossbowmen must all be in separately deployed BGs or all in mixed BGs'. Therefore either all close combat foot must be organised in battle groups of 6 or 8 bases of close combat foot, and all crossbowmen in battle groups of 6 or 8 bases of crossbowmen, or all must be organised in battle groups of 3 bases of close combat foot and 3 bases of crossbowmen or 4 bases of close combat foot and 4 bases of crossbowmen.

- Close combat foot can be Armoured or Protected, whether in separate battle groups or mixed. Crossbowmen can only be Armoured if in mixed battle groups. All the bases in a battle group must have the same armour level, but different battle groups can have different armour levels. The list gives the different points costs.

Japanese Bushi

- The army must include at least 6 bases of close combat foot and 6 bases of crossbowmen, and can have up to 32 bases of each. If in mixed battle groups, the army will include equal numbers of bases of close combat troops and crossbowmen. The special instructions for the list specify that 'The army must include at least as many Medium Foot crossbowmen bases as "close combat foot" bases.'. This means that if separate battle groups of close combat foot and crossbowmen are used, the total number of bases in the army of troops labelled "close combat foot" must not exceed the total number of bases of Medium Foot crossbowmen.

APPENDIX 2 – THEMED TOURNAMENTS

A tournament based on the "Empires of the Dragon" theme can include any of the armies listed in this book.

It can also include the following armies from our other army list books.

Field of Glory Companion 3: *Immortal Fire*
Classical Indian (Only Guptas)

Field of Glory Companion 4: *Swords and Scimitars*
Seljuk Turk (Only Eastern Seljuks)
Khwarazmian (Only before 1231)

Field of Glory Companion 5: *Legions Triumphant*
Kushan or Indo-Skythian
Hephthalite Hunnic

Field of Glory Companion 6: *Eternal Empire*
Timurid

Field of Glory Companion 7: *Decline and Fall*
Western Turkish (Not Khazars)
Abbasid Arab
Ghaznavid

INDEX

References to illustrations and maps are shown in **Bold**